SINGAPORE: THE CHAIN OF DISASTER

By the same author (in collaboration with others)

History of the Second World War: The War Against Japan
(5 vols.) (Her Majesty's Stationery Office)

SINGAPORE:
THE CHAIN OF DISASTER

Major-General S. Woodburn Kirby
CB, CMG, CIE, OBE, MC

With a Foreword by

Admiral of the Fleet the Earl Mountbatten of Burma
Supreme Allied Commander, South-East Asia, 1943–6

THE MACMILLAN COMPANY, NEW YORK, NEW YORK

The Macmillan Company
866 Third Avenue, New York, N.Y. 10022

Singapore: The Chain of Disaster was first published
in Great Britain by Cassell & Co. Ltd., London.

Library of Congress Catalog Card Number: 72-150977

FEB 8 '72

First American Edition 1971

Printed in Great Britain

Foreword by Admiral of the Fleet
The Earl Mountbatten of Burma
KG, GCB, OM, GCSI, GCIE, GCVO, DSO, PC, FRS
Supreme Allied Commander, South-East Asia, 1943–6

I never met General Woodburn Kirby but we corresponded frequently over his manuscript of the Official History of the War against Japan—so we became 'pen friends' and I learned to respect his immense capacity for assimilating facts and presenting the historical truth. He served for four years in Malaya before the war and spent two years at the War Office in the section of the operations directorate, responsible for building the defences of the naval base. Thus he lived with the military story of Singapore and got to know the main actors before its capture and, as the official historian, had the opportunity to interview those who survived while their memories were still fresh.

This book gives an authoritative account of the events leading up to the loss of Singapore and explains very clearly what went wrong. It is therefore an important contribution to military history.

I was in Singapore in 1922 when the idea of turning it into an impregnable fortress was being talked about. When I came out in 1934 it was rapidly being turned into an impregnable fortress, or rather a fortress impregnable to sea attack. I remembered that when it was decided in the nineteenth century to defend Portsmouth, in addition to seaward defences facing south, a line of forts was built on the Portsdown Hills facing north to prevent the port being taken by invading forces from inland. But I was a young destroyer captain with no possible idea that within ten years I would be the Supreme Commander charged with the recapture of Singapore.

Soon after I set up the South-East Asia Command I started investigating what went wrong in Singapore, and came to the conclusion that the chief mistake was having no Supreme Commander in the Far East, years before the war. It is true that Air Chief Marshal Sir Robert Brooke-Popham was eventually sent out as Commander-in-Chief, Far East, but much too late and with totally inadequate powers.

When I moved my Supreme Headquarters to Singapore in 1945 I began to worry about its future defence and indeed our whole military position in the Far East. I was convinced that when my time was up in 1946 a permanent post of British Supreme Commander with complete command over the three Services in the Far East should be established. This view, which I put strongly in writing from Singapore and personally at subsequent meeting in London, was rejected. Although the Commanders-in-Chief of our land and air forces were both located in Singapore, the navy, which had pressed so hard for a Supreme Command just before the war, now moved their Commander-in-Chief's shore headquarters to Hong Kong, 1,500 miles away. So there wasn't even an effective resident Commander-in-Chief's committee for the Far East in Singapore.

Eighteen years later, when I had become Chief of the Defence Staff (itself a fairly recent creation) I was able to persuade the Government to appoint a unified Commander-in-Chief for the Far East who commanded all three Services in their operations against the Indonesian confrontation. So it can be claimed that for the last few years of its existence, before we finally leave the Far East, the defence organization for this vast area is on the right lines and that the lessons of military history have not been wholly lost.

*On doit des égards aux vivants ;
on ne doit aux morts que la vérité.*

Voltaire, *Lettres sur Oedipe*

Contents

Contents

Maps

Introduction

When I was asked in 1962 to write a book on the loss of Singapore, I came reluctantly to the conclusion that it was a task I ought to undertake. I had known most of the individuals who had taken part in the preparation of Malaya and Singapore for war between 1933 and 1941 and those who were in command during the short seventy-day campaign, had discussed the problems connected with the defence of the naval base with them and had studied the problems in considerable detail.

The loss of Singapore in 1942, the greatest national humiliation suffered by Britain since Yorktown, requires explanation, more especially as the Royal Commission, which Winston Churchill undertook in 1942 to form to investigate the causes of the disaster, was never brought into being. The official histories of the Second World War have examined the loss of Singapore in the context of the larger picture of the whole of the Far East, but they are books of reference which are read by few. A number of individuals, who were present in Malaya or Singapore during the years immediately prior to the outbreak of war or who took part in the campaign and suffered years of hardship as prisoners of war, have written their reminiscences. These books all naturally tend to view the situation from the Malayan end and therefore fail to deal comprehensively with the basic causes which led to the disaster. There is therefore a gap which this book attempts to fill.

I have approached the subject with three objects in view. The first is to give a sober, disinterested and as far as possible accurate account of the events in the two decades before the war with Japan, events which made disaster inevitable, in the hope that the statesmen, politicians and Service leaders, who control the destinies of Britain in the 1970s, will not repeat the follies of the 1920s and 30s. The second is to describe in general terms the strategy of the campaign, and to show how the gallant but ill-trained and ill-equipped garrison of Malaya tried to cope with the Japanese invasion, fighting in a country not properly integrated or prepared for war and whose population remained neutral to the outcome. Furthermore to explain how it was that, up to a month before war broke out, the armed forces and civilians in Malaya lived in a land of make-believe, considering not only that the danger of hostilities was remote but also that Singapore was an impregnable fortress. The third, after weighing up all the available evidence, to try to assess and to apportion the responsibility for the humiliation of February 1942, which was to result in the end of British colonial rule throughout the Far East (with the one exception of Hong Kong) in the immediate post-war years. This humiliation was retrieved in 1945, but only in the military sense, by the defeat of the Japanese armies in Burma by General Slim's 14th Army and the reoccupation of Malaya and Singapore by the British–Indian troops of South-East Asia Command, both under the leadership of Admiral Lord Louis Mountbatten.

Glossary of Malay words

Alor	river channel or pool
Besar	large or big
Bukit (Bt)	hill
Kampong (Kg)	village
Kechil	small or little
Kota	fort
Kuala	mouth of a river
Padang	open space
Parit	ditch or drain
Paya	swamp
Pulau	island
Sungei (S)	river
Tanjong (Tg)	cape
Tinggi	high

1

Why Singapore?

Map A, pp. 4–5

In 1902, nineteen years before the events described in this volume began, Great Britain signed a treaty of alliance with Japan, since at that time both countries feared Russian encroachment on their spheres of influence. This treaty secured for Japan British neutrality at the time of the Russo–Japanese war and cemented the friendship which already existed between the two island nations, somewhat similarly placed geographically off the coasts of Europe and Asia. The treaty was renewed in 1905, but was revised in such a way that either ally bound herself to go to the aid of the other in defence of the other's interests in the Far East and India, if attacked by any power or powers; the revision made it possible for Britain to concentrate most of her naval strength in Europe, where Germany was beginning to adopt an aggressive attitude. The treaty was again renewed in 1911, at a time when Britain found herself involved in a hectic naval building race to meet the fast-expanding German naval strength.

Throughout the latter part of the nineteenth century Britain's naval strategy had been based on maintaining her navy on a two-power standard, a standard which gave her adequate strength to meet in combat at the same time the two powers with the next largest navies. Early in the twentieth century, with the introduction of the expensive Dreadnought type of battleship and with the very rapid growth of the German navy, the maintenance of this standard became much more difficult. Britain had very large commercial interests in the Far East and in Australia: Shanghai and Canton in China, Hong Kong, the Netherlands East Indies and Malaya. Bearing in mind that she had Japan as an ally, she was able to protect these by means of a comparatively small naval force, known as the China Squadron, which was based on Hong Kong, but which showed the British flag from the Yellow Sea in the north to Singapore in the south. She had installed coast defences and maintained small garrisons at Hong Kong and Singapore sufficient to beat off a small-scale raid by a hostile power; at the former she constructed a dockyard capable of repairing and refitting naval vessels of the pre-Dreadnought era.

This was the position in the Far East when Britain became involved in war with Germany and Austria in 1914. In accordance with the spirit of her treaty of alliance, Japan came to Britain's aid. The need to strengthen the British fleet in Europe had resulted in a

B

1

diminution of the strength of the China Squadron, and thus it was left to the Japanese to attack and occupy the various German possessions in the Pacific; these included the naval base at Tsingtao on the Shantung peninsula in north China and the Mariana, Caroline and Marshall islands in the central Pacific. It was, however, at this moment that Japan showed the world that her national aspirations were to dominate China and eventually to take over the role of the western powers in the Far East and so become the leading political and commercial power in eastern Asia. Two months after the capture of Tsingtao she made her 'Twenty-one Demands' on China which, had China acceded to them, would have given her a predominant position in that country. It had always been British and American policy that China should be free of access commercially to any power; this was known as the 'Open Door' policy. Thus both nations immediately urged Japan to moderate her demands. In face of this pressure Japan gave way, but nevertheless managed to obtain concessions from the Chinese in Manchuria and in the Shantung peninsula.

With the Battle of the Atlantic against the submarine menace reaching its height in 1917, Britain, who could not spare sufficient vessels to escort her convoys in the Mediterranean and the Indian Ocean against German submarines, made an agreement with Japan under which she provided the much-needed escorts in return for an understanding that, at the peace conference after the defeat of Germany, she would be ceded the groups of islands in the central Pacific which she had captured. Accordingly, when the war ended it was agreed that, with the exception of Guam, Japan should have the Mandate under the League of Nations for the Mariana, Caroline and Marshall islands, and should retain the concessions in the Shantung peninsula which she had wrested from China.

By 1919, therefore, Japanese influence, which prior to 1914 had been confined to Japan, Korea, the Ryukyu Islands and Formosa, was extended nearly as far south as the Equator and as far east as the International Date Line. She thus held, although under Mandate from the League of Nations, a chain of islands astride the tenuous line of communication from the United States to the Philippines by way of Hawaii, Wake Island and Guam. The 1914–18 war had, however, another and more far-reaching effect on British strategy in the Pacific. The German navy had been eliminated, but both the American and Japanese navies had been considerably expanded, with the result that these nations had become the second and third world naval powers, after Great Britain. Furthermore, the United

2

States was in a position easily to outbuild Britain and thus become the strongest naval power. The centre of gravity of naval power had therefore shifted from the Atlantic and Mediterranean, where it had rested before 1914, to the Pacific. The British government realized in 1919 that a British fleet ought to be maintained in the Far East, for a potential threat now existed to the sea communications between the United Kingdom and Australia and New Zealand, as well as to the security of Britain's vast commercial interest in the Far East.

Exhausted as a result of the war, and considering that no further major war was likely to occur for the next ten years, the British government came to the conclusion that it was neither necessary nor economic to maintain a fleet in both the west and the east. Furthermore, there was no British naval base with repair facilities capable of maintaining a modern fleet in the Far East. The docking and repair facilities at Hong Kong were inadequate and, in the post-war strategic situation in the Pacific, the colony was an isolated outpost which could not possibly be defended. A decision was therefore made to hold a British fleet in a central position in European waters from which the Far East could be reinforced when necessary.

It was evident that no part of the centrally located fleet could be sent out to the Far East unless a naval base was created in that area to maintain it. Under the premiership of Lloyd George the Cabinet therefore asked the Committee of Imperial Defence early in 1921 to examine the situation with a view to determining where in the Far East a suitable naval base with full facilities for the maintenance of a sizeable fleet could be established. The main line of communication from Britain to the Far East ran through the Mediterranean and the Suez Canal and thence across the Indian Ocean to Ceylon. There it bifurcated, one branch going south-east to Fremantle and thence round the south coast of Australia to Adelaide, Melbourne and Sydney and on to New Zealand, and the other going east through the Strait of Malacca to Singapore and thence to the Netherlands East Indies, Borneo, Indo-China, Hong Kong and Shanghai. Both these lines carried vast commercial traffic. The problem which the Committee of Imperial Defence had to resolve was the point from which, in the general strategic situation which then existed, both routes east of Ceylon could best be protected.

In 1921 the backbone of a fleet was the battleship, for the development of air power had not yet reached the point when air attack was considered to be a menace to the enemy. It was therefore thought

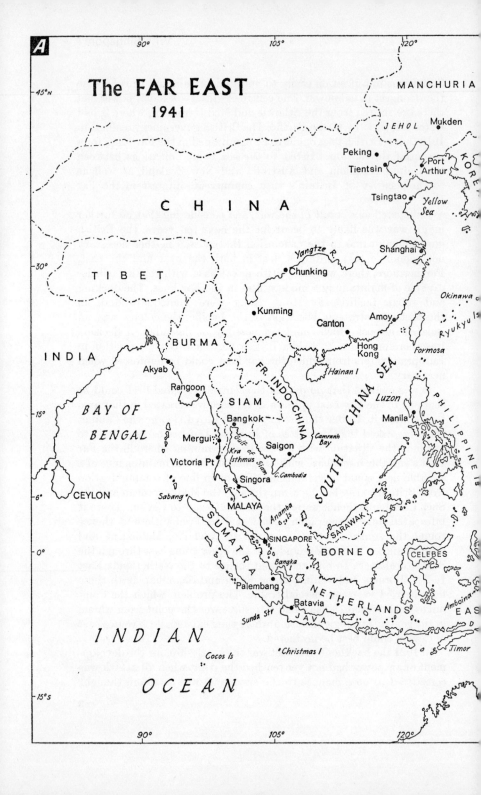

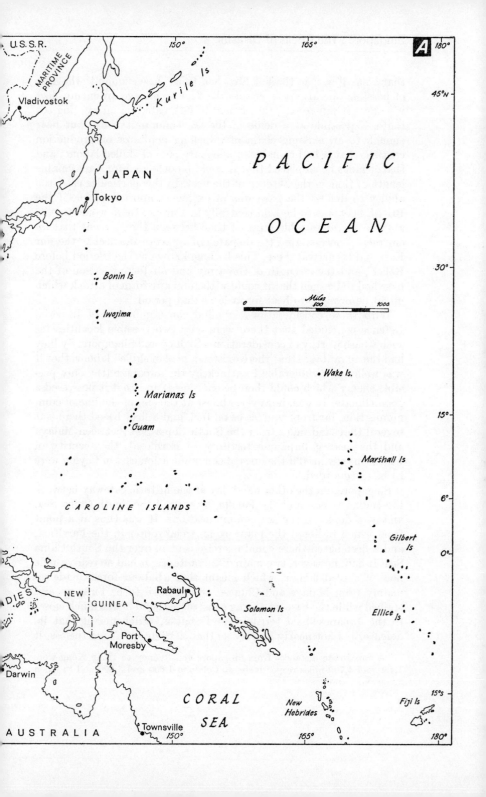

that a naval base in the Far East had to be close enough to the area of possible operations to enable the fleet to engage an enemy fleet whenever it put to sea; that it had to be located on an existing sea route, if possible at a defile in the sea communications, but near enough to an existing chain of refuelling points or oil-production centres; that it had to have an adequate pool of skilled labour; and that it must be so placed that it could be defended for a reasonable length of time in the absence of the fleet. In this particular case, the ability to defend the base was of extreme importance, for, if the British fleet was to be held centrally in Europe, there would inevitably be an undesirable lapse of time between the moment that an emergency necessitated the dispatch of a part of the fleet to the Far East and its arrival there. This became known as the 'Period before Relief', and the strength of the army and air force garrison of the base had to be such that it could withstand any form of attack which might be brought to bear for at least that period.

With these considerations in mind the Committee of Imperial Defence concluded that there were only two possible localities for such a base worthy of consideration—Sydney and Singapore. Sydney had the advantages that there existed a pool of skilled labour, that it was wellnigh invulnerable to attack by the Japanese (the only possible enemy which could then be envisaged) and that it possessed a good climate. It was, however, almost at the end of the line of communication, far from sources of oil fuel, and a fleet based there was several thousand miles from the South China Sea (between Malaya and the nearest Japanese territory in Formosa), the security of which was essential if the lines of communication east of Ceylon were to be safeguarded.

Singapore, on the other hand, lay at the historic gateway between the Indian Ocean and the Pacific, by way of the South China Sea, and at a defile on the sea communications. It was thus at a point from which radiated the many commercial routes in the Far East, and a fleet based there could exercise control over the South China Sea. It had, however, two main disadvantages: it had no ready-made pool of skilled labour, which meant that a labour force, made up mainly from Malays and Chinese, would have to be built up and trained while the base was being constructed; and it was much closer to the Japanese-held territory in Formosa, which meant that its defence was not nearly as easy as that of Sydney.[1] Nevertheless, it

[1] Approximate distances from Singapore and Sydney to Hong Kong were 1,450 and 4,700 miles respectively, to Colombo 1,600 and 5,600 and to Aden 3,600 and 7,400.

was felt at that time that Japanese bases were so far away and the country in Malaya (the greater part of which was jungle-covered) so difficult that an overland attack could be discounted; all that was considered necessary was the installation of adequate coastal fixed defences to insure against an amphibious attack on the island during the Period before Relief, which was then calculated to be seventy days. Since a fleet based on Singapore was strategically far better placed than at Sydney to protect Malaya with its rich resources of rubber and tin and the Netherlands East Indies with their oilfields, and to safeguard Britain's communications to and commercial interests in the Far East, the Committee of Imperial Defence recommended that Singapore should be the site of the new naval base which Britain had to develop.[1] This recommendation was accepted by the Cabinet in June 1921 and the information was passed to the delegates to the Imperial Conference then in session.

The balance of power in the Pacific was one of the subjects discussed at length during the Imperial Conference. It was agreed that Japan intended to expand in China, an action which neither Britain nor the United States could view with equanimity, for it would undoubtedly threaten the 'Open Door' policy for which they both stood. Furthermore, the Japanese, who had not been heavily involved in the war, had already become dangerous commercial competitors with the British in the Far East. The question which had to be settled was whether the alliance with Japan, which had been in force for some twenty years, should be continued or abandoned. The British government felt that if the alliance were discontinued, the one possible check on Japan's expansionist policy would be removed; they therefore wished to retain it. Both Australia and New Zealand agreed with this view, for they felt it was better to have Japan as an ally rather than a potential enemy, pointing out that if Japan were excluded from the alliance, she would feel herself isolated and her national pride wounded. Canada, knowing that the United States viewed the alliance with considerable hostility, opposed the views expressed by Australia and New Zealand, and suggested the convening of an international conference to settle all outstanding matters in the Pacific.

Before any action on Canada's suggestion could be initiated, the

[1] Admiral of the Fleet Lord Jellicoe had, during an extended tour of the Far East undertaken shortly after the 1914–18 war, recommended Singapore as the most suitable site for a new naval base. No doubt the Committee of Imperial Defence took note of his views when reaching their decision.

United States invited Britain, Japan, France and Italy to attend a conference at Washington to discuss proposals for reducing competition in armaments and contributing to the maintenance of peace. There is no need here to do more than set out the decisions reached at the conference. Early in 1922 the Washington Treaty, under which the contracting parties agreed to a limitation of naval armaments, was signed by Great Britain, the United States, Japan, France and Italy. Their fleets of capital ships (battleships) were to have a total tonnage of 525,000, 525,000, 315,000, 175,000 and 175,000 tons respectively; similar ratios were agreed for fleets of aircraft-carriers; and the tonnage permitted for individual replacements for naval vessels was limited to 35,000 tons for battleships, 27,000 tons for aircraft-carriers, and 10,000 tons for cruisers, which were not to mount guns exceeding 8-inch calibre. The treaty incorporated in it an article (XIX) under which Great Britain, the United States and Japan agreed to establish no new fortifications or naval bases in certain specific areas in the Pacific and to take no measures to increase existing facilities, except for the replacement of worn-out equipment. The areas covered by this article were: for Britain, Hong Kong and any insular possessions east of the 110th meridian except those adjacent to the coasts of Canada, Australia and New Zealand (Singapore was thus definitely excluded); for the United States, all her insular possessions in the Pacific except the Hawaiian islands, and those adjacent to the coasts of the USA, Alaska (excluding the Aleutian islands) and the Panama Canal zone; and for Japan, her insular territories in the Pacific, to wit the Kurile, Bonin and Ryukyu islands, Formosa and the Pescadores (the islands between Formosa and the mainland). Article XIX also covered insular territories in the Pacific which the three signatories might acquire in the future. The Mariana, Caroline and Marshall islands were not mentioned in Article XIX, since Japan was responsible to the League of Nations for the maintenance of the *status quo* in them.

The idea behind the naval treaty was to prevent an armaments race in the Pacific and the establishment by the Japanese of advanced naval and air bases in the central Pacific, but the treaty made no attempt to solve the problem of the Anglo–Japanese alliance. To replace this alliance a further treaty was signed under which Britain, the United States, Japan and France, all powers with territorial possessions in the Pacific, confirmed the *status quo* in the area, agreed to call a joint conference to resolve any dispute that might arise between them and to concert on measures to be taken if any one of them was threatened by an outside power. A third treaty was also signed, this time by nine powers, among them Britain, the United States and Japan, in which they severally bound themselves to respect the sovereignty, rights and interests of China, thereby retaining the 'Open Door' policy towards that country. When she signed this treaty Japan voluntarily gave up her concessions in the Shantung peninsula.

It is of interest to consider which power gained or lost from these series of treaties. Great Britain gained in that she avoided becoming involved in another naval building race, which at that time she could ill afford, ensured at least naval parity with the United States, and obtained the right to build the purely defensive naval base which she required to protect her interests in the Far East and from which she could, once a fleet was established there, deter any attempt on the part of Japan to seize Malaya and the oil-producing centres in the Netherlands East Indies. The United States gained in that she had taken steps to check the Japanese from defending their newly won possessions in the central Pacific which would have endangered American communications with the Philippines, and had preserved the policy of the 'Open Door' in China. Japan appeared to have gained the most, provided she followed a peaceful policy, for neither Great Britain nor the United States could construct naval bases nearer her shores than Singapore and Hawaii, and these were too far away to be of value for aggressive purposes. This fact, coupled with the possession of chains of islands in the Pacific and the right to maintain a sizeable fleet, immensely strengthened her defensive perimeter and firmly secured her communications with the mainland of Asia. She therefore had complete control of the north-west Pacific, a control which could not be challenged. The liberal and mainly civilian government of Japan which signed these treaties was well aware of the advantages they conferred on her in the way of security and peace. The pro-German military clique, temporarily eclipsed by the defeat of Germany, was far from satisfied, but saw advantages to itself provided that it bided its time in patience, since it realized that Japan had lost face both by accepting an inferior naval status and because Britain had abandoned the longstanding alliance with her in favour of the United States with whom, for various reasons, Japanese relations had been far from cordial for a long time.

Any treaty is but a scrap of paper unless there is a willingness on the part of the signatory powers to uphold it, or alternatively, to show that they have the economic and military strength and sense of purpose to enforce its observance. Although it appeared to Britain that the action she had taken had cemented her relations with the

9

United States and was a deterrent to Japanese expansionist tendencies, the series of treaties contained the seeds of trouble in the years to come. For the moment, however, it appeared that they would ensure peace in the Pacific for a considerable number of years.

2

The Wasted Years   *Map B, p. 12*

Early in 1923 a site was selected for the new naval base on the Johore Strait, just east of the causeway which links Singapore Island with Malaya (*see map B*). At the Imperial Conference that year the representatives of Australia, New Zealand and India pressed for work on it to begin as soon as possible; Britain agreed, subject to parliamentary approval of the necessary financial provisions. Before work had gone beyond the planning stage, however, Britain had a new government: her Labour Prime Minister, Ramsay MacDonald, was both an idealist and a pacifist. Under his direction Britain would rely on the collective security enunciated in the principles of the League of Nations; international disputes would be settled by conciliation and arbitration, and armaments would be limited.

One of the Prime Minister's first acts was to inform the Dominions that the Cabinet favoured ending the project and to ask them to submit their views on the subject. The Canadian government said that the matter did not affect her interests; the South African government welcomed the proposed abandonment of the project on the grounds that the cause of appeasement and conciliation among nations would be seriously undermined if the base were built. The governments of Australia, New Zealand and Newfoundland were unanimous in condemning the Cabinet's views. The Australian Prime Minister made the point that the peace of the world and the strength of the League of Nations depended to a large extent on the strength of the Royal Navy and its capacity to operate in all parts of the world. The Prime Minister of New Zealand pointed out that, although the League of Nations was an influence for peace, it could not prevent hostile action between nations. He believed that the Empire would stand as long as Britain held the supremacy of the seas but that, once she lost it, the Empire would fall. To maintain this supremacy a strong naval base at Singapore was essential.

These protests fell on deaf ears, and in the middle of March 1924 MacDonald told the Dominions that he intended to stop all work on the Singapore base. In defending his policy before the House, he said that he and his colleagues were convinced that to build a base in the Far East would have a detrimental effect on Britain's foreign policy and would leave open to suspicion her good faith in striving towards disarmament. MacDonald's policy was attacked by the Opposition, by the Navy League and by many others on the grounds that expert

11

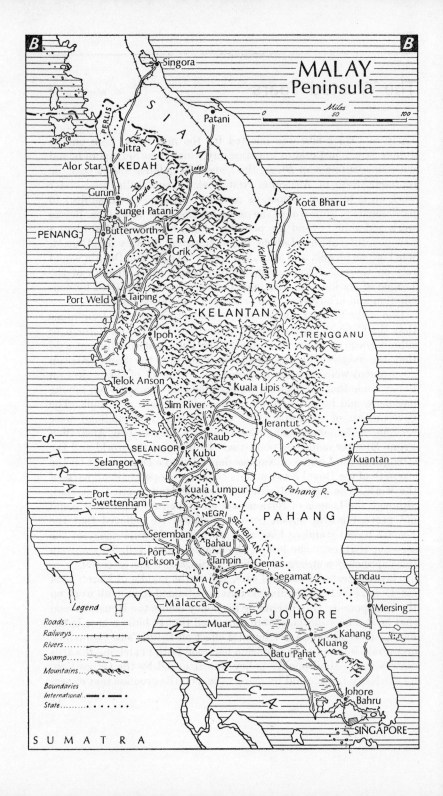

opinion had come to the conclusion that the building of a base at Singapore was the only way in which, under post-war conditions, the needs of the defence of the Empire could be met. They accused MacDonald of lack of vision, of betraying the Dominions and of repudiating Britain's duty towards the Empire.

Although MacDonald had said that he was striving towards creating conditions for general disarmament, he took steps, almost at the same time that he abandoned the Singapore base, to strengthen the fleet by laying down five cruisers and by agreeing to enlarge the Royal Air Force. He defended his apparent inconsistencies on the grounds that whereas the expansion of the navy and the RAF was being undertaken to ensure that Britain's sea lines of communication could be protected, the building of a base at Singapore would begin an armament race in the Pacific with a certainty of eventual war in that area. His policy of dependence on the League of Nations and the terms of the Washington Treaty signed only two years earlier led him to sacrifice the security of Britain's vast interests in the Far East and that of two loyal Dominions.

MacDonald's government had, however, a short life, and in November 1924, when Baldwin led the Conservative party to power with a large majority, the new government lost no time in announcing that work on the base would be continued, a decision which was welcomed by the Dominions and Colonies in the Far East. The Federated Malay States made a contribution of £2 million, New Zealand of £1 million and Hong Kong of £250,000. Owing to the cancellation of the project by the MacDonald government, and to the feeling that perhaps the fleet, which in emergency was to be located at Singapore, might never materialize, Australia decided to ensure her own defence by building up her own navy and laid down two cruisers; she therefore made no monetary contribution towards the cost of the base. Australia was not alone in expressing this view, for General (later Field-Marshal) Smuts had said that tensions in the Pacific would probably arise only when troubles in Europe would make it wellnigh impossible for the whole or even a part of the British fleet to be moved to Singapore.[1]

The decision having been taken to continue with the project, a sub-committee of the Committee of Imperial Defence was set up in 1923 to re-examine the site selected for the base, to consider the scale of defences and the rate of their construction, and the use of aircraft as an alternative weapon to the more usual fixed heavy coast defence batteries. This sub-committee recommended that the chosen

[1] Quoted in House of Commons Debates 25 March 1924: Vol. 171, p. 1284.

13

site should be developed and that an airfield and air base should be built nearby at Seletar. It then turned its attention to the probable scale of attack. Its members were well aware that, both at Port Arthur in the Russo–Japanese war and at Tsingtao in the 1914–18 war, the Japanese had landed an expeditionary force behind the defended ports and had taken them by overland attack from the rear. They were informed, however, both by the Chief of the Imperial General Staff and by General Sir Neil Malcolm (who had recently relinquished the appointment of General Officer Commanding, Singapore), that detailed military reconnaissance had shown that, owing to the difficulties of the terrain, the approach of an enemy force towards Singapore Island after a landing on the east coast of Johore would be exceptionally difficult and that generally the country favoured the defence.

The sub-committee came to the conclusion that, partly because of the difficulty of transporting and protecting an expeditionary force and partly owing to the difficulty of the terrain in Johore, the Japanese would have to attack Singapore directly from the sea, and that an attack overland was unlikely. In support of this conclusion it must be remembered that at this period there was no direct road from the most likely landing places on the east coast of Johore (Mersing and Endau) to Singapore; and that an enemy force would therefore have had to move westwards along a narrow track running through swamp and jungle to Kluang to reach a road leading to Singapore.

It is of interest, however, that Sir Neil's successor at Singapore (General Sir Theodore Fraser) held an entirely different view. He came to the conclusion in 1925 that any attack on the base would be made from Siam down the Kra Isthmus and along the western side of the Malayan peninsula, where a first-class road existed. Fraser's conclusion was correct and similar to that reached by General Sir William Dobbie some twelve years later (*see page 31*), and it was unfortunate that his view was not put before the Committee of Imperial Defence.

The sub-committee, however, came up against a considerable difference of opinion between the armed Services over the suggestion that aircraft might take the place of fixed guns. It must be remembered that in the 1920s, with the 'no war for ten years' rule extant, the three Services, having no enemy in view, had the greatest difficulty in making their case annually for funds to maintain themselves at an adequate level of efficiency. This in turn led to each Service trying to outbid the others for the funds that were available. The Royal Air Force was the worst offender in this respect, for, having seen their wartime strength waste away after 1918, they tended, under the leadership of Sir Hugh, later Lord, Trenchard, to make claims they could not substantiate, claims which brought them into head-on clashes with the other two Services.

The Air Ministry spokesmen claimed that heavy coast defence weapons were outmoded and that torpedo-bombers, protected by fighters and assisted by reconnaissance aircraft, could provide a much cheaper and more efficient deterrent against attacking naval forces. Aircraft, they rightly said, could attack the enemy ships far beyond the range of heavy guns; but they added that, thanks to the mobility of aircraft, those required for the defence of the Singapore base could be located elsewhere in peace and moved to the base only when war was imminent. This would make for economy in defence expenditure.

The Admiralty and the War Office took the opposite view. They realized that torpedo-bombers had not yet proved to be reliable deterrents, that, although it was true that aircraft were mobile in themselves, no reinforcement route to the Far East was in existence, and aircraft without proper ground maintenance staffs could not be operated efficiently. There were no transport aircraft in existence which could speedily move the maintenance staffs, and the Air Ministry would therefore have to maintain the necessary ground staff both at the base and the station where the aircraft were located in peacetime. This would be most uneconomic. Moreover, as there was no guarantee that aircraft located elsewhere could ever reach Singapore in an emergency, and because their deterrent effect was not proven, they preferred to trust in the heavy gun which, they felt, could provide, with the new fire-control techniques then being developed, an adequate deterrent against attack by enemy warships.

Faced with these conflicting views the sub-committee found it difficult to reach a decision. But in July 1926 they recommended that the first stage of the defences should provide the necessary close and medium gun defences and three 15-inch heavy guns, and that as it would be some four years before the RAF could develop aircraft capable of acting as a deterrent, the question of substituting aircraft for the remainder of the heavy guns should be re-examined later. They suggested, however, that immediate action should be taken to extend to Singapore the air reinforcement route, which then terminated at Calcutta. Yet the divergence of opinion between the Services over the capability of the air force to undertake the defence of the Singapore base against naval attack was not resolved and this was to become the cause of a lack of co-operation between the army and the RAF, a factor which was to prove highly detrimental to the defence of this vital area.

In 1927, eight years after the decision to build a base in the Far East had been taken, a committee was sent by the War Office to Singapore to make recommendations on the strength of the garrison and the number and location of the fixed defences. Unfortunately delays and difficulties resulted from a demand by the government of the Strait Settlements for a definite assurance that no part of the expenditure on the naval base would fall either directly or indirectly on the Colony's finances. Until such an assurance was received, the Governor was not prepared to recommend to his Council that the land required for military purposes should be handed over to the War Department. This attitude of mind on the part of the local government was a forerunner of an attitude which was to harden as the danger increased and to prove a bar to proper co-operation between the civilian authorities and the Services throughout Malaya. Early in 1928, the Chiefs of Staff agreed that the first stage of the defences should be begun and be completed by 1933, but they postponed the second stage—the addition of the remaining heavy guns or aircraft in lieu.

In 1928 the decision taken in 1919 that there would be no war for ten years had to come up for review, and the Cabinet, after discussions with the Committee of Imperial Defence, decided to extend the rule for the purposes of the annual estimates and to make the assumption that from any given year there would be no major war for a further ten years, an assumption which was to be reviewed annually. Shortly afterwards the Conservative government was defeated at the polls, and early in 1929 the second Labour government, with Ramsay MacDonald again as Premier, took office.

By this time the site for the naval base at Singapore had been cleared, and the contract for the graving dock had been let and was due for completion by 1935; some progress had also been made on the construction of the Seletar air base and on those portions of the fixed defences for which funds had been voted. On taking office MacDonald again embarked on a pacifist policy. Despite the failure of the League of Nations to get any international agreement on general disarmament, he relied on the Kellogg–Briand Pact to make war unlikely in the foreseeable future. In pursuance of this aim he stopped work on a number of British warships which had been laid down, a gesture which was matched by the United States; he also offered to reduce the number of cruisers allowed under the Washington treaty, and suspended further work on the Singapore naval base. He then paid a visit to the United States, where he and the President sent out invitations to Japan, France and Italy to a conference in London in 1930 to consider further naval limitations. As a result a London Naval Treaty was signed in April 1930 under which these five nations agreed not to exercise their right under the Washington Treaty to construct replacement vessels for their obsolescent capital ships until 1936; altered the ratio between Britain, the United States and Japan for cruiser tonnage to 10 : 10 : 6 and for auxiliary vessels to 10 : 10 : 7; and finally permitted parity between the three nations in destroyers and submarines. It was also agreed to call a further conference between the five powers in 1935 to discuss further naval limitation.

The London Treaty not only weakened both Britain and the United States *vis à vis* Japan, but also resulted in Britain having to scrap without replacement five capital ships, the United States three and Japan one. Since the replacements for these could not be laid down till 1936 at the earliest, the treaty favoured no one but Japan. It was, however, noticeable that during the conference there was considerable opposition on the part of Japanese naval officers to its signature. Japan signed but gave a clear warning that, when the treaty expired in 1936, she would demand parity with both Britain and the United States. The signature of the treaty resulted in the resignation of Japan's Naval Chief of Staff.

As before, Australia and New Zealand objected strongly to the further delay in the construction of the Far East naval base and the weakening of British naval power. After some heated discussion at the Imperial Conference of 1930, it was agreed that the policy of establishing a base at Singapore should be maintained, but that, apart from expenditure to which Britain was already committed, work should be suspended for five years, that is, until 1935.

Britain's economic position, greatly weakened as a result of the 1914–18 war, had never been re-established. It was partly for this reason that successive Governments had endeavoured to keep defence expenditure at the lowest possible level compatible with safety. Economic conditions in Britain were seriously worsened by the financial crash in the United States and the world slump which followed. Beset by economic difficulties the MacDonald government fell in 1931 and was replaced by a National Coalition government, and Britain was forced off the Gold Standard. Nevertheless the new government once again reversed the decision of its predecessors and allotted in the 1932 Budget funds, albeit small, for continuance of work on the base.

Thirteen years had now passed since the decision had been taken

C

to hold the British fleet in a central position in Europe and to build a strongly defended naval base in the Far East. But oblivious of the lessons of history, successive British governments had allowed British naval strength to decline to a point which would make it impossible to send a detachment to the East without taking undue risks in Europe. Moreover, there was still no adequately defended base in the area which could maintain such a fleet.

One may well ask how it was that successive governments failed to take adequate steps for Britain's security. Surely it was the *laissez-faire* attitude to defence problems, and the trend towards idealism and internationalism that prevailed after the First World War. But Britain's inability to come to terms with her reduced economic strength also contributed, for this led to a policy of cutting defence expenditure to the bone on the grounds that financial and economic risks were more serious than military risks. As a result thirteen years were wasted, at the end of which Britain found herself in the middle of an economic slump, with dangers to her security growing both in the east and west.

3

The Rise of Aggression and the Years of Appeasement

1931 was to see the beginning of the period of aggressive action by Japan, Germany and Italy which led to the Second World War. Japan had been hit by the world economic slump, as had all other nations, but she sought a different way out of her difficulties from Britain. Her markets in India had been badly hit by the abrogation of the Indo–Japanese trade agreement of 1904, and her trade with Britain looked as if it would be curtailed by the Ottawa agreements to be brought into force in 1932. Chafing under the alleged national loss of face caused by the Washington and London naval treaties, the military clique found itself in accord with Japanese industrialists, who had come to the conclusion that markets for Japan's goods as well as sources of raw materials would have to be acquired. Japan had sunk considerable capital into Manchuria from 1904 onwards but, owing to the corruption and general inefficiency of the Chinese administration, was not getting the returns she expected. The younger Japanese army officers who favoured an expansionist policy thought that the position could be radically improved if the existing administration in Manchuria could be replaced by one under Japanese control. Taking advantage of the fact that Japanese troops were acting as guards for the South Manchurian Railway, owned and operated by the Japanese, army officers in Manchuria deliberately staged an explosion on 18 September 1931, which destroyed part of the railway track near Mukden, and claimed that the Chinese had sabotaged the line. Japanese troops immediately attacked Chinese troops quartered in barracks outside the city. Following this incident Japanese troops gradually occupied strategic points in Manchuria, and by February 1932 Japan had set up the puppet Chinese state of Manchukuo under her domination. This action was taken despite the fact that Japan was a signatory power to both the Nine-Power Treaty of 1922 and the Kellogg–Briand Pact. From that moment statesmen and politicians who held liberal views and had been in control of Japan's destinies for the previous decade began to lose their power to those elements in the armed Services who favoured a policy of expansion, if necessary by the use of force.

The Chinese government appealed to the League of Nations, and this appeal was supported by the United States, although she was not a member of the League. The Council of the League called upon

Japan in October to withdraw her troops from Manchuria. No notice of the League's demand was taken. The moment had then arrived when the League of Nations, if it were not to fall into disrepute, had to ensure that action was taken against an obvious aggressor. The only powers which the League might have asked to take action with any possibility of success were the United States and Britain. The former had sunk back into her traditional isolationism after the end of the 1914–18 war and, as we have said, was not a member of the League. Britain was in no position to act; part of her fleet had mutinied on 15 September, as a result of economies introduced that year which had affected the pay of the ratings; twelve out of her fifteen capital ships were either pre-war or of the immediate post-war period and were therefore obsolescent; and, of course, the base at Singapore was in no state to maintain a fleet or to be defended against even a long-distance raid. In any case the deterioration of international relations in Europe made it inadvisable for a fleet to be sent to the Far East.

The Japanese action in Manchuria resulted in the Chinese increasing considerably the already existing boycott of Japanese nationals and of Japan's commercial interests in China, more especially those in Shanghai. A series of Chinese provocations led to a Japanese decision to take over the International Settlement at Shanghai. Fierce fighting, marked by excessive brutality, broke out, and continued for several days. The Japanese, however, met an unexpected degree of resistance.

Britain, France and Italy hurriedly reinforced their defence forces in the Settlement, and Britain took the lead in trying to prevent the incident developing into a full-scale war. Japan, however, insisted that the Chinese should withdraw their troops at least some twelve miles from their sector boundary, and this the Chinese refused to do. Realizing she would lose face if she failed to overcome the Chinese resistance, fearing that the troops she had there would be too weak to withstand an attack by the Chinese army and that her 30,000 nationals would then be at the mercy of the Chinese, Japan now decided to send an expeditionary force to Shanghai. Partial mobilization was ordered; a force of some three divisions was dispatched; and when these formations arrived in the middle of February the Japanese took the offensive. By 3 March they had forced the Chinese 19th Army to retire from the boundary of the International Settlement. After this withdrawal the British, French and Italian authorities were able to negotiate a settlement, and by May Shanghai had returned to normal.

These events in 1932 rudely shattered the hopes and ideals of those who believed in the settlement of international disputes by arbitration, and the Chiefs of Staff in London seized the opportunity to ask the Cabinet to abandon the 'no war for ten years' rule which had caused Britain's defences to fall to such a dangerously low level of efficiency. The Cabinet agreed but made it clear that, because of the extremely serious economic and financial situation, the abrogation of the rule should not be taken as a justification for larger demands for expenditure by the three Services. The Chiefs of Staff were now at last free to consider Britain's strategy and defence requirements in the event of a major conflict. One thing was quite clear: if Britain were to play an effective role in the Far East, the base at Singapore had to be completed and properly defended. The Chiefs of Staff therefore pressed for the work on the base to be accelerated.

Before any further progress could be made on the defences, the inter-Service controversy resulting from the suggestion that aircraft could take the place of fixed defences had to be settled. The need for a settlement had been foreseen, and a sub-committee of the Committee of Imperial Defence, under the chairmanship of Stanley Baldwin, had been set up in December 1931. Its task was to examine the whole question of the security of defended ports throughout the Empire with special reference to the employment of air forces in that role. The Air Ministry put forward similar arguments to those submitted in 1926, but with greater force, for it had now been shown that with the improved performance of aircraft and the introduction of new techniques in the use of bombs and torpedoes against warships, aircraft could provide an effective defence against seaborne attack far beyond the range of fixed defences. The Admiralty and the War Office pointed out that any overseas base had to be safe against surprise whether by bombardment or assault, and attacked the Air Ministry's thesis of the mobility of aircraft. In the particular case of Singapore, they contended that Japan might well strike without warning and at a time when Britain was engaged elsewhere. Any defences to be installed at Singapore should, they maintained, be of a permanent nature.

The final decision was that the coast defences should be organized on the basis of co-operation between the three Services: the gun was to retain its place as the main deterrent against naval attack, but the RAF was to take part in all aspects of the defence of the base, including reconnaissance, fighter defence and offensive action against enemy warships. This recommendation was approved towards the

end of 1932, and early the following year it was agreed that the first
stage of the defence programme and the construction of the naval
base should be accelerated, a second airfield should be built and
additional air force squadrons provided for Singapore. Thus, fourteen
years after the decision was taken that a base in the Far East was
necessary, it looked as if the base would really come into being by
about 1937–8, though the full scale of fixed defences would not even
then be ready for action.

During 1933 Britain's strategic position changed even more for the
worse. The refusal of the Japanese to withdraw from Manchuria,
coupled with the Shanghai incident, led the Assembly of the League
of Nations to name Japan as an aggressor. In consequence Japan
gave the statutory two years' notice of her intention of withdrawing
from the League. The Chiefs of Staff now warned the British government that unless there was a considerable increase in the Service
estimates over a number of years, the serious accumulated deficiencies caused by the 'ten years' rule would make it impossible for
Britain to be ready to meet the grave emergencies which might arise
in the near future.

With Germany's repudiation of the Versailles Treaty, Italy bent
on colonial expansion, and Japan already an active aggressor in the
Far East, the British government at long last took the decision to
rearm. Nevertheless the government continued to assert that the
economic and financial hazards were greater than the military risks,
and a severe limit was placed on defence expenditure. Priority was
given to the strengthening of the navy and the RAF at the expense
of the army, which was to be a small, highly mobile force, primarily
for home defence. There was now no possibility of Britain being able
to make up the accumulated deficiencies in her defences in under a
decade. She had now to play for time.

*

The years of appeasement which were an inevitable consequence of
Britain's weakness now began. Since Germany had repudiated the
Versailles Treaty in 1934, there was no reason why she should not
once again embark on a vast naval building programme. Britain's
weakness, which had helped to make that repudiation possible, now
forced her into the position of trying to limit German naval expansion. She therefore signed a treaty in June 1935 under which Germany had the right to build up to 35 per cent of the surface tonnage
of the Royal Navy. The British government claimed that this treaty
was another step towards the limitation of armaments and the

maintenance of peace. But in fact there was no other course, and the expansion of the German navy meant that the bulk of the British fleet would have to be held in home waters.

This was the situation when the conference on the limitation of naval armaments took place in London at the end of 1935. Of the five powers attending, Japan and Italy were not prepared to agree to any limitations on their naval tonnage. Many Japanese had since 1922 felt resentment at the inferiority inherent in the 10 : 10 : 6 ratio of the Washington Treaty. The nation had made up its mind after 1930 to pay whatever price might be necessary to rid itself of this stigma. Thus, as already indicated by their representatives at the 1930 conference, Japan demanded parity with Britain and the United States. When this was refused, she declined to take any further part in the conference, and immediately set to work to increase the size of her naval forces.

In 1936 Nazi Germany re-occupied the Rhineland. Since at that time German rearmament was in its infancy, this action was a deliberate gamble on the part of Hitler, taken because he realized that neither Britain nor France had the means or the will to oppose it. Britain had no alternative but to accept the position, and France was morally too weak to use such strength as she had. In the same year Italy began to align herself with Germany. In the Far East, from the time of the signature of the London Naval Treaty in 1930, there had been political unrest in Japan. In essence this unrest was a struggle to settle whether Japan's armed forces were to be subservient to civilian ministers or whether their leaders were to dictate Japan's foreign policy. The conflict came to a head in February 1936, and a new government was formed subservient to those who favoured an expansionist policy. By August this new government had formulated its policy in accord with the views of the Services. This was based on establishing a firm footing on the Asian mainland, and an expansion to the south.

At this time there was no identity of views between the Japanese army and navy on foreign policy. The former tended to see the main enemy as Russia and was intent on gaining and maintaining control of Manchuria and north China, whereas the latter, realizing that its supplies of oil fuel were dependent on the goodwill of the United States and the Dutch, tended to look southwards towards the Netherlands East Indies. Both Services shared equally in the funds made available for 'defence' and both were prepared to accept a policy which would ensure that Japan was a controlling, or what they termed a stabilizing, force in eastern Asia.

Japan's actions from 1931 onwards had tended to isolate her diplomatically from all the western nations, except resurgent Germany. On the surface Japan had something in common with Germany, for both nations felt that they had been treated as inferiors after the First World War, though in totally different ways. Moreover, both had a fear of Communism, and thus of Russia. This led them to sign an Anti-Comintern Pact in 1936 which was to be binding for five years. Under it both powers agreed to exchange information on Communist activities and to collaborate in any measures necessary to counteract Communist influence. There was also a secret clause under which, if either of the two powers was threatened by or actually attacked by Russia, the other would do nothing which might assist the latter, while both would consult on what action should be taken to protect their common interests. Furthermore, neither party was to conclude a treaty with Russia which was not in accord with the spirit of the secret clause.

It was against the background of these events in Europe and the Far East that an Imperial Conference was held in London in the summer of 1937. The representatives from Australia and New Zealand, perturbed by the turn of events in the Far East, asked for an appreciation of the situation as seen by the British government, and an assessment of the help they could expect to receive in the event of a Japanese attack. In their appreciation the Chiefs of Staff considered that the most probable enemies were likely to be Germany first, Japan second, and Italy third. They made it clear that with France as an ally in a war against Germany a British fleet at least equal to the strength of the German fleet would have to be held in home waters, and that the size of the fleet available for the Far East could be determined only in the light of events at the time. If Britain were faced with war against Germany, Japan and Italy at the same time and her only ally was France, they considered that France could neutralize the Italian fleet and command the western part of the Mediterranean, but that in the eastern end British interests would be insecure. They could not countenance the surrender of British sea power in the Far East, for if they did, Japan could attack Singapore at her leisure and might succeed in capturing it. Its loss would expose the whole of Australasia, South-East Asia and India to attack, and endanger the sea routes to Australia and New Zealand. It was their opinion that the survival of the British Empire depended on the security of the United Kingdom itself and on that of Singapore, and that the situation in the eastern Mediterranean should not be allowed to interfere with the dispatch of a fleet to the Far East.

The basis of Britain's strategy should therefore be to establish a fleet at Singapore as soon as possible after the outbreak of war with Japan; this fleet would have to be sufficiently strong to protect Singapore and serve as a deterrent to any threats that Japan could make against the Empire's interests in the Far East. The period before the arrival of the fleet at Singapore, termed the 'Period before Relief', should be taken as seventy days, but the strength and time of arrival of the fleet in eastern waters would have to depend on naval and political considerations.

The British government accepted these views and, although Australia and New Zealand continued to press for a fleet to be stationed at Singapore in peacetime, decided to adhere to the policy of retaining the main fleet centrally in European waters. Thus the Dominions had to be content with the promise that the defence of Singapore was second only to that of the United Kingdom, and that a fleet would be sent to the Far East in the event of war with Japan.

Even before the Imperial Conference was over, an event took place which was to worsen Britain's strategic position, for in July 1937 war broke out between Japan and China. As Japan's action in going to war was in contravention of the 1922 Nine-Power Treaty, the remaining signatory powers called a conference at Brussels in November. This Japan refused to attend. The conference proposed a cessation of hostilities and offered mediation to obtain a just settlement in the dispute. But Japan took the line that events in China were the concern of no one but herself, and ignored the conference proposals. She had, since 1931, taken a number of gambles, all of which had come off successfully, and she felt certain that she could continue with her expansionist policy safe from interference from either Britain or the United States. She then set to work to undermine British and American influence in China by a number of staged incidents designed to humiliate their nationals in the eyes of the Chinese. These incidents culminated in December in attacks on British and American gunboats in which an American gunboat was sunk in the Yangtse River. Although there was strong evidence that the attacks were deliberate, both Britain and the United States accepted her explanations that the attacks were the result of a mistake. However, the incident did bring about secret and confidential talks between the Admiralty and representatives of the American Navy in London early in 1938, at which co-operation between them in the event of war with Japan was discussed. It was agreed unofficially that the best form of co-operation would be for the British to station a fleet at Singapore and the Americans another at Manila. It was also agreed that both nations should have mutual use of all their existing bases in South-East Asia and the Pacific. The size of the British fleet was not specified, and the Admiralty made the proviso that the British fleet would go to the Far East only if Italy were neutral.

In May 1938 the Japanese landed troops at Amoy in south China, and in October at Bias Bay, thirty miles from Hong Kong. They occupied Hainan Island, some three hundred miles south of Hong Kong, in the following February. These moves, which effectively isolated Hong Kong, the base of the British China Squadron, showed how right the British government had been in 1921–2 to consider Hong Kong an indefensible outpost and to concentrate on Singapore as Britain's base in the Far East. Japan was now, however, very much nearer to Singapore and it would not be difficult for her to seize bases in Indo-China from which she could launch an attack on Malaya. The danger to Singapore, once remote, had now come much nearer.

Meanwhile, events in Europe led to another review of Britain's strategic position. The Chiefs of Staff now assumed that Britain might find herself involved in war with Germany, Italy and Japan simultaneously, and although they realized that the only way in which Japanese threats to South-East Asia could be met was by the dispatch of a fleet to Singapore, they were forced to admit that its strength would have to depend on the state of events in Europe and on the naval reserves available. How right they were was shown in March, when Germany marched into Czechoslovakia and Italy occupied Albania.

In February 1939 the Prime Minister of Australia, J. A. Lyons, asked whether the British government could give an assurance that, in the event of war with Japan, Britain would send a fleet to Singapore in time to contain the Japanese fleet and ensure that Japan could make no major act of aggression against Australia. Chamberlain replied in March that it was Britain's intention to prevent the fall of Singapore, to keep open the Imperial sea communications and to ensure that Japan could undertake no major operations against Australia or India. It was therefore Britain's intention to send a fleet to Singapore but, since she would be fighting against a combination of powers not previously envisaged, the size of the fleet would depend on the date Japan entered the war and the naval losses sustained by the British and enemy fleets up to that time. From this reply it was evident that the order of priority of possible enemies had changed and was now Germany, Italy and Japan.

In June, when another crisis flared up at Tientsin, the Admiralty made it clear that, if war came, the fleet which could be sent to Singapore could not include more than two capital ships unless British interests in home waters and the Mediterranean were to be prejudiced. Alarmed at this, Robert Menzies, who had just become Prime Minister of Australia, asked for the same assurances as his predecessor. Chamberlain sent exactly the same reply as he had sent Lyons, in March the same year.

4

Preparations for the Defence of the Naval Base

1934–9   *Map B, p. 12, and Map H, pp. 218–19*

It could be argued that with her naval strength at its lowest ebb, and with the threat of war with Germany, and possibly Italy, making it unlikely that a fleet could be sent to the Far East and based on Singapore, Britain's wisest course would have been to abandon the Singapore project in 1933–4. Then, by arrangement with the Australian government, such funds as were available could have been spent on developing Sydney as the Empire's naval base in the Far East. Such an argument would have been fallacious, for not only did Malaya export at that time about a third of the world's supplies of rubber and some six-tenths of the world's tin, but Singapore was the nodal point on the line of communications between Europe and the Netherlands East Indies with their riches in oil, rubber and many other valuable raw materials. Japan had already shown her aggressive tendencies and her determination to be the leading Asian power, but she had no supplies of oil, rubber or tin at her disposal. It was therefore evident that she would cast covetous eyes on both Malaya and the Netherlands East Indies, and to have left such rich prizes completely undefended would have been utterly foolish. The development of a properly defended naval base at Singapore and the location of powerful naval squadrons there would not only provide a defence for Malaya but could also give protection to the Netherlands East Indies. There was no other answer but to press ahead with the construction of the naval base and to ensure that the means existed to defend it against a Japanese attack in the absence of a fleet for the Period before Relief, at that time still seventy days.

When the decision was taken in 1933 to complete the naval base and the defences at Singapore, the purse strings were at last loosened and progress became more rapid. The Admiralty pressed ahead with the contract for the graving dock at the naval base, with the construction of workshops, accommodation for ammunition and other stores and with gathering and training a suitable labour force. The Air Ministry proceeded with the construction of airfields and accommodation at Seletar, Sembawang, and Tengah on Singapore Island (*see map H, pp. 218–19*), and with the airfields on the reinforcement route from India. The War Office, which was responsible for the defence of the naval base, worked on the assumption approved by the Committee of Imperial Defence that the most probable form of attack was a naval expedition and an amphibious assault on Singapore Island. They therefore set to work to complete the fixed gun defences and provide accommodation for the British battalions which were to form the mobile garrison of the island, and for the Royal Artillery and Royal Engineer units required to man the defences.

The fixed defences were to consist of two fire commands: the Changi Fire Command in the east consisting of three 15-inch, three 9.2-inch and eight 6-inch guns, and the Faber Fire Command in the south and west with two 15-inch, three 9.2-inch and ten 6-inch guns. These, with an elaborate rangefinding and fire-control system, effectively covered the east and west entrances to the naval base in the Johore Strait and Keppel Harbour, the commercial port of Singapore. All the fixed defences were provided with armour-piercing shell for use against ships, although a small proportion of shell suitable for use against land targets was provided for the 9.2-inch and some of the 6-inch batteries. Many of the 6-inch guns had inevitably a limited field of fire to seawards because of their particular tasks, but the 9.2-inch and the modern 15-inch guns had an all-round field of fire; there was, however, no fire-control system developed to cover the north of the island, since this was to be defended, if attacked, by mobile formations. The defence of Singapore against aircraft was based on the new 3.7-inch anti-aircraft gun which had an adequate ceiling and hitting power, though these guns would not be available at the earliest before 1939.

*

With the growth of military activity at Singapore, there had grown up among the more senior members of the colonial administration an anti-military bias. Fortunately, this was not shared by the commercial and industrial community at large. The general attitude of the members of the colonial administration was that the soldiers and airmen were acceptable provided that they kept to their traditional areas. The demand for land for the fixed defences, for airfields, for new barracks and hospitals in various parts of the island as well as requests for buildings or land for amenities such as canteens, clubs and recreational grounds was opposed by the Malayan government as an infringement of the perquisites of the European civil population. It is difficult to give a reason for this attitude, but perhaps it sprang from the fact that very few of the senior Malayan civil servants of the time had taken any part in the 1914–18 war, having of necessity been retained in their civilian posts. Thus they had little understanding of the military outlook or of the problems which faced the Services in building up the defences of the base.

By 1936 the first stage of the fixed defences was nearing completion. The 9.2-inch and the 6-inch batteries had been installed and considerable progress had been made with the construction of the 15-inch batteries. In August that year Major-General (later Lieutenant-General Sir) William Dobbie assumed the appointment of General Officer Commanding, Singapore. One of his first actions was to persuade the War Office to appoint a defence security officer. This was rendered very necessary in view of the mounting interest Japan had taken in Malaya since 1923. Not only did a Japanese company own an iron mine in Trengganu and export the ore in Japanese ships, but there were numerous Japanese-owned rubber estates managed by retired Japanese officers, especially in Johore. Japanese nationals ran most of the photographic shops as well as the barbers' shops in Singapore and other towns in Malaya.

Colonel Hayley Bell, who had been brought up as a boy in Japan, spoke Japanese and understood the Japanese mind, began an investigation into the Japanese espionage activities in Malaya in October 1936 in close co-operation with the Inspector of Police and the existing British intelligence services in the Far East. In the next two and a half years, he not only uncovered an extensive Japanese espionage system but also made what proved to be an accurate assessment of future events. The information he provided was so disturbing and so unwanted by the civil administration that in May 1939, at the special request of the Governor, Hayley Bell was sent back to the United Kingdom, and the excellent organization he had built up was disbanded.

Dobbie's next action was to review the problem of defending the new base in the light of the current situation. Up to this time it had always been assumed that the probable form of attack was a landing on Singapore Island under cover of a naval bombardment, that air attack would be limited to carrier-borne aircraft, and that not only would an enemy be unable to land on the east coast of Malaya during the north-east monsoon (October to March) but also that the difficulty of the country inland was such that it provided an automatic defence for the base from the north. Dobbie had to consider whether these assumptions still held good.

Another factor also had to be taken into account. All airfields up to this date had been built, mainly for commercial reasons, on the western side of the central range of mountains in Malaya, while Alor Star and Port Swettenham had been built as part of the reinforcement route for military aircraft from India. With no fleet readily available to retain command of the sea, the air forces based on Malaya had to be prepared not only to reconnoitre the Gulf of Siam but also to take the offensive against any enemy forces approaching Malaya. Since the aircraft then available had a very limited range, a demand arose for airfields located in eastern Malaya. On the advice of the Air Officer Commanding, Far East, the Air Ministry decided to take over a private landing ground at Kota Bharu and to build airfields at Gong Kedah in Kelantan and at Kuantan, and a landing ground at Kahang between Mersing and Kluang. With his very small peacetime army garrison the General Officer Commanding, Singapore, was not in a position to protect these airfields which, in order to get the maximum range, had been sited, without consulting him, in areas unsuitable for defence and highly vulnerable to enemy landings, since they were close to the coast.

During the north-east monsoon of 1936–7, exercises to test the feasibility of landing on the east coast between October and March were carried out. These not only proved that landings were possible but that they were indeed more probable at that time of the year, as bad visibility would limit air reconnaissance and reduce the efficiency of any air attack on an enemy fleet and its transports. In November 1937, Dobbie (whose Chief of Staff was Colonel A. E. Percival, later to become the General Officer Commanding, Malaya) sent the War Office an appreciation of the methods Japan would use should she decide to attack the naval base. Later events were to show how prescient he was. In his view the Japanese would first secure advanced air bases in Siam or Indo-China and would probably then land at Singora and Patani in southern Siam and at Kota Bharu in Malaya, although additional landings might be made subsequently at Kuantan and Mersing. The Japanese troops would then advance along the main road and railway on the western side of Malaya with the object of attacking Singapore Island from the north. The conclusion was that the security of the naval base depended on holding north Malaya and Johore, and that this would mean a greatly increased garrison.

In July 1938 Dobbie warned the Chiefs of Staff that the greatest potential danger at that time was a landing in Johore near Mersing followed by an attack on Singapore from the north, as in his opinion the country in Johore was quite passable to infantry. Since the task of the garrison was the defence of the naval base and not merely the defence of Singapore Island, it would have to be prepared to fight in Johore as well as on the beaches of the island. To do this he asked for funds to begin work immediately on skeleton defences in Johore and on Singapore Island, for he was sure that there would be no time to undertake the work after a war had broken out.

In addition to beach defences on the island and defensive positions covering Singapore City, Dobbie proposed to provide a line of pill boxes running from the Johore River through Kota Tinggi towards Kulai and thence south-westwards to Pontian Besar. This line was sufficiently far to the north to prevent enemy artillery from shelling the naval base and would also protect the reservoir and pipeline which ran over the causeway to Singapore, supplying two-fifths of the island's daily requirements of water. The pill boxes were to be protected by obstacles and backed by a road grid of twelve-foot laterite roads through the rubber and jungle. It was proposed that army engineers should build the pill boxes and that rubber companies should be asked to provide the roads, for which they would be paid cost price. Dobbie felt that this plan would provide a flexible defensive position from which counter-attacks could be quickly mounted. A sum of £60,000 was eventually allotted to him to provide defences on Singapore Island, Penang and in Johore; how this sum was to be divided was left to Dobbie. In the event some £23,000 was allocated to the Johore line, and pill boxes were built along the Johore River and from Kota Tinggi for a short way to the west. But £60,000 was insufficient to complete the line or to build the roadways. At this point Dobbie was succeeded by Major-General L. E. Bond, who decided that the defence of Singapore meant defending the whole of Malaya, which in turn would require a larger garrison. As a consequence work on the Johore defensive position was allowed to lapse.

In view of Dobbie's report, the War Office decided that the Indian Army battalion normally stationed at Taiping, which was due to be relieved as soon as the Malay battalion then being raised was ready for action, should remain in Malaya. Thanks to Dobbie's foresight it was at last realized that the defence of the naval base involved the defence of the whole of Malaya with its long and vulnerable coastline. This, however, meant a very great increase in the size of the army and air force garrison over and above that available in January 1939.

It is of interest to note that for a number of years from about 1930 the Directing Staff and students at the Imperial Defence College in London carried out a war game based on Japan attacking British territory in the Far East (the United States remaining neutral) but Britain being forced by the situation in Europe to retain a large proportion of her fleet in home waters. Year after year the students, as the result of examining Japanese military history, came to the conclusion that she would attack without a previous declaration of war during the north-east monsoon and would effect a landing or landings well to the north of Singapore in southern Siam or northern Malaya with the object of gaining control of existing airfields in those areas, and then advance southwards towards Singapore along the main road and railway. They therefore agreed with Dobbie's appreciation, and the results of their work were always at the disposal of the Service ministries.

*

Since it was now evident that the peacetime garrison in Malaya and the Straits Settlements was far too small, the sources from which reinforcements could be found require examination. Britain, with a tiny regular army whose modernization and re-equipment was well down the list of priority when rearmament began and with her other commitments, could not possibly find the troops and aircraft required. The only alternative source was the Indian Army.

The Army in India was organized to undertake the duties of internal security throughout the country, to defend India's North-West Frontier against incursion by an invader through Afghanistan and to keep the peace among the warlike tribes along that frontier. It consisted of British and Indian infantry, the former mainly on internal security duty, a large number of cavalry regiments, fine bodies of well-trained horsemen but quite unfitted to the type of warfare which might be met in the middle of the twentieth century, and a small quota of British artillery regiments. There were only six squadrons of aircraft equipped with obsolescent aircraft, and with its very limited budget the Indian government had not attempted to fit the army for a major war. In the early days of 1937, not only was the horizon of General Headquarters, India, limited to the North-West Frontier and tribal expeditions, but the economic crisis of the thirties had forced it to eat up its reserves. As a result the Indian arsenals were nearly bare and, if it had been required to mobilize that year, formations fit to take part in operations other than those on the North-West Frontier would not have been forthcoming.

In the latter part of 1937, the growing world crisis, coupled with the realization that Britain had embarked on a rearmament programme in 1934, opened Delhi's eyes to the dangers of the position,

D

and plans were hurriedly made to reorganize and modernize the army to fit it for modern warfare. But it was soon found that this was quite beyond India's limited financial capabilities. In the spring of 1938, on the plea that the existing Indian Army was adequate for internal security and the defence of India's frontiers, but totally unfitted for service outside India, the British government was asked for financial aid, and a plan for a complete reorganization was submitted. Both the Minister for the Co-ordination of Defence (Lord Caldecote) and the Chancellor of the Exchequer (Sir John Simon) accepted the fact that a modernized Indian Army would be of considerable value should the Empire become involved in a major war, but they were not in a position to earmark funds for the purpose without first obtaining the consent of the House of Commons. It was therefore decided that a commission, under the chairmanship of Admiral of the Fleet Lord Chatfield, should be sent to India to examine her proposals and submit recommendations.

When the commission's report was placed before the Cabinet in June 1939 it was agreed that Britain should provide India with weapons and equipment costing some £34 millions over a five-year period. In return the government of India contracted to maintain a small Indian Navy for local defence, and to provide military and air units for her internal security and the defence of her frontiers. In addition she would maintain an external defence force, to be known as the Imperial Reserve, consisting of three infantry brigades and an unspecified number of air squadrons; these were to be equipped on a higher scale than troops earmarked to remain in India, and were to be ready to proceed overseas in an emergency. The size and nature of the military and naval forces were specified in some detail but the size of the RAF in India and of the Indian Air Force was left to be decided at discussions in London during the autumn of 1939.

*

By the middle of 1939 it was evident that the war clouds were gathering, and in July the Chiefs of Staff raised the hypothetical length of the Period before Relief from seventy to ninety days, and asked the Governor to consider the implications of stocking six months' supplies for the civil population of Singapore and Malaya. Realizing that the army and RAF garrisons might have to face an attempt by the Japanese to capture the base, unaided and without command of the sea, they also decided to reinforce Singapore. India was asked to send one of the infantry brigade groups of her Imperial Reserve and two bomber squadrons to Malaya, while two other bomber squadrons were sent from Britain. When the remaining two infantry brigade groups of the Imperial Reserve were sent to Egypt about the same time, India was denuded of all the formations she had earmarked for overseas.

When war with Germany broke out in September 1939, the regular garrison of Malaya consisted of nine battalions (12th Indian Infantry Brigade of three battalions and a mountain artillery regiment, four British battalions and one Indian and one Malay battalion) and eight RAF squadrons (four bomber, two torpedo-bomber and two flying-boat squadrons) with ninety first-line aircraft.[1] This was a sizeable force, but one which was quite inadequate to hold the whole of Malaya against the scale of attack which the Japanese could bring to bear. In addition there were local volunteer forces. They were far below strength and their training and equipment fitted them only for static roles.

War in Europe naturally altered the situation in the Far East. There was the immediate possibility that Japan would seize the opportunity to strike at both Hong Kong and Singapore; her forces already surrounded Hong Kong and were so placed in south China that she could seize airfields in Indo-China and an advanced naval base at Camranh Bay from which a short-range attack on Malaya could be launched. In August the possibility of her doing so was enhanced, as the Admiralty had been forced to withdraw most of the important ships of the China Squadron to reinforce her fleets in home waters and the Mediterranean. In these circumstances the Period before Relief was increased in September from 90 to 180 days.

There was, however, one hopeful sign which indicated that Japan intended no immediate action, for on 5 September she asked Britain, France and the United States to withdraw their garrisons in China so as to avoid incidents. The British gunboats, of which there were about twenty on the Yangtse and other rivers, were withdrawn in October and most of them sailed to Singapore, where they were converted to minesweepers. At the same time the British garrison at Tientsin was reduced to a company, but no change was made elsewhere. When representatives from the Dominions met in London in November 1939, those from Australia and New Zealand once again raised the question of the dispatch of a fleet to the Far East, in view now of the probability of Italy entering on Germany's side. In reply, the First Lord of the Admiralty, Winston Churchill, made it clear

[1] Although the RAF had ninety aircraft, they had no fighters and the torpedo-bombers were obsolescent; they would have been no match for their possible Japanese opponents.

that Britain could not contemplate the dispatch of a fleet to the Far East on the mere threat of a Japanese attack. But, although Britain's interests in the Mediterranean were very great, he said, if it came to a choice, they would have to take second place to the security of the two Dominions. Britain would neither allow Singapore to fall nor permit a serious attack on either Dominion. These were brave words; unfortunately Britain did not have the means with which to back them.

5

The Preparation of Malaya for War

1939–40   Map B, p. 12

To understand fully the events of the years 1939–40 a knowledge of the inhabitants of Malaya and Singapore and of the organization of their government is necessary. The population of Malaya and Singapore, which covers an area about the size of England, excluding Wales, was in 1940 roughly five millions. This was made up mainly of Malays and Chinese in approximately equal proportions, a comparatively small European and Eurasian community, a larger number of Indians and a few of other nationalities, including Japanese. Most of the British other than those employed on government service were in commerce. Until the British rule was established the indigenous Malays were constantly at war with each other, but a hundred years of *Pax Britannica* had led them to become a peace-loving, pleasant but rather indolent people. The Malays provided the ruling classes in the many separate Malay states, but the bulk of them were agriculturists and fishermen. The Chinese were the shopkeepers and, attracted by trade, had emigrated from China. A small proportion had been born in Malaya and their link with their home country was slight. A larger number were, however, immigrants who looked to China as their home, and among them were some who had Communist leanings. They congregated mainly in the towns, though there were Chinese shopkeepers in most Malay villages. Some Chinese owned tin mines and many worked in them. The Indians were mainly Tamils, who provided the indentured labour on rubber estates, and Sikhs, attracted to service in the police and similar occupations. Since the end of the First World War the Japanese had bought land and established rubber estates, usually in areas of strategic importance. They owned iron mines on the east coast of Malaya, exporting the ore in their own ships. Most were engaged in some form or other of espionage. As the Malays did not show any nationalistic tendency, and most of the Chinese, like the British, did not regard Malaya as their home, there was no natural patriotic fervour among the population which would have caused them to fight willingly for the security of the country.

Pre-war Malaya comprised the Straits Settlements, which included Singapore Island, Malacca, the island of Penang and Province Wellesley, a narrow strip of territory opposite Penang; the Federated Malay States of Perak, Selangor, Negri Sembilan and Pahang; and the Unfederated Malay States of Perlis, Kedah, Kelantan, Trengganu and Johore. The Straits Settlements were a Crown Colony, governed directly from Singapore, while the Federated Malay States were administered from Kuala Lumpur by a Federal Government, although they enjoyed a considerable degree of self-government under their own sultans, each having a British Resident. The Unfederated Malay States were governed by their own sultans assisted by a British Adviser. In 1939 Sir Shenton Thomas was the Governor and Commander-in-Chief of the Straits Settlements, and High Commisioner of the Federated Malay States and, through the British Advisers, had a considerable measure of control over the Unfederated Malay States. There were therefore a very large number of separate bodies and individuals who had to be consulted and whose agreement had to be obtained before any measure affecting Malaya as a whole could be introduced. The machinery of government was thus complicated and cumbersome and in no way fitted for war.

*

For many years the General Officer Commanding, Singapore, had been in charge of the defence scheme, which he controlled through a Defence Committee with one of his staff as secretary. The Committee had a number of sub-committees dealing with the various military and civil matters affecting defence, including one dealing with the supply of food under war conditions for the population of Malaya. The Royal Navy, the RAF and the civil administration were represented on these sub-committees as necessary, but the overall control lay entirely in the hands of the General Officer Commanding.

In August 1938 a Malayan civil servant, Mr C. A. Vlieland, was given the task of looking into the problem of providing food supplies for Malaya should the British Empire become involved in war. Vlieland, a Balliol man, had not been in the forces in the First World War. But he had studied military geography, and also considered himself to be something of a military strategist. Realizing that he had to be *au fait* with the military plans for the defence of Malaya to conduct his inquiry, he asked that these should be placed at his disposal. When the request was granted, he saw immediately that the defence scheme covered only southern Johore and Singapore Island.

Vlieland held the view, already expressed by General Fraser in 1925, and by General Dobbie and Colonel Percival in 1937, that if Japan were to attack Malaya, she would do so by way of Siam. He therefore considered that the defence scheme should cover the whole of Malaya. Justifiably, he also resented the fact that its planning had been almost entirely in the hands of the army, and was determined that the civil administration and the three Services should all have their say. He disliked, however, any system which depended on the action of committees and considered that responsibility for defence should be placed squarely on the shoulders of specially designated executive officers. He also considered that the Governor, since he also held the courtesy title of Commander-in-Chief as was usual in British Colonies at that time, should be responsible for the defence scheme, although this was a role which few, if any, Governors were fit to assume.

With these factors in mind, Vlieland prepared and submitted to the Governor a paper in which he advocated the abolition of the existing Defence Committee and its replacement by a newly constituted body. The Governor, as Commander-in-Chief, should become the chairman of the new body, the civil administration being represented by a Secretary for Defence who, with a small secretariat, should co-ordinate the action of all civil departments in Malaya on defence matters, and the three Services being represented by their own commanders. He proposed, however, that this new Defence Committee, which would become the War Committee on the outbreak of war, should be a purely consultative body with no secretary, no agenda and no minutes and that its members should be free to take action or not as they pleased within their own spheres of responsibility. The Secretary for Defence would have direct access to the Governor without going through the usual channels on all matters connected with defence, and would be empowered to deal directly with the British Residents or British Advisers in each of the Malay States, each Resident or Adviser being able on his own initiative to make decisions on behalf of his State with the knowledge that covering authority or the necessary legislation would automatically follow.

The Governor accepted this scheme and appointed Vlieland to be Secretary for Defence. General Dobbie, who was then General Officer Commanding, Singapore, offered no objection to this reorganization, while the Air Officer Commanding, Far East (Air Vice-Marshal J. T. Babington), welcomed it, as it gave him and his Service a much greater say in the formulation of policy. This new organization came into being at the end of 1938.

Vlieland's action to widen the scope of the Defence Committee and to get it removed from the sole control of the General Officer

Commanding, Singapore, was sound, for the problem of defence concerned the civil administration throughout Malaya as well as the three Services, and the defence of the naval base depended on the defence of the whole country. The appointment of a Secretary for Defence was also a sound move, for at one stroke it overcame the cumbersome and complicated governmental system of administration in Malaya, and should have made it possible for decisions on all matters affecting defence to be put into effect throughout the country without delay. But the system had obvious weaknesses, as the means to defend the whole country were not available. It would also inevitably break down unless the chairman were strong enough to hold the members of the committee together and weld them into a team.

In September 1939 the Defence Committee automatically became the War Committee. It then consisted of Sir Shenton Thomas, Mr Vlieland, Major-General L. V. (later Sir Lionel) Bond, who had relieved Dobbie on 1 August 1939, Air Vice-Marshal Babington, and later, when Headquarters China Squadron was transferred to Singapore from Hong Kong, Admiral Sir Percy Noble, the Commander-in-Chief, China Squadron. Since this War Committee proved to be a far from effective body during 1939 and 1941, it is necessary to spend a little time in considering its members and their opinions on defence.

Sir Shenton Thomas, who had spent most of his colonial service in Africa, had been appointed Governor and Commander-in-Chief in 1934, his first post in the Far East. Before he took this up the War Office briefed him on the defences of Singapore. To the Director of Military Operations (Major-General, later Field-Marshal, Sir John Dill), Sir Shenton Thomas said that he would do his utmost to further the War Office aims, and gave the impression that nothing would deter him from getting the defences finished as early as possible. Unfortunately Thomas proved to be a man who was inclined to be influenced by the opinions of those with whom he was in daily contact, in this case his senior Malayan civil servants and in particular the Colonial Secretary. This trait of the Governor's became evident early in 1935 when the staff officer who had been present throughout the interview between General Dill and the Governor was sent from the War Office on a tour of inspection to examine with the local military authorities the structure and layout of the fixed defences at each defended port in the Far East and to make recommendations for their alteration or improvement as necessary. While this officer was in Singapore he was asked to a luncheon party at Government House. During the meal the Governor said to him in a voice that could be heard by all present, 'I wish you —— soldiers would go away; your presence here and your efforts to build up the defences will only bring war to this country. We should be much better off without you', or words to that effect. This pronouncement in public showed clearly that the Governor had absorbed the views of the local government officials and either forgot or failed to realize the strategic importance of Singapore which had been explained to him in London. His failure to grasp the fact that an undefended Malaya with its untold riches would be a temptation to the Japanese boded ill for the future relations between the civil and military authorities. Events were to show that the Governor was a weak chairman of the War Committee, incapable of enforcing measures which would prepare Malaya for an invasion.

The army and air force representatives on the War Committee were men who held very different views on the best method of defending Malaya, and all, unfortunately, were personally antagonistic to each other. General Bond, although a man of sterling worth and character, was lacking in personality, kept himself aloof and was inclined to exercise control from his office chair. He seldom, if ever, studied his problems on the spot. Although he knew that his predecessor had been convinced that the Japanese would attempt to seize Singapore by attacking Malaya from the north through Siam, he took the view that as he could not undertake the defence of the whole of Malaya with the very small forces at his disposal at the end of 1939, his immediate task was the close defence of Singapore Island and southern Johore. At first he showed no interest in the defence of Malaya as a whole and refused to consider the defence of the new RAF airfields on or near the east coast of Malaya and close to the northern frontier with Siam.

The new Air Officer Commanding, Far East (Air Vice-Marshal Babington), was a disciple of Lord Trenchard and held the extreme view that, in the absence of a fleet based on Singapore, the defence of Malaya and thus of the naval base could and should be undertaken solely by the RAF. In his opinion the army's task was to defend the airfields from which his aircraft would have to operate and which had been sited so that they provided the maximum range. He refused to accept the fact that Bond's force had no alternative but to concentrate on the defence of the south, and apparently he failed to realize that the obsolete aircraft at his disposal could not possibly undertake the tasks he expected of them. Furthermore, he was personally jealous of the fact that Bond, as General Officer Commanding, Singapore, was a member of the Legislative Assembly and had the courtesy title of 'His Excellency' whereas he, the Air Officer Commanding, Far East, with wider responsibilities, did not enjoy such privileges. In consequence, at a time when close co-operation was essential the divergent temperaments of the two men and their entirely different approach to their common problem led to constant friction. In mitigation, however, it must be stressed that responsibility for this state of affairs really lay with the Service ministries in London, who had appointed men who were incompatible. It must also be remembered that for years the War Office and the Air Ministry had themselves been at loggerheads over the theory expounded by the RAF that aircraft could undertake unaided the defence of defended ports overseas. Consequently, it was to be expected that each would appoint a man who believed sincerely in the views they themselves held on this subject.

The Secretary for Defence had a position of great power. As secretary of the Defence Committee, not only did he have direct access to the Governor, the chairman of the Committee, and was thus in a position to persuade him to adopt his views, but he was also able to initiate, or fail to initiate, action by the civil administration on defence matters. Had Vlieland carried out his duties purely as Secretary for Defence and executive head of the civil administration for defence matters, Malaya, by 1941, might have been well organized to meet a Japanese invasion. Unfortunately Vlieland, holding strong views on the necessity of defending the whole of Malaya, and incensed by Bond's apparent unwillingness to spread his meagre resources throughout the country, entered into matters which lay outside his sphere of responsibility. He allied himself with Babington, with whom he was on very friendly terms and whose views he accepted, and set out to try to impose those views on Thomas and Bond. He had, as will be seen, no difficulty in getting the Governor to accept them, with the result that the War Committee was divided into two opposing camps and everything that Bond suggested was opposed. In these circumstances the Committee accomplished little of value.

*

In September 1939, Sir Shenton Thomas was instructed to give priority to the export of the largest possible quantities of rubber and tin from Malaya. Britain's urgent need of American dollars for the purchase of essential supplies of food, raw materials and military equipment from the USA made this necessary. At this time Malaya was Britain's best potential dollar earner, since she then produced

42

38 per cent of the world's rubber and some 60 per cent of the world's tin, a large proportion of which was exported to Canada and the United States. Receipt of this instruction in Malaya increased the difficulty of co-operation between the civil and military authorities, for the former became intent on increasing production and exporting Malaya's raw materials, while the latter had the task of preparing the country to resist a possible invasion, and this inevitably involved considerable interference with the life of the civil and commercial community.

The divergent interests of the civil and military authorities soon brought about a clash over the use of the available European manpower. From the civil point of view manpower was needed to increase the numbers available to manage the rubber and tin industries, to run processing plants and to handle the growing volume of exports. In addition, the inevitable expansion of government services caused by war requirements made increasing calls on the diminishing European community, for the younger men were now leaving the country in order to take part in the European war. On the military side General Bond, with his shortage of forces, naturally began to press for the introduction of compulsory service so that the Volunteer Forces (which composed on paper not an inconsiderable part of the available military strength) could be expanded and trained. Furthermore, there was a need for Europeans with a knowledge of the country and an ability to speak Malay to organize civil defence on a voluntary basis. It soon became evident that the resources of European manpower were insufficient to meet the needs of the forces, the civil administration and industry.

The first clash over the use of European manpower occurred in September 1939, when at Bond's request the Governor decided that the Volunteer Forces should be mobilized. When he heard of the decision Vlieland objected, and the Governor changed his mind. Unable to decide what to do, the Governor referred the matter to the Colonial Office for a ruling at the end of February 1940. In a dispatch he expressed the opinion that not only would the application of conscription adversely affect the production of rubber and tin, but that the organization of the Volunteer Forces was in itself unsound since many of their members would in any case have to be exempted for civil defence and other duties. As things stood in 1940 the existence of Volunteer Forces organized into military units was unsound, for their units could never be fit for a mobile role whatever training they could be given; indeed the available Europeans would have been better employed as liaison officers with the military units, to most of which the country and the people were strange. But with insufficient forces at his disposal, Bond had no alternative but to press for their mobilization.

At the same time as he sent his dispatch Sir Shenton Thomas took the opportunity to air his views on how Malaya and the base should be defended; these tallied in every respect with those held by Babington and Vlieland. If the Japanese were to attack with any prospect of success, he said, they would first have to overcome the naval and air defences. In the absence of a fleet stationed at Singapore, a successful defence depended on the action of the RAF aided by any submarines and other naval vessels on the station. He therefore advocated a large increase in the RAF garrison, even if this was to be at the expense of the army garrison. He concluded by saying that he was convinced that the threat to peace in the Far East would be greatly reduced and might completely disappear if the policy he advocated were adopted. There is no doubt that in the absence of a fleet the strengthening of the RAF was essential for the security of Malaya. The view that the RAF alone could secure Malaya and that the role of the army was purely that of guarding the airfields from which the RAF would operate was, however, fallacious.

On 13 March Babington followed up the Governor's memorandum with one of his own to the Air Ministry. In it he pointed out that the Far East defence policy had always been based on the dispatch of Britain's main fleet to Singapore. Since this was no longer possible, the defence of the base, which required the defence of the whole of Malaya, now fell on the RAF. Once the Japanese had gained a foothold in Malaya, he said, the fate of the base was sealed. He therefore asked that the RAF garrison should be greatly increased, and that it should be agreed once and for all that the defence of the base necessitated the defence of the whole of Malaya. Once this truth had been accepted, the army would be released from its localized role and could be used to support a defensive organization based primarily on air power. Like Thomas, Babington wanted the army to be used to protect the air bases from which a strengthened air force could prevent the Japanese from approaching the Malayan coasts.

When these dispatches were discussed in London the Foreign Office took the view that, as Japan had been at war with China for some three years, she was in no position to embark on a war with the British Empire. They also stated, erroneously, that there was an internal crisis in Japan which would tend to prevent the Japanese army leaders from further adventures. They therefore considered that the threat to Singapore was remote and that measures to guard against such a threat should take second place to economic considerations. The War Office took a more realistic view, arguing that Britain's involvement with Germany vastly increased the possibility of Japan taking the opportunity to expand her influence southwards and, furthermore, that if the Allied forces in Europe sustained any reverse there would be a very rapid deterioration of Britain's security in the Far East. The Air Ministry, while accepting the need for an increase in the strength of the RAF in Malaya, said that there was little they could do to help, because they were heavily involved in expanding Britain's air strength to meet the menace from the German air force. They had plans in hand to increase the strength of the RAF in Egypt and India; and any accretion in strength there would enable Malaya to be quickly reinforced in an emergency.

In April 1940 the Overseas Defence Committee's reply to the Governor's dispatch was received in Singapore. Although the security of Singapore, it said, was vital to the safety of the British Commonwealth in the Far East, Britain was not in a position to spare forces for areas where the danger was not imminent. There was thus no immediate possibility of increasing the strength of the RAF in Malaya and, indeed, it might become necessary to reduce it temporarily. The task of those in Malaya was to do the best with what they had. Although economic considerations were to be given first priority, the Governor was to devise some method of improving the efficiency of the Volunteer Forces without jeopardizing the output of rubber and tin.

Supported on this occasion by both Bond and Babington, Thomas felt that Malaya's problem had not been fully understood and, since he was about to embark on an eight months' spell of leave, he asked the Colonial Office to give him the opportunity of discussing the problem with them in London. At the same time he pointed out that the available European manpower was not sufficient to release men for the Volunteer Forces and to provide for the essential increase in the civil administration and the civil-defence services.

General Bond, meanwhile, had also written a memorandum on the defence of Malaya, in which he pointed out that the problem of defence had been entirely altered by the increase in the Period before Relief to 180 days, and by the fact that the Japanese were in control of south China and Hainan Island. They were now in a position to assemble an expeditionary force there ostensibly for use against China, and could easily establish air bases in Siam and Indo-China, from which to cover an attack on Malaya. The whole of Malaya must therefore be held, and this demanded a large increase in the garrison.

He assessed that to hold the whole of Malaya he would require at a minimum three divisions, two tank battalions, two machine-gun battalions and a pool of 20 per cent reinforcements. If an invasion of southern Siam were contemplated to forestall a Japanese descent through that country on to Malaya's northern frontier, he would require at least a further two divisions. This appreciation was the very first realistic attempt to show the authorities in Britain what was really required in the way of military formations to make the naval base secure.

Bond realized that it would be difficult for Britain at that time to produce forces of this magnitude, and so, in deference to the views held by Thomas and Babington, he suggested an alternative. In it he proposed that the RAF should be made absolutely responsible for the detection and the destruction of any enemy expeditionary force at sea or, if that were to prove impossible, at least to prevent a Japanese base being established within striking distance of the vital airfields in Malaya. In such a case the army's task would be the defence of Penang and the areas containing the northern group of airfields (which also included the rice-growing area in the north), the defence in depth of the likely points of attack on the east coast (Kota Bharu, Kuantan, Endau and Mersing) so as to protect the main north–south communications, and the anti-aircraft defence of all airfields and other vital points. To carry out this alternative plan he would require some seventeen battalions and a company of tanks, a force nearly double his existing strength. But, he warned, the adoption of this alternative with its consequent reduction in army strength depended entirely on a speedy increase in the strength of the RAF garrison and on its equipment with up-to-date aircraft capable of meeting the Japanese air force on equal terms.

Bond's and Thomas's memoranda were considered in London on 16 May, six days after the end of the 'phoney war' period in Europe. Although note was taken of Bond's request for a larger garrison, the Overseas Defence Committee agreed that the overall war situation was such that no reinforcements could possibly be sent to Malaya at that time. In the circumstances the Committee suggested again that some form of conscription of manpower for the Volunteer Forces ought to be put into effect in Malaya without, if possible, affecting the output of rubber and tin. In this reply, sent on 18 May, Bond was told that the Chiefs of Staff were reviewing the strategical situation in the Far East as a matter of urgency. With German forces invading France, Belgium and Holland no other answer could have been given.

The reply had the immediate effect of enhancing the tension between Bond on the one hand, and Babington and Vlieland on the other. Bond told Malaya's War Committee that, although he fully realized the need to defend the whole of Malaya, he could do no more with the troops at his disposal than defend southern Johore and Singapore Island, provide a battalion for Penang, and another for the vital Alor Star airfield. He also said that in his opinion the naval base could not be made secure for more than two months at the outside. Babington insisted that what military garrison there was should be deployed in northern Malaya to secure the airfields in Kedah, as the security of Malaya depended largely on the rapid arrival of additional squadrons by way of the reinforcement route from India. Both commanders were right in the views they expressed: Bond because he could not possibly disperse his small force to protect airfields from which an air force might operate if it were to arrive, and Babington because he felt that the length of time Singapore could be held would be determined by Britain's ability to retain air superiority over Malaya.

In the absence of Sir Shenton Thomas on leave in the United Kingdom the chairman of the War Committee was now the Acting Governor, Mr S. W. Jones. Unlike the Governor, Jones felt that military matters were best left to military men and was not therefore prepared to impose any views on them. Feeling that he was not competent to judge the merits of the case put forward by Bond and Babington and much less to decide between them, he submitted the conflict between them to London for solution by the Chiefs of Staff. In forwarding the divergent views of Bond and Babington, Jones did say that while he sympathized with Bond's desire to concentrate his available forces, his proposals would result in an attempt to hold Singapore Island with troops alone, while the Japanese would have command of the sea and be able to establish aircraft on the mainland. When this happened any aircraft remaining could only offer a short-term defence. Finally, Jones stated, the main reason for Bond's and Babington's disagreement lay in the weakness of the forces available for the defence of Malaya, and the only solution to this problem was the dispatch of reinforcements as soon as possible.

The Far East

April–October 1940   *Map A, pp. 4–5*

The fall of France and Italy's entry into the war in June 1940 drastically altered Britain's strategic position in the Far East. Without a European ally the Royal Navy not only had to fight the battle of the Atlantic single-handed to ensure the flow of food and raw materials to the United Kingdom, but had also to take over the task of neutralizing the Italian fleet in the Mediterranean. In addition they had to escort convoys to the Middle and Far East, which now had to travel round the Cape of Good Hope. Moreover, the disastrous campaign in Flanders, ending in the withdrawal of the British Expeditionary Force from Dunkirk with enormous losses of stores and equipment, together with the imminent possibility of an attempted invasion of Britain by Germany, not only tied the British army to the shores of the United Kingdom, but also reduced almost to vanishing point the possibility of arms and equipment being sent abroad except to the Middle East theatre, now threatened by Italy. The urgent need to expand the RAF to defend London and other vulnerable points in the United Kingdom against the coming short-range air attack precluded any possibility of aircraft being available to reinforce the Far East. There was no possibility of a strong fleet reaching Singapore whatever term was set for the Period before Relief, and the finding of army and air reinforcements for Malaya was to be by no means easy.

In these circumstances the expansionist elements in Japan must have been tempted to strike quickly while the opportunity existed. Fortunately for Britain several factors made Japan hold back: the situation in China was unsatisfactory and prospects of its improvement unpromising; the Japanese navy was unwilling to embark on a southern adventure which might easily bring about a conflict with the United States; neither the army nor the navy were at the time prepared for such a war; and any weakening of the *Kwantung Army* in Manchuria might have resulted in Russia invading that country, which since 1931 had become vital to Japan's economy.

In July 1940, however, expansionist and militarist elements in Japan forced the resignation of the Japanese Cabinet and replaced it by one which was under their complete control. General Hideki Tojo became War Minister and Yosuke Matsuoka Foreign Minister; both were committed to an expansionist policy. The policy adopted for the time being by the new Cabinet was to be twofold: to gain control of the Southern Region (a vast area including Indo-China, Siam, Malaya and the Netherlands East Indies), if possible without recourse to war, and to bring hostilities in China to a successful conclusion as early as possible. This meant attempting to force the Dutch to provide more oil and other raw materials, gaining control of French Indo-China, bringing pressure to bear on those helping China, coming to some diplomatic understanding with Russia which would ensure the security of Manchuria, obtaining a closer relationship with Germany and Italy, and preparing the nation to use force if necessary to take advantage of any further development in Europe unfavourable to Britain.

The first action on these lines was a demand that Britain should close the Burma Road from Rangoon to Chunking, along which military supplies were reaching China, and withdraw her garrisons from Shanghai and Tientsin. After consulting the Dominions, the British government told the United States, who were supplying China with most of the war material passing along the Burma Road, that unless they obtained clear assurances of American support the road would have to be closed. This support was not forthcoming, and the British Ambassador in Tokyo was instructed to explore the possibility of reaching some settlement without accepting the closure of the road, but in the last resort to agree to it as being imposed by *force majeure*. Not only did the Ambassador report that there was no hope of getting the demand withdrawn, but he also warned that there was a real danger of Japan declaring war if it were not met. On 18 July 1940 the road was closed for a period of three months.

No sooner was this matter settled than on 6 August Japan demanded that the Governor-General of French Indo-China should give her the right to move troops into that country and control the airfields in its northern half. On instructions from London, Admiral Sir Percy Noble did his best to persuade the French naval Commander-in-Chief (Admiral Découx) to transfer his squadron to Singapore and espouse the Free French cause, as well as to allow the normal commercial flow of rice to Hong Kong and Singapore to continue. But Découx, loyal to the Vichy French regime, flatly refused these British overtures; shortly afterwards he was appointed Governor-General. This meant that the diplomatic battle for Indo-China was now lost, and as Vichy France was under the control of Germany, it was an easy prey for Japan. On 23 September 1940 Japanese troops entered the northern part of the country, where they were in an ideal position to threaten not only Siam but also southern

E

Indo-China, a base from which they could easily launch an attack on Malaya.

Four days after her troops had moved into northern Indo-China, Japan signed a Tripartite Pact with Germany and Italy, which recognized Japan's right to establish a new order in the Far East. The pact bound the contracting parties to assist each other by economic, political and military means should any one of them be attacked by a power not involved in the China Incident or in the European war, a clause which was clearly aimed as a warning to the United States. Although the United States had not been prepared to support Britain over the Burma Road, she did react to this Tripartite Pact, and on 16 October 1940 she placed a control on the export of all grades of steel and iron scrap, on the grounds that these raw materials for steel production were required for home defence. Since Japan was dependent on the import of steel and iron scrap, her inability to obtain supplies from the United States forced her to begin to use the stockpiles she had accumulated and made her more dependent on those areas in Asia from which she could still obtain supplies.

*

Meanwhile, the Chiefs of Staff in London had been reviewing Britain's strategic position. They accepted that the Japanese intention was the eventual control of the resources in the Far East and the exclusion of all western influence from the area. They recognized that to accomplish this she would have to capture the Singapore naval base, which would remain a potential threat to a southern drive so long as a British fleet was in being anywhere in the world. They considered, however, that the danger to Malaya was not immediate; in their view Japan's next likely step would be to penetrate into southern Indo-China and possibly Siam, and follow this by attacking the Netherlands East Indies to obtain bases from which to attack Singapore. Penetration into Indo-China and Siam could be opposed, they considered, only by unobtrusive economic measures designed to delay rather than prevent any southward movement. But, should Japan invade the Netherlands East Indies, Britain was bound to offer full military support to the Dutch.

In the changed circumstances, the defence of the Singapore base had assumed even greater importance than before. The problem now was how to defend it without command of the sea, since the dispatch of an adequate fleet to the Far East was now out of the question. Calculations by the Chiefs of Staff showed that to defend Malaya properly without the fleet at least twenty-two air squadrons, with a total of 336 first-line modern aircraft, were needed. As there were only eight squadrons with some 88 obsolete aircraft in Malaya, they recommended that every effort should be made to send two squadrons of reconnaissance and two of fighter aircraft to Malaya by the end of 1940, that the existing squadrons should be brought up to strength and equipped with modern aircraft as soon as possible, and that by the end of 1941 the whole of the twenty-two squadrons should be *in situ*. They considered that once all these squadrons had reached Malaya the army garrison could be safely reduced to six brigades but, until the squadrons had arrived, the garrison should be increased (as General Bond had already suggested) to three divisions and attached troops.

Where these additional formations were to be found was the next problem. None could be spared from the United Kingdom, and India had already sent the last of her Imperial Reserve overseas. The Chiefs of Staff therefore recommended that Australia, already committed to sending divisions to the Middle East, should be asked to provide and as far as possible to equip a division for Malaya, and that Bond should be instructed to make preparations to receive it, as well as another division should one be made available. They further recommended that food reserves for the proposed garrison and the civil population in Malaya should be built up, and that, as soon as the garrison had been strengthened, conversations with the Dutch in the Far East should begin with a view to drawing up an Anglo–Dutch defence scheme. At the same time they accepted that, despite the loss of face, the British garrisons in north China would have to be withdrawn, since they were tactically in a hopeless position and could be better used elsewhere. They said that, since the garrison of Hong Kong could not hope to withstand a Japanese attack for any length of time, it should be considered an outpost, the loss of which would not affect the position in the Far East.

These recommendations, submitted to the British War Cabinet on 15 August, were approved on the 28th, and the commanders of the three Services at Singapore were then instructed to prepare a co-ordinated tactical appreciation based on that of the Chiefs of Staff. In drawing it up they were to assume that the Japanese had established bases in north and south Indo-China and had the use of Camranh Bay, and they were asked to state what forces were required.

Meanwhile, on 2 July the Colonial Office had told Jones (the Acting Governor) that the defence of Malaya should be at five days' readiness and that Australia was being asked to send a division and two squadrons of aircraft to Singapore as soon as possible. The arrival of these reinforcements would, they hoped, help to settle the differences of opinion on defence held by the army and air force commanders, which they agreed had arisen through lack of resources.

*

With the departure of the Governor on leave to the United Kingdom, the situation in Malaya's War Committee drastically altered. Until then Babington and Vlieland had expounded the theory that defence depended solely on air power and the holding by the army of the whole of the Malayan peninsula. Thanks to Vlieland's influence over the Governor, this view had prevailed, and Bond's views on many matters were not heeded. Vlieland has since claimed that steady progress had therefore been made towards objectives on which all but Bond agreed, and that Bond's desire to concentrate on the close defence of Singapore could be overcome. But in retrospect this claim does not seem to be valid. Bond's appreciation, sent to London before Sir Shenton Thomas's departure on leave, far from supporting the close defence of Singapore, showed that his ultimate objective, subject of course to the means to do so being provided, was the defence of the whole of Malaya. That steady progress in preparing the country for war had not been made is shown by the fact that, despite Vlieland's lip-service to the idea of holding all Malaya, the civil-defence organization, which was being very slowly developed, was confined solely to the Straits Settlement.

Jones, the acting chairman of the War Committee, not being under Vlieland's influence, acted impartially, and for the first time General Bond's views received a fair hearing. As a consequence, policy decisions made by the Committee under Sir Shenton Thomas's chairmanship were often reversed, and Vlieland began to lose hard-won positions. Disagreement at the highest level continued, however. Sir Percy Noble, who attended the meetings of the War Committee when he was at Singapore, had begun even before the fall of France to have serious doubts about the efficacy of the plans and arrangements being made in event of war in the Far East by both the military and civil authorities. He was well aware that the antagonism between Bond and Babington was preventing proper co-operation between the Services, and after the war he declared that although there were faults on both sides, the blame for the situation lay mainly with Air Vice-Marshal Babington. Admiral Noble was also aware that great dissatisfaction existed among the unofficial members of the Legislative Council with the way in which the civil administration was then tackling the problem of defence, and that there was a strong feeling that the Governor should be replaced. Admiral Noble had already formed his own views on the Governor, whom in private he considered to be a pleasant companion and a charming host, but in office no leader.

After the fall of France Noble expected that the Governor, realizing the added danger to Malaya, would quickly return to his post, and he was horrified and alarmed when July passed and it became obvious that Sir Shenton Thomas had no intention of cutting short his leave. He also saw that Jones was not sufficiently strong to take the measures necessary for the safety of Malaya and that the antagonism between Bond and Babington grew no less. Reluctantly, therefore, he came to the conclusion that it was his duty to take some action. He hesitated, he has recorded, to send a cable to the Admiralty, for he realized that their Lordships would probably discuss the matter with Sir Shenton Thomas, who was then in London, and that no action would result. At that moment, however, he was told that he was to hand over command of the China Squadron to Vice-Admiral Sir Geoffrey Layton and return to London to take over the appointment of Commander, Western Approaches.

As soon as Admiral Noble reached London he obtained an interview with the Secretary of State for the Colonies (Lord Lloyd) and told him of the extremely unsatisfactory state of affairs in Malaya. Asked for his recommendations on how to improve the situation, he proposed that both Bond and Babington should be replaced as soon as possible by experienced younger men who could co-operate with each other, that Thomas should remain as Governor, since he had a detailed knowledge of the very complicated administrative set-up in Malaya, but that a carefully selected senior officer from one of the three Services should be placed in supreme authority over the head of the Governor and the General and Air Officers Commanding. By this means and this alone, Noble continued, could proper co-ordination be achieved and the safety of Malaya be ensured. As is now known this was the solution imposed in Ceylon by the Prime Minister when in 1942 he appointed Vice-Admiral Sir Geoffrey Layton to be the supreme commander there. Had Noble's suggestion been adopted and the right man appointed supreme commander in Malaya, its story might have taken a different course. Unfortunately, Lord Lloyd was taken ill next day and died shortly afterwards, and nothing was done.

Back in Singapore Admiral Layton was quickly struck by the complete ineffectiveness and apparent futility of the War Committee of which he found himself a member. He saw that the antagonism and professional feud between General Bond and Air Vice-Marshal Babington was resulting in a lack of co-operation between the Services and inaction on many matters of importance, and that the personality of the Acting Governor was such that he was not fitted to guide the deliberations of the Committee. However, Layton was a man of action once he had decided that action was necessary, and early in October he cabled the Admiralty, told them of the position as he saw it, and asked that steps should be taken to relieve Babington who, in his opinion, was a more forceful character than Bond and less justified in the attitude he had adopted.

Simultaneously with the dispatch of an instruction on 2 July 1940, that the defences of Malaya should be put at five days' notice, the Colonial Office had asked for information on the stocks of rice. Twelve days later they told Jones that all possible steps should be taken to increase food stocks to the utmost extent practicable and that the War Office considered that the storage and milling capacity for rice should be dispersed throughout the country. He was therefore to consider arrangements for the distribution of food stocks in the closest liaison with Bond. On the advice of the Secretary for Defence, Jones replied that the stocks then held amounted to two months' supplies of rice and that to disperse stocks then (especially as they were being increased) would be very difficult and involve immense expenditure of man-hours and time. Informed of these developments by the War Office, Bond cabled London at the end of July to say that Jones's reply had been drafted without consultation with him. Early in August the Colonial Office reaffirmed the necessity of increasing stocks as rapidly as possible and dispersing them, but no action was taken in Malaya. About the middle of September, as the result of an inquiry from the War Office, Jones was asked to report on the measures taken or actively in hand for the redistribution of stocks of rice to safer areas. Jones replied on 2 October that no action had been taken or was contemplated and that, until additional rice mills were available in other areas, there were serious objections to the removal of rice stocks from the north. He added that the policy of retaining stocks in the north appeared to be consistent with the views expressed in the appreciation by Chiefs of Staff, which pointed to the fact that the whole of Malaya should be held rather than only Singapore Island. This latter statement appears to have been made on Vlieland's advice, for on 20 September he had written to Bond saying that now that there were troops located in Kedah, Alor Star was safe and therefore the reorganization of the rice stocks was unnecessary.

It was at this stage that Admiral Layton entered the fray. On 4 October he telegraphed the Admiralty (and the War Office) pointing out that Jones had failed to consult with either Bond or himself when drafting his telegram of the 2nd, and that neither of them agreed with the views expressed therein, as if Japan were to occupy Siam it would be strategically unsound for an important part of the reserve food stocks to be held in or near the front line. Two days later, having expressed surprise that Jones had failed to consult the local military authorities, the Colonial Office instructed him to reconsider the position in consultation with them, and to examine in particular the advisability of locating the largest store of food near to an important airfield.

Only then was positive action taken. About the middle of November Jones reported that, after a reconsideration of the problem with the Services, he had arranged for the transfer of rice from Perlis and Kedah to storage being erected in fourteen centres in Perak, Selangor, Negri Sembilan and Johore. Within the next two or three weeks this storage would be filled with 39,000 tons of transferred rice and 15,000 tons from the Netherlands East Indies. It is of interest to note that at a meeting of the War Committee on 16 November it came to light that the Secretary for Defence had failed to inform the Food Controller in Malaya that stocks had to be built up to 180 days; a decision taken a year earlier. Furthermore it appeared that he considered that the military pressure to disperse these stocks was but a further indication that Bond had no intention of holding the whole of Malaya and was still proposing to concentrate on the close defence of Singapore.

The Chiefs of Staff, now aware of the divergence of views between Bond and Babington as well as the lack of any comprehensive defence scheme covering Malaya, Burma and the Bay of Bengal, recommended that the Prime Minister should appoint a Commander-in-Chief, Far East, and on 17 October Air Chief Marshal Sir Robert Brooke-Popham was selected to fill the post. It should be noted that this was purely a service appointment made on the recommendation of the Chiefs of Staff. Probably owing to the death of Lord Lloyd, no action was taken between the Services and the Colonial Office to ensure that there was better co-operation between the military and civil authorities in Malaya. Sir Robert had had a distinguished career in the Royal Air Force and, after his retirement in 1937, had been appointed Governor and Commander-in-Chief of Kenya; in September 1939 he had been reinstated on the active list. When appointed Commander-in-Chief, Far East, he was sixty-two and, having been away from the RAF for some time, could not be said to be entirely *au fait* with sea, land and air warfare in the form it had taken in Europe and the Middle East. He was also very dependent on his staff, for he had developed a habit of falling asleep at any time of day and often in the middle of a conference at which he presided, therefore often missing much of the subject under discussion. Although a man of great charm, he had clearly passed his prime and was not a forceful enough personality to deal with this complicated and difficult situation.

Under his directive Brooke-Popham was made responsible for the operational control and training of all British land and air forces in Hong Kong, Borneo, Malaya and Burma. The General Officers Commanding in these territories and the Air Officer Commanding, Far East, were to be subordinate to him, but he was not to relieve them of their administrative and financial responsibilities. They were, as before, to correspond directly with their own Service departments in London. In practice this meant that, although he could deal with matters of major policy, he could not be held responsible in detail for the training of the troops, the preparations for war in the administrative plane or, in fact, for operations in any of the territories. He was, however, made responsible for the co-ordination of the defence plans of all the territories and for the operation of the RAF squadrons based on Ceylon and for reconnaissance over the Bay of Bengal. He was neither given control over naval operations in the Far East, which were to remain the responsibility of the Commanders-in-Chief, China and East Indies Stations, under the general direction of the Admiralty, nor over the Far East Intelligence Bureau, although it was to provide him with intelligence. He was to co-operate with the naval commanders and with the Australian and New Zealand Defence Departments. All matters of general policy were to be referred to the appropriate Service departments in London. As regards his position with the civil authorities in the territories included in his command, he was given no power at all, for the Service chiefs in each territory were to remain responsible for co-operation with the authorities in their commands. Finally he was told that in all his dealings in the Far East he was to be guided by the fact that British policy was to avoid war with Japan, and that the defence of the Far East would have to be based on air power until it became possible to send a fleet to Singapore.

It will be seen at once that this directive did not give Brooke-Popham the power to enforce decisions necessary for the defence of each of these territories, and in this respect he simply became an

extra cog in an already cumbersome machine. His overall task of co-
ordinating defence throughout the Far East relieved the local commanders of many matters which would have been a burden to them,
but he had to carry out his task without any control over the naval
forces in the area. His presence, and that of his staff of seven, in no
way improved the position in Malaya, Hong Kong, Borneo or Burma,
for although he could deal with the Chiefs of Staff as a corporate body
or in their individual capacities, the officers in command in each
territory still remained responsible to their own Service ministries
and the civil authorities to the Colonial Office. In retrospect not only
was the selection of Brooke-Popham unwise in itself, but the directive he was given was faulty. Malaya was the key to the defence of
the Far East and yet nothing whatsoever was done to overcome the
difficulties pointed out quite clearly by Noble and Layton and to
ensure that some dynamic action was taken to force all those in
Malaya to prepare the country to meet a possible, indeed probable,
invasion. A great opportunity to improve the situation in Malaya had
been missed. What was required at that juncture was the appointment as supreme commander in Malaya of a younger man of dynamic
personality with the necessary powers to galvanize the customary
peacetime somnolence of Government and Services alike; and there
were clearly many in Malaya at that time who would have welcomed
such a man, especially if he had the authority to ensure that the
Service Ministries in London and the Colonial Office could not tie the
hands of the local authorities.

*

No sooner had the Chiefs of Staff completed their strategical
review in August 1940 than they set to work to try to find reinforcements for Malaya. Two British battalions were withdrawn from
China and sent to Singapore, where they arrived in September. At
the same time, India agreed to send 11th Indian Division Headquarters and two infantry brigade groups, without artillery, to
Malaya. The divisional headquarters and one brigade arrived in
Singapore in October 1940, and the second brigade in November;
this with 12th Indian Infantry Brigade group already in Malaya
produced a complete Indian infantry division, although with only
one (mountain) artillery regiment, and provided a useful accretion of
strength, although the troops had had very little training and none
whatsoever for warfare in close or jungle country.

The arrival of these reinforcements, which brought the strength of
the army garrison up to seventeen battalions (the equivalent of

nearly two divisions without artillery), together with the fact that the Battle of Britain had been won and the possibility of an invasion of the United Kingdom had passed, made it possible for the British government to take a stronger line in dealing with Japan. The reaction of the United States to the signing of the Tripartite Pact showed that American policy in the Pacific was becoming more sympathetic, and thus, when he took the decision to reopen the Burma Road on 18 October, the Prime Minister told the President in advance of his proposed action. He went further and suggested to the President that, as actions would speak much louder than words, an American naval squadron might be sent on a friendly visit to Singapore, a visit which could be used for technical discussions on naval and military problems affecting both nations in the Far East, and to which the Dutch might be invited. The President's advisers felt that the dispatch of a naval squadron to Singapore might precipitate action by Japan and that it was not a favourable moment to provoke trouble.[1] Nothing therefore came of this first real attempt to get an agreed defence plan should war break out in the Far East, but discussions were held in Washington on means whereby Britain, Australia, New Zealand, the United States and the Dutch could exchange information on the forces available in the Far East to meet Japanese aggression. The Burma Road was duly reopened and there was no reaction from Japan.

By this time Layton, Bond and Babington had completed their tactical appreciation, which was sent to the Chiefs of Staff on 16 October. In it they agreed that, in the absence of a fleet, air power would have to be the main weapon of defence for Malaya, and concluded that Japan would attack from bases established in Siam and southern Indo-China, from where heavy bombers would be within range of Singapore. Their recommendation was that the Chiefs of Staff should consider whether, if the Japanese entered Siamese territory, British forces should advance into the Siamese southern provinces in the Kra Isthmus to deny the use of sea and air bases close to the Malayan frontier and to provide some protection for the airfields on the air reinforcement route. Excluding any reinforcements required for an advance into Siam, they recommended that the first-line strength of the air force should be increased as quickly as possible to thirty-one squadrons with 566 aircraft (220 more than the number proposed by the Chiefs of Staff) and that only when that air strength had been reached could the military garrison be reduced

---

[1] It is now known that the dispatch of an American naval squadron to Singapore would in all probability have triggered off Japanese action.

from the three divisions asked for by Bond to twenty-three battalions (five more than the Chiefs of Staff had suggested in their own estimate), that three more battalions would be required for the defence of British Borneo and that three flotillas of motor torpedo boats were required to prevent enemy forces from moving by sea along the coasts of Malaya.

At the end of October 1940, a conference was held at Singapore with Admiral Layton in the chair and attended by General Bond, Air Vice-Marshal Babington and Mr Vlieland as well as by staff officers from Australia, New Zealand, India and Burma, a naval officer representing the East Indies Station and the American naval attaché from Siam as an observer. Its task was to consider the defence problem in the Far East in the light of the appreciation by the Chiefs of Staff and the local commanders in Malaya, in preparation for discussions which it was hoped would be held with the Dutch and possibly with the United States. The conference started by assuming that, in the event of war with Japan, the Dutch would be involved from the beginning, but that the United States would remain neutral unless attacked. Until naval forces strong enough to take the offensive were available, it was evident that the only possible course was to remain on the defensive and concentrate on the protection of those points which were vital. The one place which had to be held was Singapore; the defence of Malaya was thus of first priority, but until reinforcements of aircraft and troops, over and above those which had already arrived or had been earmarked, reached Singapore, the defence of Malaya for any length of time would not be possible. It was therefore necessary that India, Australia and New Zealand should be asked to help Britain to find the necessary formations and squadrons. Note was taken that India would have four divisions ready for overseas service during 1941; although their destination was the Middle East, the conference thought that there should be no difficulty in diverting one or more of them to Malaya, and furthermore that it would be possible, provided the Australian and British governments agreed, for Australia to provide an Australian brigade group for Malaya by the end of 1940. The conference accepted the figures given in the commanders' appreciation for the army and air garrisons of Malaya as adequate but pointed out that serious deficiencies existed,[1] and that much

---

[1] These deficiencies were six battalions, six artillery regiments, six infantry brigade anti-tank companies, three engineer field companies, three light tank companies as well as a large number of heavy and light anti-aircraft guns and searchlights.

greater army reinforcements than these would be needed unless the number of aircraft reached the required figure of 566. It also recommended that Burma should be reinforced by seven battalions and an air squadron which should be located at Rangoon. The conference urged that these deficiencies should be met soon, that special efforts should be made to increase the number of aircraft in Malaya and that, whether aircraft could or could not be made available, arrangements should be made to enable aircraft to be concentrated at any point in the Far East, Australia and New Zealand by the construction of advanced operational bases complete with their ground staff. Finally the conference drew up an agenda for staff discussions with the United States and the Dutch.

7

The Far East

November 1940–April 1941   *Map A, pp. 4–5*

Even before they had signed the Tripartite Pact with Germany and Italy, the Japanese had begun their attempts to persuade the Dutch in the Netherlands East Indies to supply them with larger quantities of raw materials, especially oil. Early in September 1940 a mission to Batavia, led by Kobayashi, a member of the Japanese Cabinet, demanded that the Dutch should give Japan oil concessions in the Netherlands East Indies and supply Japan with three million tons of oil a year, for the next five years. This quantity of oil represented some two-fifths of the total Dutch production and five times as much as Japan normally obtained from the Netherlands East Indies.

The Dutch told Kobayashi that this was a matter for him to discuss with the commercial companies concerned. Meanwhile, when the British and United States governments heard of the mission, they brought diplomatic and commercial pressure to bear on the companies, urging them to sell only crude oil to Japan, and that in quantities similar to those supplied before 1940. As a *quid pro quo* Britain and America said they would purchase the whole of the Dutch output of aviation petrol, thus ensuring that none would be available to Japan. In the event, the companies refused to grant oil concessions to Japan but on the basis of a six-month contract agreed to supply about half of the oil and other raw materials that the mission had demanded, but no aviation petrol. Only too anxious to obtain what he could, Kobayashi signed an agreement on 12 November 1940 with the companies concerned, and thereby achieved some increase in supplies of oil fuel, bauxite, tin and rubber.

The amounts fell far short of what the mission had hoped to obtain, and Kobayashi's failure to persuade the Dutch to provide Japan's full requirements had the effect of spurring the Japanese government to further action. In January 1941 another mission, headed this time by Yoshizawa, also a Cabinet minister, was sent to Batavia. This mission was authorized to demand large quantities of raw materials, prospecting rights for oil and other minerals, the right of admission to the country of a greater number of Japanese, the right to maintain a fishing fleet in Dutch waters with ancillary shore-based fisheries and the use of Japanese vessels for Dutch coastal traffic. Clearly these demands were but the first phase in a Japanese plan to acquire an economic hold on the Netherlands East Indies, and the Dutch flatly refused to consider them.

Rebuffed by the Dutch, the Japanese now intensified their efforts to gain control over French Indo-China and Siam. The moment was propitious, as the Siamese had decided to take advantage of French weakness to attempt to regain from French Indo-China the border provinces which had at one time been part of their territory. In January 1941, after clashes between Siamese and French troops on the frontier, Siam threatened to invade French Indo-China, unless the border provinces she claimed were returned to her. This provided Japan with an opportunity to step in and offer to act as a mediator. Despite warnings from the United States that to accept Japanese mediation might be dangerous to their own security, the Siamese government took the line that Japan was not seeking favours and accepted the offer. A cease-fire agreement was signed on board a Japanese cruiser in Saigon harbour on 31 January. Japan had gained a diplomatic victory, but to improve her position further she decided to force both Indo-China and Siam to sign political, economic and military treaties with her. These treaties were to be framed in such a manner that French Indo-China would have to grant Japan the right to locate troops and aircraft in her southern as well as her northern provinces, to construct new airfields and to make use of existing port and other facilities, while Siam would have to sell all her surplus rice to Japan. The treaties were to be drawn up and signed, if possible, by April 1941.

*

The general trend of Japanese intentions at this time became known in Washington, for their diplomatic code had been broken. By this means it was learnt that on 14 February the Japanese Foreign Minister, Matsuoka, had told his Ambassador in Washington that the price of avoiding war in the Pacific was to be the recognition by the United States of Japanese overlordship in the western part of that ocean. By the same means it was learnt that Japan was considering the acquisition of military bases in southern Indo-China, to be followed by an attack on the British base at Singapore with the eventual object of incorporating the whole of the south-west Pacific within the Greater East Asia Co-Prosperity Sphere.

Japan now set to work to try to resolve her position with Russia and at the behest of the navy, anxious if possible to avoid a conflict with the United States which it realized might end in disaster, decided to try to obtain some agreement with her over the Pacific by diplomatic means. In February 1941 a Japanese naval officer, Admiral Nomura, who was known to have many acquaintances among Americans and who had been displaced in the Cabinet by the extremists in 1939, was appointed Japanese Ambassador to the United States. His instructions were to open negotiations to obtain a settlement in the Pacific as soon as possible. As regards Russia, steps had already been taken in November 1940 to try to open negotiations with her through the intermediary of Germany. These efforts had met with no success, for at that time Hitler was already contemplating an attack on Russia and was only interested in trying to persuade Japan to make an immediate attack on Singapore. Since Japan was not prepared to risk a war with Britain and the United States until she knew where she was with Russia, she took little notice of the pressure from Germany, and Matsuoka, after a visit to Germany, made a direct approach to Moscow. Eventually on 13 April 1941 Russia and Japan signed a Neutrality Pact under which should either party be attacked by one or more powers the other would remain neutral. The pact was to run for five years, a year's notice to be given should either party wish to withdraw from it. Japan felt that the pact would ensure the security of her Manchurian frontier while she was engaged in setting up her Greater East Asia Co-Prosperity Sphere in the Southern Region, while Russia, realizing by this time that she might be attacked by Germany, felt that it would provide some security for her eastern frontiers.

By April 1941, therefore, Japan considered that she had secured her vulnerable Manchurian flank and that by diplomatic action she might be able to prevent the United States from interfering with her plans for an advance, without recourse to war, into the Southern Region. Furthermore she had already got into a position from which she could move her troops into southern Indo-China without much difficulty and force Siam to act as she wished. These actions were necessary preliminaries to her bringing pressure on Britain in the Far East, as they would put her into a position to threaten or invade Malaya should she eventually find such a course was necessary. The appreciation by British Chiefs of Staff that Japan would adopt a step-by-step advance to the south was proving to be right.

*

Sir Robert Brooke-Popham, the new Commander-in-Chief, Far East, arrived in Singapore on 18 November 1940, set up his headquarters at the naval base alongside that of the Far Eastern Intelligence Bureau, and lost no time in letting the Chiefs of Staff have his views on the situation in the Far East. On 7 December he told them that as appeasement would only be interpreted as weakness a policy of firmness should be adopted and closer relations with the Netherlands East Indies, China and Siam developed. He suggested that the British government should make it clear to Japan that, if she attacked the Dutch, she would be involved with Britain, and that China should be encouraged to fight on by providing her with air support, by developing the communications between Burma and China, and by sending a mission to Chunking to establish closer relations with Chiang Kai-shek. Brooke-Popham said that he was considering the plan, already mentioned in the commanders' tactical appreciation, whereby British forces would occupy the southern provinces of Siam on the Kra Isthmus, if Japan, under the guise of affording protection, moved into Siam. This, he said, would offer considerable strategic advantages and was not likely to lead to war, but it would necessitate a larger garrison for Malaya. Since the most potent factor in restraining Japan from further southward aggression was Anglo–American co-operation, he advocated that the firmer tendency towards Japan recently shown by the Americans should be encouraged. Finally, he warned the Chiefs of Staff that the British position in the Far East would be greatly weakened if Japanese forces were moved into southern Indo-China or Siam.

When the Chiefs of Staff met on 13 January 1941 they were faced with a minute from the Prime Minister in which he pointed out that he did not approve of the diversion of forces to the Far East, and that the political situation in that area did not at that time warrant the maintenance there of large forces. In view of this minute, it is of some interest to see what line of thought the Prime Minister had followed in relation to the Far East since the fall of France and the entry of Italy into the war. In September 1940 he had expressed the opinion that the defence of the naval base depended on the British Fleet, and that the fleet in the Mediterranean, which had been strengthened recently, could, if so ordered, reach Singapore quite quickly. Even if the Japanese had landed in Malaya and were in the process of besieging the 'fortress', the fleet would not be deprived of its relieving power. The defence of Singapore had therefore to be based on a local garrison capable of holding the 'fortress' and on the potentialities of sea power. He was not prepared to entertain the idea of holding the whole of Malaya. In his opinion, the Japanese were cautious people, and the danger of a rupture with Japan was, therefore, remote; furthermore they were unlikely to commit a large portion of their fleet so far away from their home waters, for they would have to take account of the American fleet in the Pacific. Therefore, he preferred that all Australian forces available for overseas should be directed to the Middle East rather than to Malaya.[1] Unfortunately he had come to believe that Singapore Island was a veritable fortress, and it seems that he had also failed to grasp the strategic importance of Malaya and the Kra Isthmus to the defence of the naval base. Not until January 1942 was he to realize how fallacious this belief was.

Towards the end of December 1940, in a letter thanking the government of Australia for their offer to send troops to Malaya, the Prime Minister admitted that it would be impossible for the fleet to leave the Mediterranean at that time, unless Britain were to forgo all that had been gained there. Meanwhile, it was necessary to accept the anxieties in the Far East. In his opinion, however, the United States would become Britain's ally, should Japan enter the war, and this would drastically change the balance of naval strength in the Far East. Despite the views expressed by the Defence Conference of October, he went on to say that Britain could not spare aircraft to lie idle in Malaya on the remote chance of an attack by Japan when they should be playing their part in Europe. The broad policy of the British government was to build up as large a fleet, army and air force as possible in the Middle East and keep it in a condition to prosecute a war in that area or to reinforce Singapore should circumstances in the Far East change for the worse.[2]

These views made it clear that at the end of 1940 and for some considerable time to come the dispatch of a fleet to the Far East was not possible, and that the Prime Minister was basing his strategy in that area not on making Malaya so strong that the Japanese would hesitate to attack, but on the policy of sending naval, military and air reinforcements from the Middle East theatre if Japan were to commit an act of war.

*

Even before he sent his first appreciation to the Chiefs of Staff the Commander-in-Chief, Far East, had begun his attempts to coordinate the defences of the Far East with the Dutch, Australians and, if possible, the Americans. Although it had not been decided in London whether Britain would or would not go to the assistance of the Dutch should Japan attack the Netherlands East Indies, the

[1] Winston Churchill, *The Second World War*, Vol. II, pp. 591–2.
[2] Churchill, *The Second World War*, Vol. II, p. 627.

staff conversation with the Dutch, which it had been agreed at the October Defence Conference should be held, took place at Singapore at the end of November. The Dutch announced that, without entering into political commitments, they were prepared to co-operate, and there was a complete exchange of military information. Since combined operations between the British and Dutch air forces appeared to be the only practicable form of co-operation, it was agreed that the area from the Bay of Bengal to the Timor Sea should be divided between the two air forces for reconnaissance purposes. The results of the discussions were sent to London, where they were approved in principle by the British government and the Dutch émigré government. Both governments agreed that a common Anglo-Dutch code should be brought into use, joint facilities organized at certain airfields, liaison officers interchanged, a joint plan for supervising Japanese nationals throughout the area drawn up and put into force, and that Britain should provide arms and equipment for the Netherlands East Indian forces as and when this became possible. It was also agreed that pressure should be brought to bear on the Portuguese government in order to ensure that the Japanese were given no further concessions in Timor.

Early in December 1940 the British and American Chiefs of Staff agreed to hold secret discussions, the outcome of which in March 1941 was the 'ABC1' plan. This plan was based on the premise that should both powers be involved in war, their primary strategic objective would be the defeat of Germany. The United States agreed therefore to increase her naval forces in the Atlantic and the Mediterranean, so that Britain could reinforce her naval forces east of Suez. In the event of Japan going to war with them, the strategy of both powers in the Far East would be purely defensive, the American Pacific Fleet being used to weaken Japanese economy and divert her strength from the south-west Pacific. This plan, though accepted by both governments, did not commit the United States to enter the war against Germany or specify the circumstances in which she might do so. However, it did have the advantage that an agreed strategy was now in being to cover the situation in which the United States might be involved in war with either Germany and Italy, or Japan, or all three powers. Two points need to be noted: first, that the defeat of Germany was the primary object and that the defeat of Japan was only of secondary importance, a fact which was to govern all strategy when the war with Japan did break out; and, second, that, while the move of American naval forces to the western Atlantic reduced the military threat to Japan, it enhanced the importance of curbing her activities by economic means and thereby, as will be seen, affected the course of events in the second half of 1941.

As a follow-up to the Singapore Defence Conference of October and the Anglo–Dutch conversations of November 1940, the Commander-in-Chief, Far East, convened a conference on 22 February 1941, with the object of producing a combined Anglo–Dutch–Australian plan for the defence of the interests common to all three powers. The conference assumed that Japan would not attack either Australia or New Zealand initially, that it was improbable that she would attack Malaya and the Netherlands East Indies simultaneously, but that her most likely course of action would be an attack on Malaya from bases established in Indo-China and Siam. The conference produced what became known as the ADA Agreement. The importance of collective action against Japanese aggression was stressed, as well as the need for a clear understanding of what actions by the Japanese would constitute an act of war. These were defined as: first, an act of war against the territory of any of the associated powers; second, the movement of Japanese forces into any part of Siam west of longitude 100° East or south of latitude 10° North; third, the movement of any large numbers of Japanese warships which from their position and course made it evident that they were making for the east coast of the Kra Isthmus or the east coast of Malaya or had crossed to the south of latitude 6° North between Malaya and the Philippines; and fourth, an attack on the Philippines. A plan for mutual air reinforcement between Australia, the Netherlands East Indies, India and Malaya was drawn up, and the Australians undertook to maintain an air striking force and army units at Darwin in readiness to support the Dutch in Amboina and Timor. It was also agreed that the existing bases in Amboina, north Celebes, and North Borneo were to be held, arrangements made for their reinforcement and for the protection of sea communications in the area.

This agreement went much further than anything accepted up to that time, and was about all that the Commander-in-Chief could have hoped to achieve. The most important point in it was the definition of an act of aggression, but this the Chiefs of Staff refused to accept, saying that a decision to co-operate with the Dutch could only be taken by the British government when Japanese aggression actually took place. This meant that Japan would retain the initiative and be able to choose the moment of aggression. The Australian government felt that the conference had failed to produce a properly co-ordinated naval plan, and requested that a further conference should be held as early as possible to establish such a plan in co-operation with the United States.

The next move came in April, when the Commander-in-Chief, Far East, held a conference of British, American and Dutch commanders and their staffs, attended by Australian, New Zealand and Indian representatives. Their object was to discuss a combined plan in the event of Britain, the United States and the Netherlands East Indies finding themselves at war with Germany, Italy and Japan. The conference agreed that the key to the situation lay in the Philippines, as American submarines and aircraft based on Manila could dispute control of the south-west Pacific. It was assumed therefore that any Japanese assault on Malaya and Borneo would be accompanied by an attempt to capture both Hong Kong and Manila, but it was unlikely that she would take any action of this nature until she had secured complete military and political control over southern Indo-China. It was also assumed that attacks on Burma, Sumatra, Java, Australia and New Zealand would not be attempted until Japanese operations to secure the Philippines (especially Luzon), Hong Kong, Malaya and Borneo had been successfully completed. Events were to show that this was an accurate appreciation of Japan's course of action.

The conference also agreed that, until Britain could build up a fleet in the Indian Ocean, she could only adopt a defensive policy in the Far East. The American delegates expressed the view that Singapore, though of great importance, was not vital and that its loss, though undesirable, could be accepted; they made it clear, however, that they did not expect to be able to hold the Philippines for long against a determined attack and anticipated having to withdraw from the whole of the Philippine archipelago.

The conference recommended that the American Asiatic Fleet, based on Manila and Hong Kong, should operate against the flank of any Japanese southward advance, while the American Pacific Fleet, based on Hawaii, should operate against Japanese communications with the mandated Pacific Islands and endeavour to support British naval forces east of Australia and New Guinea. Another recommendation was that the British Commander-in-Chief, China Station, should have unified control over all the naval forces of the associated powers in the eastern theatre, other than those operating under the Commander-in-Chief, US Asiatic Fleet, but that part of this fleet should come under his orders at the beginning of hostilities and the remainder under his strategic direction when Manila became untenable. The strategic direction of the air forces of the associated powers should be exercised by the British Air Commander-in-Chief, Far East; the Dutch military forces should defend the Netherlands East Indies, but their naval and air forces should be made available as necessary to reinforce the British; and the Australians should reinforce Amboina and Dutch Timor. The conference finally reiterated the views expressed by the ADA conference on what should be considered as constituting an act of hostility on the part of the Japanese. These recommendations became known as the ADB Agreement.

The Chiefs of Staff accepted the recommendations of the conference with two exceptions: Hong Kong, they said, was more of a liability than an asset and could not be considered as an advanced base for the US Asiatic Fleet, and they again refused to agree that any specific Japanese move should be considered as a *casus belli*, on the grounds that, until the United States clarified their action on the outbreak of war in the Far East, it was inadvisable to do so. The American Chiefs of Staff, however, rejected the recommendations out of hand, for they disliked both its political and strategical implications. They thought that its acceptance might lead to their Asiatic Fleet, when placed under the command of the British, being deployed in waters which were of no strategic value to the United States and that the proposed dispositions of the British naval forces would give insufficient support for that fleet. The conference therefore failed in its object.

Immediately after it, further conversations were held to clarify matters which had arisen as a result of the ADA conference held in February 1941. A plan, later the basis of a plan known as PLENAPS, was drawn up for use in an emergency which defined the distribution of, and the operational areas for, the British and Dutch naval and air forces. Thus it was that by the end of April 1941 an Anglo–Dutch plan was in existence but, although the Americans knew of it, they were not prepared to undertake any agreed role in the Far East.

*

The wide divergence of opinion over British strategy in the Far East between the Prime Minister and the Chiefs of Staff, which had begun in 1940, continued during the following year. At the end of April the Prime Minister, in a directive dealing with the reinforcement of the Middle East, reaffirmed his view that Japan would be unlikely to enter the war unless Germany successfully invaded Britain, which was by that date extremely unlikely, and that even if the Middle East were lost she would not necessarily act. He felt there was no need to make any further arrangements to improve the defences of Singapore and Malaya beyond those already in progress. His views, he said, were to be accepted by the Services as a guide and should they cease to be valid his Ministers would be responsible for notifying the Services in good time.[1]

After considering the Prime Minister's directive, the Chiefs of Staff, in a reply sent early in May, emphasized that 'good time' when dealing with the Far East would be at least three months, since that was the shortest period in which reinforcements could possibly reach Malaya.[2] In the course of correspondence between the Chief of the Imperial General Staff (Field-Marshal Sir John Dill) and the Prime Minister, the former pointed out that it had always been an accepted principle that in the last resort the security of Singapore should come before that of Egypt, but that the defences of Singapore were still considerably below standard. While calculated risks had to be taken in war, the error of whittling away the security of vital points had to be avoided. If the need arose Britain would have to cut her losses in areas which were not vital before it was too late.[3] In reply, the Prime Minister said that the defence of Singapore required only a fraction of the troops required in the Middle East; but that he had already stated the political data upon which the defence of Singapore should be based, namely, that the United States would probably come into the war as an ally, but in any case Japan would not be likely to 'besiege' Singapore at the outset of a war since such an operation would be far more dangerous to her and less harmful to Britain than sending her naval forces to raid the Eastern trade routes.[4] While agreeing with the Prime Minister that Singapore required only a fraction of the troops required in the Middle East, Dill then pointed out that the small addition required to the garrison of Singapore would scarcely affect the strength of the Middle East defences. Prophetically he added that if Britain were to wait until an emergency arose in the Far East, she would be too late.[5] Churchill did not heed Dill's plea, and, as he has himself said, his views prevailed and the flow of reinforcements to the Middle East continued unabated.

[1] J. R. M. Butler, *Grand Strategy*, Vol. II, pp. 77–78.   [2] Ibid., p. 579.
[3] Churchill, *The Second World War*, Vol. III, p. 375.   [4] Ibid., p. 376.
[5] Butler, *Grand Strategy*, Vol. II, p. 581.

8

Events in Malaya

November 1940–April 1941 Map B, p. 12

While talks continued in London, in Malaya Sir Robert Brooke-Popham, the new Commander-in-Chief, Far East, reacted quickly to the problems of the defence of the naval base, the unhappy situation which existed among the members of the War Committee and between the Services, and the general lack of drive in preparing the country for war which this had caused.

When Brooke-Popham assumed command on 18 November 1940, Bond had his forces disposed with two brigades on Singapore Island, 12th Indian Brigade group in the vicinity of Mersing, 11th Indian Division (6th and 8th Brigades only) around Alor Star in north Malaya, and two unbrigaded battalions at Penang and Taiping. These dispositions clearly showed that it was his intention to hold the whole of the peninsula, if adequate reinforcements were forthcoming. Although the air force still consisted of only some ninety partly obsolescent aircraft, mainly located on Singapore Island, arrangements were being made to receive reinforcing squadrons in 1941. Little more could be done until both army and air reinforcements arrived.

During 1941, however, the strength of the garrison was to be increased considerably. The promised Australian brigade group was due to reach Singapore in February 1941 but, before it left Australia, the General Staff there came to the conclusion that the staff of a brigade was insufficient to handle an Australian force in an overseas theatre. It was therefore decided that Major-General H. Gordon Bennett, the commander of 8th Australian Division, should be sent to Malaya to set up an Australian headquarters. He arrived by air with a skeleton staff on 4 February, and 22nd Australian Brigade Group following by sea arrived on the 18th. General Bond arranged that the Australian headquarters should be set up at Kuala Lumpur and that the brigade be deployed in the Port Dickson–Seremban area, some two hundred miles north of Singapore. Thus Bennett found himself in the peculiar position of commanding a division, one brigade of which was in Malaya, a second at Port Darwin (in readiness to reinforce Amboina and Timor) and a third in New South Wales. It was intended at that time, however, that an Indian formation should relieve 22nd Brigade and that 8th Australian Division, less its brigade at Port Darwin, should be concentrated in the Middle

71

East. Bennett was far from being satisfied with the position in which he found himself, for it was clear to him that in the event of war his one brigade would be used to reinforce 11th Indian Division, and that he would be left with nothing to command. At the end of February the Australian Deputy Chief of Staff, who was in Malaya on a visit, told him that he must either arrange with Malaya Command to let him have a specific area to command or, failing that, return to Australia and take command of the greater part of his division. Early in March, Bennett reacted by asking that a second brigade, a machine-gun battalion and a pioneer battalion should be sent to Malaya, and that his staff be strengthened. Initially his request was turned down, but towards the end of the month Army Headquarters in Australia arranged for the whole of his divisional staff, with some administrative and base units, to join him. The build-up of an Australian force had begun.

Meanwhile, the Chiefs of Staff had arranged with India that 9th Indian Division, less its artillery, should be sent to Malaya by March or April 1941. Unfortunately, just as the division was embarking, a crisis developed in Iraq and one of its brigades had to be diverted there, leaving the division with only 15th and 22nd Indian Brigades. It seemed, therefore, that by the end of April Bond would almost have the twenty-six battalions, the minimum he had asked for on the assumption that the air force would be built up to a first-line strength of 336 aircraft. Arrangements were already in hand to send five artillery regiments from the United Kingdom before the end of 1941, thus increasing the scale of supporting artillery to one regiment per Indian brigade, and to provide an anti-tank regiment for Malaya.

*

Brooke-Popham, who became an *ex officio* member of the War Committee, quickly sized up the position, which he found had not been exaggerated by either Noble or Layton. He found an early opportunity of taking Vlieland to task over his unwillingness to co-operate with Bond, making it plain that his sympathies were entirely with Bond and that Vlieland's task was to confine himself strictly to organizing such civil measures as were considered necessary and to avoid interfering in matters which were properly those of the Services. The Governor, Sir Shenton Thomas, returned from his eight months' leave in December 1940 and resumed the chairmanship of the War Committee, but the previous pattern of its deliberations was not resumed. The reasons for this would appear to be that the presence of a very senior air force officer as Commander-in-Chief, Far

East, reduced Air Vice-Marshal Babington's power as a member of the Committee, and that the Governor had been briefed during his stay in the United Kingdom on Britain's strategic position. He was now aware that it was the Chiefs' of Staff intention to hold the whole of Malaya, to rely on air power to keep the Japanese at a distance, and to send reinforcements, all matters which he himself had advocated.

Shortly after the Governor's return from leave, Brooke-Popham asked him to remove Vlieland from the post of Secretary for Defence on the grounds of lack of confidence and threatened to resign if no action was taken on his request. Then, backed by Bond and Layton, he charged Vlieland at a War Committee meeting with consistently refusing to co-operate with Bond and with deliberately using delaying tactics over the initiation of measures necessary for the defence of the civil population. Instead of going to Vlieland's aid as in the past, Thomas sat silent throughout the meeting and did not support him. Next day Vlieland tendered his resignation as Secretary for Defence and then asked to be allowed to resign from the Malayan Civil Service. Both requests were granted, and he returned to the United Kingdom in February 1941. When he left, Mr C. W. Dawson was appointed secretary of the War Committee.

In preparation for the Anglo–Australian–Dutch Conference in February, Brooke-Popham had attended a meeting of the Australian War Cabinet, where he made some surprising statements. They were told that he expected Hong Kong would be able to hold out for some four months against a Japanese attack, although the Leased Territories on the mainland would have had to be abandoned shortly after the outbreak of hostilities; and that, in Malaya, Singapore Island would be held even if the Japanese succeeded in occupying Johore. He went on to express the view that Japanese aircraft were not very efficient, that the Japanese were not air minded, and that the air force in Malaya would be able to inflict sufficient damage on them to prevent the RAF squadrons from being put out of action. He based the last statement on the belief that the American Brewster Buffalo fighters, with which the new fighter squadrons for Malaya were to be equipped, would prove to be more efficient than any Japanese fighter; a belief which later proved wrong. Neither the Australian War Cabinet nor their Chiefs of Staff were as confident as Brooke-Popham; indeed the Australian Chiefs of Staff warned that events pointed to Japan having already made up her mind to control Indo-China and Siam, and urged that any Japanese movement into southern Siam in strength should be treated as a *casus belli*. To this

Brooke-Popham agreed, saying that any such movement would justify retaliation.

The Australians clearly were not prepared to accept Brooke-Popham's palpably over-optimistic statements. They knew that the Chiefs of Staff considered Hong Kong more of a liability than an asset and could see that Singapore Island, with no prepared defences on the landward side, could not hold out for long once Johore was in enemy hands. The only effect of Sir Robert's statements was to undermine Australia's confidence in the ability of the British forces to hold the Far East.

In April the British military attaché in Tokyo (Colonel G. T. Wards) visited both Hong Kong and Malaya, and, while he was in Singapore, was asked to give a lecture to the officers of the Singapore garrison on the Japanese army, a subject he was competent to speak on since he had studied it at close quarters for some time both in Japan and China, and had taken part in some of its manœuvres and exercises. He told his audience that he rated it as a first-class fighting machine and emphasized the extreme physical fitness of the Japanese troops, their marching prowess, their ability to move by day or night and find the way about in difficult country despite obstacles, the efficiency of the unit and sub-unit commanders, especially in the infantry, which made them capable of fighting in close country, and the fanatical patriotism of all ranks and their readiness (amounting almost to a desire) to die fighting rather than to face the disgrace of being taken prisoner. He also pointed out that the Japanese General Staff consisted of a body of highly trained, conscientious and hardy officers, second to none in their keenness, *esprit de corps* and ability to handle large formations over immense distances. He went on to say that during his stay in Singapore he had found that, in the formations and units he had visited, it was generally believed that the Japanese never operated by night, that they were poor mechanics, drivers and air pilots and that, as their expeditionary force appeared unable to beat the grossly inefficient Chinese armies, it was ridiculous to consider them as any danger to Malaya. These views, he stressed, were wholly false and highly dangerous. He ended by drawing attention to the Japanese passion for secrecy and also for collecting information about others, and observed that, whereas the British in Malaya knew little about Japanese military matters, the Japanese were bound to have a very detailed knowledge of British strength and dispositions in Malaya—a statement which it is now known was only too true.

However, at the end of the lecture, the General Officer Commanding, General Bond, rose to say that, '. . . while the lecturer has told you that the Japanese army is very efficient and that the Japanese know all about us in Singapore, this is far from the truth. . . . What the lecturer has told you is his own opinion and is in no way a correct appreciation of the situation. I will now tell you that every morning the telegrams which the Japanese Consul-General sends to his government in Tokyo are placed on my office table and from these I know exactly what the Japanese are up to and just how much or how little they know about us. If this is the best that the Japanese can do, I do not think much of them and you can take it from me that we have nothing to fear from them.'

These remarks were received with accord, and the meeting broke up. The lecturer was so astounded that he stopped Bond before he could leave the room and said that, with due respect, he was quite certain that he had in no way exaggerated the efficiency of the army which British troops might soon have to meet in battle. He regretted profoundly that Bond disagreed with his views and that to under-estimate one's enemy was highly dangerous. The gist of Bond's reply was that 'we must not discourage the chaps and we must keep their spirits up'.

Why did both Brooke-Popham and Bond so underestimate the value of the Japanese army? The reason must lie in the intelligence reports they received from the Far Eastern Intelligence Bureau and from the Intelligence Departments of the Services in London, who based their views mainly on information received from China, where Japanese troops were in contact with the Chinese. Their observers there consistently underrated the Japanese, whom they judged incapable of overcoming the very inefficient Chinese forces. They failed to realize that, whenever or wherever it suited the Japanese to advance and occupy areas, such as north China and the Yangtse Valley, they swept everything before them, but that the immensity of the country and the limitations on the number of troops employed made it impossible to conquer the whole country.

There is, however, another factor to be taken into account—that of local opinion in Malaya. Japan had failed to attack when war broke out in 1939 and she had not taken an obvious opportunity of attacking when Britain was at her weakest immediately after the fall of France; thus, as the months rolled by, it began to be felt that the danger from Japan was over.

*

Early in 1941 the Commander-in-Chief, Far East, came to the conclusion that neither Air Vice-Marshal Babington nor General

Bond was capable of carrying the responsibilities of his command. Babington was due to be relieved in the normal course of events in April, but Bond had not yet come to the end of his normal tour of duty. Brooke-Popham, therefore, in March 1941, asked the War Office to replace Bond as soon as possible. On 24 April Babington was succeeded by Air Vice-Marshal C. W. H. Pulford, and on 14 May Lieutenant-General A. E. Percival replaced Bond.

The departure of Vlieland, and of Bond and Babington in April and May 1941, three of the main actors on the Malayan stage, provides a convenient opportunity to review the period from September 1939, when the European war broke out. Enough has already been said to show how much precious time had been wasted during those nineteen months and how little real preparation had been made to render Malaya fit to withstand invasion. The reason why these vital months were so largely wasted can be summed up in the words used by St Paul, 'If the trumpet give an uncertain sound, who shall prepare himself to the battle?' The uncertain sound of the Malayan trumpet was due primarily to three factors: first, the colonial administration had been given two tasks by London—the production of the maximum amount of dollar-earning raw materials, which in the circumstances in which Britain found herself had to be given first priority, and, at the same time, the preparation of the country to withstand invasion—tasks which to the authorities in Malaya appeared to be conflicting; second, that, since Britain's naval, army and air strength was insufficient to defend her world-wide interests, the Far East took bottom place in the order of priority for troops and equipment; and third, that the organization of, and the clash of personalities within, the War Committee stifled all initiative in the task of preparing the country for war.

*

From September 1939 onwards the Europeans and the upper strata of the Malay, Chinese and Indian communities were only too anxious to assist in the British war effort, or to play their part in any defence measures which the authorities deemed necessary, provided that the reasons for such measures were explained to them. What they required was a clear lead, but this they did not get, except in so far as the production of rubber and tin was concerned. Nevertheless, all nationalities and classes made generous financial contributions to various war funds. Cash contributions to the British Treasury made by the Straits Settlements and Malaya between September 1939 and December 1941 amounted to some seventeen million pounds, which was more than two-thirds of all the contributions made by the Colonial Empire. Of this sum one million pounds was voluntarily subscribed to a Bomber Fund and to the Malayan Patriotic Fund designed to raise money for the British Red Cross and other war charitable organizations, the bulk being contributed by Chinese residents in Malaya. All nationalities gave voluntary service freely: a Local Defence Corps, a Corps of Air Raid Wardens, an Air Observation Corps, an Auxiliary Fire Service, a Medical Auxiliary Service and other forces were raised and staffed by volunteers, including women. These organizations began in the Straits Settlements and were eventually extended throughout Malaya, but their strength was inadequate, they lacked essential equipment, and consequently their training was insufficient for the tasks which they would inevitably have to face.

9

The Road to War

April–December 1941 *Map A, pp. 4–5*

The road which the Japanese followed towards war between April and December 1941 and the British and American reactions to the various steps they took during that period must now be described. The period can be divided into three distinct phases: the first from April to July, when Japan was still trying to gain her goal without recourse to war and went ahead with her plans to gain complete control over Indo-China and Siam, plans which she had hesitated to put into effect earlier in the year. The second, which began at the end of July, was when, as a result of her occupation of southern Indo-China, Britain, the United States and the Netherlands froze her assets; this lasted until October, when she decided that she had to face war with Britain and the United States rather than abandon her plans for southward expansion. The final phase was when, having committed herself to war, she had to await the right moment to launch her offensives.

By the middle of April 1941 the Japanese Foreign Minister, Matsuoka, had succeeded in obtaining Russia's signature to the Neutrality Pact, which gave a considerable degree of security to Japan's vulnerable Manchurian flank, and the Japanese government had refused to be dragooned by Germany into making an immediate attack on Singapore. Clearly the moment had come for her to review her future policy. Although she had failed in her attempts to gain economic control of the Netherlands East Indies and to bring that area within the Co-Prosperity Sphere, she had made considerable progress in her plans to control Indo-China and Siam. She now had to judge whether, with her Manchurian frontier temporarily secure and Admiral Nomura installed at Washington, she could safely go ahead with her plans to absorb southern Indo-China and thereby hasten her southward advance. On 16 April, three days after the signing of the Neutrality Pact, it was decided in Tokyo that the plan to gain control of the Southern Region should be proceeded with, but, since the navy was not in a position to sustain a long war and still remained doubtful whether war with Britain and the United States could be prosecuted successfully, there should be no recourse to war unless Britain, the United States and the Netherlands threatened her by encirclement or by the imposition of further commercial embargoes.

Then suddenly a number of events happened which entirely

altered the situation. On 17 June the Yoshizawa mission was with-drawn from the Netherlands East Indies without having obtained any of the additional oil supplies or any of the concessions which Japan had demanded. (*See page 61*.) On the 20th, because of domestic shortages, the United States placed an embargo on the export of oil from the American eastern seaboard, except to Britain and certain other countries in the Western Hemisphere.

On 22 June Germany invaded Russia. To Japan, the German invasion of Russia came as a complete surprise and something of an blow to her pride, as Hitler had given no inkling of his plans. There were three courses Japan could now follow: she could join Germany and, despite the recently signed Neutrality Pact, attack Russia; she could dissolve the Tripartite Pact and strike a bargain with the United States in return for her neutrality; or she could take advan-tage of the fact that her Manchurian frontier was far more effectively guarded by Russian involvement in the west than by the Neutrality Pact and press on with her aims in the Southern Region. The decision, as always, lay with the Services: the army leaders, with large forces already in a position of stalemate in the interior of China, were not at all anxious to get involved in another continental war in the vast areas of Siberia; the navy leaders knew that war with Russia would not solve their problem of obtaining oil and raw materials for Japanese industry, and feared that involvement with Russia would not only give the United States and Britain the oppor-tunity to diminish even more the flow of essential resources to Japan, but would also give them more time to strengthen their defences in the Southern Region. On 25 June it was decided at a Liaison Con-ference between *Imperial General Headquarters* and the Cabinet that Japan, while adhering to the Tripartite Pact, would not join with Germany in an attack on Russia, at least for the time being, and that she would press ahead without delay with her plans to gain military control over southern Indo-China, if necessary using force.

The Japanese Government now began to place the country on a war footing, while their armed forces began to prepare their plans for an offensive drive into the Southern Region. Yet despite the definite character of these preparations, both *Imperial General Headquarters* and the Cabinet wished diplomatic conversations to continue with the United States until the outcome of the German invasion of Russia was clearer and the occupation of southern Indo-China had been completed.

On 21 July the Vichy French Government notified Japan that it had no alternative but to submit to the Japanese demand to occupy

French Indo-China. Three days later President Roosevelt proposed that Indo-China should be considered as a neutral country from which Japan could obtain all the food and raw materials that she required. Japan ignored this proposal, and by the end of July her troops had occupied the whole of southern Indo-China. The President riposted on 26 July by freezing all Japanese assets, thus bringing all commercial transactions between the two countries to an end. Despite the fact that Britain had no assurance of American military support should the stopping of all trade drive the Japanese into military action against British possessions in the Far East, she immediately followed suit by giving notice of the termination of all existing trade treaties with Japan. On 28 July the Dutch, although without any assurance of British or American support, bravely followed them and took similar action.

Japan now held bases from which she could attack the Philippines, Borneo and Malaya at short notice, with comparative ease and without running too great military risks. On 31 July a message from the new Japanese Foreign Minister, Teijiro Toyoda, to his Ambassador in Berlin was intercepted and decoded. In it he said that the economic position resulting from the actions taken by the United States, Britain and the Netherlands would become so serious that it could not be endured for long, and that immediate steps would have to be taken to break asunder the chain of encirclement which was being woven around her. From this message it should have been evident that the storm would break in the comparatively near future.

*

By attacking Russia, Germany greatly relieved the pressure on Britain, but this had a most unfortunate effect on Britain's preparations for the defence of her position in the Far East. Britain was now not alone in her struggle against Germany, but she could not afford to see her unlikely new ally defeated, as at first seemed to be possible, and felt it incumbent on her to give Russia such aid as was in her power. The only aid she could offer was in materials, and a considerable proportion of American aid in the form of weapons and equipment as well as of British production was therefore diverted to Russia and sent by the perilous sea route to Archangel; incidentally adding yet another burden to the already overstrained British navy. The Prime Minister decided that Britain's priorities were now: firstly, the defence of the United Kingdom and the defeat of the U-boat threat to the Atlantic trade route; secondly, the support of the campaign in the Middle East theatre and the Mediterranean; thirdly, the dispatch of supplies to Russia; and lastly, the defence of British possessions in the Far East. A sidelight on the Prime Minister's views is provided by the report given to the Australian government by Robert Menzies on his return in June 1941 from a visit to London. He said that he found in London a considerable amount of complacency regarding defence in the Far East and the Pacific, and that the Prime Minister was inclined to dismiss from his mind problems of defence the further they were from the heart of the Empire in London.

*

The second phase in Japan's road towards war began at the end of July. It was now evident that the freezing of her assets by the United States, Britain and the Netherlands, which had followed her occupation of Indo-China, would soon severely affect Japanese industry, as the stockpiles which had been built up over the previous decade would now have to be used.

At the end of the month another Liaison Conference was held in Tokyo; as usual this was dominated by the Services. The Imperial Navy representatives, who had always been very anxious to avoid war with the United States, now changed their attitude. To them the supply of oil was the vital factor. By April 1941, as a result of over-buying over a number of years, some 49 million barrels of oil had been put into reserve, of which the greater part was held for naval purposes. From August onwards it would be necessary to draw on these reserves, which the navy estimated would last for only two years of war even with such supplies as could be obtained from the Netherlands East Indies after their capture. Unless imports of oil were resumed rapidly, Japan would inevitably find herself facing an economic collapse, and the longer the delay in obtaining fresh supplies, the less would be her chances of success if she embarked on war. There were, therefore, only two courses which she could take: either to begin negotiating to get the trade embargoes lifted without delay, or to go to war and seize the oilfields in the Netherlands East Indies. The navy preferred negotiations to war, but was prepared to fight if negotiations did not bring speedy results. The army, however, refused to countenance any agreement with Britain and the United States which would in any way interfere with Japan's freedom of action to move southwards or against Russia, and was thus in favour of abandoning the negotiations in Washington and making war.

Prince Konoye, the Prime Minister, was himself anxious to avoid

G

81

war, and welcomed the fact that the navy proposed speedy negotiations with Washington. He therefore sent a Note to the United States on 6 August, so couched that it appeared to be a reply to Washington's Note of 21 June about the talks with Nomura early that year. Konoye demanded that all trade restrictions on Japan should be removed, that American aid to China and to British and Dutch garrisons in the Far East should cease, as should all American defensive preparations in the Philippines, and that the United States government should agree to Japan having permanent preferential economic and political status in Indo-China. The only *quid pro quo* offered was that Japan would neither move nor maintain troops in any area in the south-west Pacific other than Indo-China. On 8 August Nomura was told that the Japanese Note showed little willingness to meet the American proposals of 21 June, since there was only one concession offered.

With Japan's reserves of oil diminishing daily, the time available to find a diplomatic solution and to avoid war was rapidly running out. On 8 August Konoye proposed that he should meet the President in an urgent endeavour to find a means of saving the situation. The United States, while not refusing to countenance such a meeting, replied that, until preliminary discussions had been held to define more precisely the fundamental questions on which agreement could be sought, such a meeting would have little point.

Konoye's failure to obtain agreement to a meeting and the lack of progress in the diplomatic field brought about a demand by both the army and navy for a decision to go to war before the cessation of trade began to sap Japan's power. This led to another Liaison Conference early in September, and a compromise was reached to the effect that a time limit should be set for the diplomatic discussions to produce results, but that all plans for hostilities should be completed without delay. This solution was submitted to an Imperial Conference on 6 September, and it was confirmed that the navy and army would complete their preparations for war by the end of October. Meanwhile, diplomatic discussions with the United States would proceed with the idea of obtaining agreement to Japanese demands, which were to be similar to those of 6 August, with the exception that they would be modified by an undertaking not to use Indo-China as a base for operations other than against China, and that, if these discussions did not bear fruit by the end of October, the decision to go to war at the appropriate moment would then be taken. The navy and army felt justified in forcing the issue, since they were convinced that diplomatic conversations would produce no solution, and that weather conditions for a southward advance and for the delivery of an attack on Pearl Harbor were favourable only till the end of December. They also felt that it was essential for the oilfields in the Netherlands East Indies to be occupied at the earliest possible moment and all their southern conquests (which included the capture of Singapore) to be completed before the spring of 1942 made it possible for Russia to attack the *Kwantung Army* in Manchuria. A time limit to the diplomatic discussions had now been set.

On 24 September *Imperial General Headquarters* demanded that a decision on war or peace should be taken by the middle of October, and three days later in Washington Nomura submitted a Note which was in effect a redraft of previous Notes. On 2 October the United States reiterated her willingness for a meeting between the heads of state, provided that some agreement could first be reached on the principles on which a real settlement could be built, but pointed out that the Japanese proposals as they stood could not be accepted as a basis of negotiation.

With the Japanese Cabinet unable to make any radical changes in the national policy and with the United States unprepared to mortgage the long-term future by agreeing to the Japanese terms, there was now no real hope of any settlement satisfactory to both parties being reached. Konoye, anxious to avoid committing the country to a war which might well end in defeat, felt that his only course of action was to resign, and did so on 16 October. He was replaced as Prime Minister by General Hidaki Tojo, who had been the Minister for War in his Cabinet, and Shigenori Togo became Foreign Minister. The military had now taken absolute control in Japan, and war was inevitable.

*

The British and American reactions to Japan's actions now deserve examination. Late in July 1941 the President intimated that he would like to meet the British Prime Minister, and it was arranged that they meet in Newfoundland on 9 August. During the course of their conversations the two men discussed the Japanese Note of 6 August. The President explained that, although the Japanese conditions were entirely unacceptable, he was prepared to continue negotiations, since by so doing he could gain time (a month or possibly longer) to improve the defences in the Far East, a clear indication that he expected war with Japan in the comparatively near future. At Churchill's request he agreed to include in his reply to the Japanese a statement that the British and American governments were acting in close accord and a warning that, if there were any more encroachments by Japan, a situation would be produced in which the United States would have to take counter-measures even though these might lead the two countries into war. Fearing that the State Department would try to tone down the warning, which the Prime Minister considered to be the vital part of the President's reply, Churchill extracted an undertaking from Roosevelt that he would insert the warning in the agreed wording. He did this because he felt confident that the Japanese would hesitate if they realized they were facing a combined Anglo–American front. Unfortunately, when the reply was handed to Nomura on 17 August, the State Department had so toned down the warning that it had little force and entirely failed to show a combined front to the Japanese.

One may well ask why Roosevelt failed to keep his undertaking to Churchill. The President was facing certain constitutional difficulties: as Commander-in-Chief of the American armed forces and Chief Executive he could conduct a war, but he was unable to commit the United States to war—only Congress could do that. Opinion in the United States was not ready in August 1941 to intervene in the European war or to get involved in war with Japan; so hesitant was it that the repeal of the Neutrality Act, which might well have led to fighting in the Atlantic between American and German vessels, was passed in the United States Senate by only a very small majority, and another bill which authorized compulsory military service and the expansion of the American army was passed in the House of Representatives by only a single vote. The President could advance only as fast as public opinion would permit, and, as he could not allow it to be said that the British were trying to drag the country into war, he had to move cautiously.

Sir Robert Craigie, the British Ambassador to Japan, had warned the Foreign Office during August that a further southward advance by Japan was impending. This could only be read as an indication that an attack on either Malaya or the Netherlands East Indies was a distinct possibility. This warning, coming on top of those received through the intercepted diplomatic messages, was one that should not have been ignored.

*

The final phase in Japan's road to war began with the fall of the Konoye Cabinet and its replacement by the Tojo Cabinet. Tojo examined the position with the Services in the latter half of October and soon realized that both the army and navy wished Japan to go to war before she was weakened by the cessation of imports. At an Imperial Conference held on 5 November it was agreed that all military plans should be perfected by 1 December, and that the final decision when to go to war would be taken on 25 November, if no agreement had been reached with the United States by that date. Meanwhile, Japan's final proposals should be submitted in Washington. These final proposals were to be in two parts, called Plan 'A' and Plan 'B'. Plan 'A' said that provided the United States forced Chiang Kai-shek to make peace with Japan by threatening to withdraw all support unless he did so, Japan would within two years of the restoration of peace withdraw all her troops from China except from Hainan, north China and Mongolia (where they would remain for twenty-five years), and also from Indo-China as soon as peace with China had been brought about.

Plan 'B', which was to be submitted only if the United States refused to accept Plan 'A', was drawn up with the idea that it would permit Japan, Britain, the United States and the Netherlands to avoid war while remaining in complete disagreement in the Pacific. It proposed that Japan and the United States should agree not to take any military action in any part of South-East Asia other than Indo-China; if the plan were accepted, Japan would not only remove her troops from southern Indo-China, but also from the whole of Indo-China as soon as peace had been established with China or an equitable peace throughout the Pacific had been agreed. In return for these concessions on the part of Japan, the United States was to restore the commercial relations with Japan which had existed before 26 July, and to co-operate with Japan to enable both countries to obtain all that they required in goods and commodities from the Netherlands East Indies. No mention was made of the Tripartite Pact.

Plan 'A' was received in Washington on 7 November. Well aware from intercepted messages that Japan's diplomatic actions were by then limited to a date in November, the United States rejected the plan, and on the 15th told Nomura that the American government was not prepared to consider any representations couched in the form of an ultimatum. Nomura now saw that war, with its probable serious consequences for his country, was wellnigh inevitable and on 18 November suggested to both the Japanese and American governments that a solution lay in an agreement under which Japan withdrew her troops from southern Indo-China in return for the raising of the commercial embargoes (that is, a return to the pre-July position). Nomura was told in Washington that his proposal was worth discussion, but Tokyo told him that only the acceptance of Plan 'B' would satisfy Japan; the date for the deadline was however put forward to 29 November. Numura therefore presented Plan 'B' on the 20th.

The United States realized that she could not accept Plan 'B' without giving way on the fundamental principles for which she had always stood. Furthermore, the plan left Japan a full member of the Tripartite Pact and thus a potential enemy to both Britain and themselves, and contained no pledge that Japan would pursue a peaceful course in South-East Asia in the future. Nothing therefore could be gained by accepting it, and so on the 26th Nomura was told that it was unacceptable. At the same time he was given counter-proposals similar to those of 21 June.

In Tokyo an Imperial Conference was held on 27 November, at which Tojo made it clear that Japanese requirements could not be met by diplomatic means and said that, since from the standpoint of military strategy and national power it was inadvisable to delay any further, there was no alternative to war. This view was accepted and the next day all Japanese military and naval commanders were told that they were to take warlike action on 8 December.

*

It is of interest to consider the reactions of the British and American governments to the Japanese actions during this third phase in 1941. Although Churchill still held the view that a Japanese attack on Malaya was unlikely, the fact that the Konoye government fell and was replaced by one which was clearly under the complete control of the military caused him to ask the Admiralty about the feasibility of sending one capital ship and an aircraft-carrier to the Far East. The Admiralty, holding to the views they had expressed in August, replied that Japan would not be deterred by the presence of one modern British capital ship, as she could easily afford to detach four of her modern ships to protect a southward advance. However, a larger number of capital ships in the Indian Ocean, even though some were obsolescent, would force the Japanese to detach the greater part of their fleet to cover an advance to the south, and this move would lay them open to attack by the American Pacific Fleet.

Supported by the Foreign Office, who pointed out that the arrival of a modern British capital ship at Singapore would have a considerable political effect, the Prime Minister expressed the opinion that a powerful and fast striking force should be sent at once to the Far East to act as an effective deterrent to Japan. He proposed that the *Prince of Wales* (one of the three modern capital ships) should be dispatched, since in his opinion the main danger in the Far East lay in raids by fast Japanese warships on the trade routes, against which the obsolescent fleet proposed by the Admiralty would be useless. At a meeting of the Defence Committee on 20 October the Admiralty agreed as a compromise measure to send the *Prince of Wales* to Cape Town, where its advent would have considerable publicity value. A decision on the battleship's eventual destination could be taken on her arrival. Meanwhile the battle-cruiser *Repulse*, on convoy escort duty, had arrived in Durban on 3 October and had sailed on to Ceylon.

Despite this compromise agreement, an Admiralty signal was sent to all concerned on 21 October to the effect that the *Prince of Wales* would shortly be leaving for Singapore. The *Repulse*, which was on the way to Ceylon, was then ordered to accompany the *Prince of Wales* to Singapore. The Admiralty insisted, however, on the dispatch of the aircraft-carrier *Indomitable* (already earmarked for the Eastern Fleet) to provide a balanced squadron. Unfortunately, she ran aground on 3 November in Kingston Harbour in Jamaica, and had to be docked for repairs. It would appear that the Prime Minister, despite opposition from the Admiralty based on naval strategic and tactical factors, used political pressure to force the Admiralty to put his plan into action.

Owing to the unfortunate accident to the *Indomitable*, the *Prince of Wales* and the *Repulse* (the former flying the flag of the Commander-in-Chief designate, Eastern Fleet, Admiral Sir Tom Phillips) arrived at Singapore on 2 December without any carrier-borne air cover, and at a time when the RAF in Malaya was still far below the minimum strength deemed necessary for the defence of Malaya. The fact that the Admiralty's views were overruled resulted in two of Britain's best capital ships being hostages to fortune at Singapore, the moment Japan began hostilities. Japan's naval and air strength was quite adequate to neutralize the two ships and, owing to the weakness of the RAF in Malaya, the naval base did not offer them a safe refuge. Phillips's only prudent course of action, should war break out, would have been to withdraw as rapidly as possible from Singapore to become, as the Admiralty had always wished, the nucleus of an Eastern Fleet capable of retaining command of the Indian Ocean. Thus, in retrospect, Churchill can be considered to have committed a grave error of judgment. It would have been to Britain's advantage had he left the decisions on naval strategy in the hands of his professional advisers.

Beyond the dispatch of the naval squadron to Singapore, Britain took no action between October and December 1941 to strengthen her defences in the Far East, and the Prime Minister and the Chiefs of Staff may well be considered guilty of unjustified complacency. There were, however, a number of reasons which might explain why nothing was done in these fateful months. So long as the government gave priority to both predominance in the Middle East and aid for Russia before security in the Far East, the Air Ministry could not find the additional aircraft for Malaya. The War Office could take military reinforcements (including tanks, of which there were none in Malaya) only from the Middle East; moreover there was a desperate shortage of shipping and it was thought at the time that all formations in that theatre were required for the offensive to be launched in November with the object of relieving Tobruk. Furthermore, on the outbreak of war between Germany and Russia, the Japanese had mobilized their army in Manchuria, sending five hundred thousand men and an additional division to bring the army in that country to its full strength of fourteen divisions. The British Intelligence Service had therefore come to the erroneous conclusion that Japan was preparing to attack Russia from Manchuria with a force of twenty-nine divisions and that the continuation of their southward advance would be postponed at least until the late spring of 1942—a view which they held until mid-November 1941, when Japanese preparations for an attack on Malaya became patently obvious.

The Prime Minister and the Chiefs of Staff knew that defence in the Far East was inadequate and could be improved only by taking risks elsewhere. They were, it seems, prepared to risk the security of Singapore, which they had always said was vital to British interests, largely because they could not bring themselves to believe that the Japanese would risk involving themselves in a war with Britain and the United States which could end only in their defeat, or would be prepared to undertake operations in the Southern Region so long as the American Pacific Fleet was in a position to act offensively against her. No doubt they felt that American naval strength would act as a deterrent to Japan and provide a defence for Britain in the Far East until she was able to build up her own strength in the area. The possibility of a Japanese attack on Pearl Harbor without a declaration of war, neutralizing the American Pacific Fleet and deliberately bringing the United States into the war, clearly never crossed their minds.

Like Britain, the United States took little action to improve her position during the third phase of Japan's road to war. The flow of reinforcements to the Philippines continued and in November, as soon as the air reinforcement route by way of Australia was usable, some thirty-five Flying Fortress bombers were flown to Manila. Although from intercepted Japanese diplomatic telegrams it was evident to Washington that war was likely any time after the end of November, the Americans took no special precautions. They were thus caught utterly unprepared when Japan struck on 8 December.

10

Conditions in Malaya

May 1941 *Map B, p. 12, and Map C, pp. 100–1*

A new era began in Malaya with the change of the army and air
commanders in April–May 1941, and by chance this happened to
coincide with the first of the three phases of Japan's road towards
war described in the previous chapter. Meanwhile, early in May,
Headquarters III Indian Corps, with Lieutenant-General Sir Lewis
Heath as its commander, arrived in Singapore. Heath, who had commanded 5th Indian Division with conspicuous success in the Eritrean
campaign in the Middle East, was given the operational control of
northern Malaya (*see map C, pp. 100–1*). Under his command he had
the two brigades of 9th Indian Division in Kedah, 11th Indian
Division, also of only two brigades, on the east coast at Kota Bharu
and Kuantan, and the two unbrigaded battalions at Penang and
Kroh, the garrison of Penang, and the four battalions of the Federated Malay States Volunteer Force, which had not been mobilized;
his headquarters were at Kuala Lumpur. Major-General F. Keith
Simmons, in command of the two brigades (five battalions) on Singapore Island and 12th Indian Brigade in Johore, was responsible for
the defence of both Johore and Singapore Island. Major-General
Gordon Bennett, with the solitary brigade of his 8th Australian
Division, was in general reserve in the Port Dickson area.

Since the weakness of the RAF, which in theory was to carry the
main onus of the defence, would render it incapable of this task, it
was obvious that the defence of Malaya would fall almost entirely on
the army garrison. We must therefore consider the position facing
General Percival when he assumed command in May 1941, and see
what action he was able to take.

The army garrison, whose fighting strength during 1941 would rise
to some 80,000 men, was made up of British, Australian, Indian and
Malay formations. It was not therefore a homogeneous force, for the
organization and administrative requirements of the units of each
national contingent differed, especially as the Indian contingent
contained Gurkhas, Sikhs, Punjabis, Jats, Garhwalis, Baluchis,
Dogras and Hyderabadis and units from the Indian States, all of
which required special treatment. Clearly the problem of administer-
ing this heterogeneous force was immense. Yet the size and organization of the command headquarters at Fort Canning in Singapore
had changed so little since 1939 that at the time Percival took

over it was no larger than that of a normal corps headquarters.

The shortage of staff at Fort Canning made it virtually impossible for staff officers to visit the field formations; they therefore tended to be out of touch with the troops and to handle the problems that arose on a more theoretical than practical basis. Moreover, the standard of the staff throughout Malaya, with the exception of the newly raised III Indian Corps Headquarters, had tended to decline since 1939. Good officers, who had been recalled either on promotion or to fill vacancies in Britain and the Middle East, were not replaced by officers who had gained experience in the active theatres in France and the Middle East, the General Officer Commanding, Singapore, usually being told to fill vacancies by promotion from within his command. This was a short-sighted policy which could only have been condoned if it had been quite evident that Malaya was a backwater to which war was unlikely to come. It was a policy that General Bond should have taken every possible action to get altered, but he had made little effort to do so; nor had the War Office. In the seven months left to him before war broke out there was little Percival could do to improve this situation.

Percival was also faced with another difficulty in that the rates of pay and tax of officers on the British and Indian establishment were very different. It might happen therefore that the transfer of an officer to an equivalent or even higher appointment in another formation would involve him in a severe reduction in emoluments. This could even result in a British service officer appointed as a first-grade staff officer with an Indian formation drawing less net pay than a third-grade staff officer serving under him. It was therefore almost impossible in practice to ask an individual to accept such a transfer. The same difficulty applied, though in a different degree, to the transfer of Australian officers to appointments carrying British rates of pay. Thus Command Headquarters, which was on a British establishment, could not be staffed with the best officers available. It would have cost the Treasury little to make an exception in the case of Malaya, especially as the transport of replacements from Europe was far from easy, and the resulting gains in general efficiency would have been considerable.

The fact that Fort Canning was required to act as both a command and an army headquarters with insufficient staff to undertake the load placed upon it had some unfortunate results. For example, there was no training directorate with a senior and experienced officer in charge; instead, training was in the hands of a comparatively junior officer of the staff duties department, which was already heavily

overloaded with the task of organizing and equipping the heterogeneous force of many nationalities, each with its own type of war
establishment. Moreover, the newly raised Indian formations reached
Malaya only partially trained, and neither these formations nor the
British battalions from China nor the Australian formations had had
any experience or training in warfare in close country almost entirely
covered by trees or jungle. For this reason, the training department
at Command Headquarters should have been one of the strongest,
staffed by men of experience in this type of warfare. This again was a
matter which Bond should have fought for from 1939 onwards, for all
those competent to judge agreed that to train and acclimatize fully
trained troops to the conditions of terrain and climate in Malaya
would require at least three months of intensive effort; with semi-
trained troops it would take much longer. The same factors applied
to the organization of the very important intelligence branch at Fort
Canning. This was in the hands of one second-grade and one third-
grade staff officer who, because of their rank, had no direct access to
Percival.

The question of training is one of such importance that it requires
detailed consideration. The British battalions in Malaya had all been
on garrison service overseas in either Singapore or China for some
considerable time and had little training in the type of country to be
found in Malaya. With the exception of the three battalions of 12th
Indian Brigade, which went to Singapore in 1939, the Indian units
were all newly raised. As the Indian Army undertook its various
stages of expansion, every unit was required to give up a proportion
of trained officers, NCOs and men to act as a nucleus around which a
new unit could be formed, a process known as 'milking'. It is easy to
see that the standard of efficiency of all units of the Indian Army
steadily declined as each stage of the expansion took place. For the
first expansion in 1940 all existing units were 'milked' to form six
divisions and one armoured division, and for the second and third
expansions the units formed in the earlier expansion were succes-
sively 'milked'.[1] Thus the units forming 9th and 11th Indian
Divisions in Malaya (including those of 12th Brigade) were required
to send back to India a proportion of their strength which was
replaced by internal promotions and an influx of men who had had
only recruit training. Furthermore the units forming 9th and 11th

[1] The first expansion produced 6th, 7th, 8th, 9th, 10th and 11th Infantry
Divisions and 1st Armoured Divisions; the second expansion produced 14th,
17th, 19th, 20th and 34th Infantry Divisions and 2nd Armoured Divisions; and
the third expansion produced 23rd, 25th, 36th and 39th Infantry Divisions.

Indian Divisions had been trained on the assumption that they would be sent to the Middle East for desert warfare and were fully mechanized, which made them unfitted for warfare in close country. The Australian units, too, had been destined for the Middle East and had been equipped and trained with that end in view. The re-training of all arms on arrival in Malaya was thus of the utmost importance, in particular for the infantry, which, in enclosed country, is the key arm in battle.

This question of training for the specific type of warfare to be expected was given the most careful consideration in the Middle East theatre. Elaborate training centres and schools were established, through which all formations and reinforcements passed; they all also received intensive training for some time before being allowed to take part in active operations. The divisional commander of 4th Indian Division in the Western Desert has since said that he would rather have committed his division into action understrength than have it brought up to strength by men who had not been through the full course at these training centres.

In Malaya, with the exception of an officers' school at Changi, no such training centres were established. No doubt this was because the War Office did not meet Bond's request for twenty per cent of the establishment of each unit to be sent to Malaya, to be held there as a pool from which battle casualties could be replaced, and perhaps because Malaya was always kept, on the Prime Minister's orders, at the bottom of the order of priority for men and equipment. The units had with them on arrival only their quota of ten per cent first reinforcements, and these were quickly absorbed and seldom replaced. The training of all the troops was therefore left in the hands of formation commanders, whose units were often widely dispersed and, as will be explained, often called upon to act as labourers. Moreover, Indian units, after undergoing one and in some cases two 'milkings', often had to begin again with elementary training. It must also be remembered that the supporting artillery regiments did not arrive from the United Kingdom until the latter part of 1941, thereby rendering any form of combined training of formations impossible. The exceptions were 12th Indian Brigade and the two brigades forming 8th Australian Division, who arrived in Malaya as brigade groups complete with artillery, engineers, transport, supply and medical services. But even the artillery accompanying 27th Australian Brigade was only equipped with mortars and some obsolescent guns, and was re-equipped only just before the outbreak of war with Japan.

The training instructions issued by Command Headquarters were based upon those extant in the United Kingdom and envisaged a linear type of war more suited to Europe in the 1914–18 war than to Malaya in 1940–1. Yet the problem of warfare in forest and jungle-type country such as that which prevailed in Malaya was studied extensively by the military training directorate at General Headquarters India in 1940, as a result of which a number of training memoranda were drawn up. These all stressed that three conditions applied in modern warfare: the predominance of the mobile arm; the existence of open flanks, and the need to ensure adequate means of supply for the mobile arm. In mountainous, forest- and tree-covered country the infantry would become the mobile arm, and if it were possible to keep infantry formations and units supplied, perhaps by air or by highly trained porter units, so that they would remain mobile, the three basic conditions could be met. The method of conducting a campaign would therefore be to establish well-defined, well-sited and well-stocked bases at strategic points, from which mobile infantry columns could move and strike in any direction.

The memoranda explaining how this was to be done were sent to Malaya between the autumn of 1940 and April 1941. They got no further than Command Headquarters, due perhaps to the paucity of training staff, or because air supply was not possible, or the raising of porter units too difficult, or because it was easier to follow the British pre-war training manuals. Whatever the reason, the training instructions issued in Malaya remained inadequate.

Information regarding the Japanese that was given to formations was both faulty and conflicting. Command Headquarters, basing their facts on those supplied by the War Office and the Far Eastern Intelligence Bureau, no doubt believed that Japanese troops reacted badly to surprise, would not be jungle trained, were weak in unit training and that their junior officers lacked initiative. This view was communicated to the troops, so it is not surprising that in general the need for really intensive training was not grasped. In contrast, the Australian troops, before embarking for Singapore, were issued with information about the potential enemy which made it clear that the Japanese troops were well trained and equipped, had great physical endurance, could be self-supporting for several days, could move across country at great speed, were extremely ruthless and would do their utmost to mislead their opponents about their intentions. The surprise and dismay among the Australians when they received the training memorandum and other information issued in Singapore and the effect these had on their confidence in the British High

Command can be imagined. Both British and Australian training pamphlets did however stress that it was necessary for troops to be trained in movement through jungle or forested country, since the untrained man would have little chance against men trained in that type of terrain.

Another factor which affected the training of the troops was a lack of labour. The first call on labour had to be given to the production and export of rubber and tin, the Services having to do with what could be spared. In view of the proposed expansion of the garrison, the RAF had to give first priority to the construction and maintenance of airfields and the building of hutted accommodation in their vicinity, while the army had to provide accommodation for the new formations as they arrived. All labour surplus to the industrial needs of the country was absorbed in these and similar tasks, with the result that troops had to undertake the construction of beach and field defences to the detriment of their training. More than one brigade commander was therefore forced to make official representations that his troops were rapidly becoming pioneers and not infantry. This would not have mattered so much had the troops been highly trained in the first instance, but as it was the loss of training time was serious.

It can be said that in May 1941 the standard of training was far too low in practically every unit, little if any formation training had taken place and commanders had little practice in handling their formations in the field, especially in the co-operation of all arms in battle. The army in Malaya at that time was in no way a match for the highly trained and war-experienced Japanese troops that it was to meet in battle.

With the arrival of Lieutenant-General Percival a new spirit entered every sphere of activity, including training. The new General Officer Commanding realized that, as some nine-tenths of Malaya was covered with jungle, rubber or palm trees, infantry was the predominant arm and success depended on the initiative and skill of the junior commanders of that arm. He therefore concentrated at first on the development of the training of junior leaders. He had to face the fact that a considerable portion of the time of many units would have for the time being to be taken up with the construction of defences, since he could not find any quick solution to the labour problem. In September, however, finding that work on the approved defences had made considerable progress, he issued instructions which ensured that more time could be given to training and less to construction. After the arrival of the artillery regiments towards the end of 1941, he intended to use January, February and March 1942 (the months when the north-east monsoon was at its height and he could afford to leave the beach defences unmanned) for a series of formation exercises on the basis of opposing a Japanese attack on Malaya through southern Siam. As events turned out war came before these formation exercises could be carried out, and before even the training of the majority of the smaller formations could be completed.

There were, however, three formations (22nd and 27th Australian and 12th Indian Brigades) whose training was far in advance of all others. Because of the role they had been allotted, these three, unlike 9th and 11th Divisions, were not dispersed and could train as formations. The Australians had not had to suffer 'milking' and, being a separate national force with a considerable amount of freedom from the control of Command Headquarters, were able to train to some extent as they thought fit, working mainly on the lines of the training instructions issued to them from Australia. The 12th Indian Brigade, constituted with one British battalion (2nd Argyll and Sutherland Highlanders) and two Indian battalions, had been together as a formation for some two years and, largely on the initiative of Lieutenant-Colonel (later Brigadier) I. M. Stewart commanding the British battalion, had not only evolved tactics to meet known Japanese methods but had trained extremely hard in the jungle country around Mersing on the east coast. The fact that these formations were better trained than the others was amply borne out during the course of the campaign.

One of the factors that cramped General Percival's initiative and progress in the preparations necessary to defend Malaya was the close financial control exercised by the Treasury through the War Office over army expenditure. (In effect the same control was exercized over the RAF expenditure through the Air Ministry.) Despite the fact that the Empire had been at war since 1939, there had scarcely been any significant relaxation of this detailed control and thus the army (and air force) authorities in Malaya could not initiate urgent defence measures quickly. Although there was some relaxation of control on the subject of maintenance of existing services, all new projects costing over a fixed and comparatively small sum had to be referred to London for prior financial approval. In 1941 it was agreed that although projects costing less than £20,000 need not be referred to London, all others had to be. This procedure made it virtually impossible for many important projects to be put in hand quickly, for postal delays were serious and detailed plans and estimates could not be sent by cable or wireless. Thus, if the War Office or Air Ministry raised objections or asked for detailed explanations about any particular project, delays mounted and it was seldom that financial permission to launch a project was given under six months.

The following examples show how the close financial control from London delayed preparations being made in Malaya for the country's defence. Early in 1941 Command Headquarters wished to purchase locally a quantity of earth-moving machinery. But War Office approval had to be obtained for the expenditure of the necessary funds. On the ground that the required equipment could be supplied from the United Kingdom and shipped to Singapore, financial approval for local purchase was not given, and by the time war broke out not a single item of this equipment had reached Malaya. In consequence at the eleventh hour the Chief Engineer, Malaya, had to requisition what he required. Another example was the demand for pumping machinery required to create an artificially flooded area to cover the left flank of the defensive position being built at Jitra to guard the Alor Star area. The War Office agreed that an order should be placed in Australia for petrol engines and in Singapore for pumps, but after so long a delay that the plant was only being delivered at the moment that Japan launched her attack. Thus the left flank of the Jitra position was never protected by a flooded area. Percival was helpless, just as General Bond before him had been, and had to do his best with the situation as it existed.

The problem of the provision of labour has already been touched on, but it is advisable to examine the position more closely. An army always has a desperate need for a large and disciplined labour force. The army in Malaya was no exception; in fact the need in that theatre was greater than in others, for the garrison was always insufficient to carry out its task properly. This need was in general recognized, and India, as part of her expansion programme, raised a large number of properly organized and disciplined labour units from the non-martial races and offered them to the War Office. Owing to the demands of industry, labour in Malaya was expensive and scarce and much of it could not have been drafted into disciplined companies. Bond asked for and got two Indian labour companies at the end of the year, but a subsequent request for a third to build the defences at Penang was turned down by the War Office on the ground that its dispatch would interfere with India's programme for sending labour companies to the Middle East. Instead, Bond was told to make arrangements to use the large resources of local labour, which they said were available in Malaya, if and when a threat to Penang should arise.

The position regarding labour was not as easy as the War Office supposed it to be. A large number of rubber estates employed Tamil labour brought from India, and each estate had its own Tamil community with the wives and families. It would scarcely have been possible to raise disciplined labour companies from this source. The tin mines and some of the rubber estates employed Chinese, and it might have been possible to raise Chinese labour companies, given adequate pay and provided the language difficulty could have been overcome. The Malay community provided the labour for the fishing industry and generally for the smallholdings. It would have been possible to have formed Malay labour companies on lines similar to those employed in raising the Malay regiment, but it would have taken time. All depended, however, on the rates of pay and on the allowances paid to the wives and families.

In June 1941, by which time Percival had succeeded Bond, the War Office agreed to the raising of six local labour companies with a rate of pay of 45 Malayan cents a day (about one shilling and a half-penny in 1941 money). Percival soon realized that this rate of pay would not attract labour into what was a form of military service, and that labour obtained through civilian sources on some form of contract was likely to be very unreliable. Furthermore, the Labour Controller for Malaya advised him against recruiting companies in the country, since such action would be detrimental both to industry and to civil-defence measures. However, the Controller put forward a scheme under which labour could be obtained for the Services at a rate of pay of $1·10 (two shillings and sevenpence) a day plus rations and accommodation. Percival put this scheme to the War Office, who refused to pay the proposed daily rate. Meanwhile in June he had made a further request for three Indian labour companies, but this was also refused on the grounds that all such Indian companies were required in the Middle East.

In desperation, since there was surplus labour in Hong Kong, Percival then asked the Hong Kong government to allow him to raise three labour companies for use in Malaya. Agreement with the Hong Kong government was quickly reached, and in October 1940 Percival asked the War Office for early approval of the scheme, saying that the first company could be ready in a month from the receipt of approval and the others would follow at monthly intervals. It was found, however, that to obtain reliable English-speaking platoon commanders it would be necessary to pay them at the rate of

$2·75 (six shillings and threepence) a day. Sanction to pay this rate had to be obtained from the War Office, who referred the matter to the Treasury for decision. Having had no reply Percival told the War Office on 18 November that, in view of the urgent need to get labour he proposed to begin recruiting on 24 November. The War Office replied next day that a rate of $2 a day for platoon commanders was the maximum that could be paid, as the companies were to be raised on the Indian establishment.

Thanks to financial control by the War Office and the Treasury, who refused to accept the opinion of those who knew the local market, including their own representative at Command Head-quarters, all efforts to raise labour companies failed, and on the out-break of war the only disciplined labour available were the two Indian labour companies.[1] There is little doubt that, with the assistance of the civilian government in Malaya and the commercial companies, and given a free hand to fix suitable rates of pay and service, Percival could have organized a plan to transfer labour on mobilization from industry to disciplined companies under the aegis of either the excellent and very helpful Public Works Department or the Volunteer Force Organization. Many European planters and officials of the tin mining companies, with their knowledge of labour and ability to speak Malay and/or Chinese, would have been better employed in this way than in the units of the Volunteer Forces.

*

The position which Air Vice-Marshal Pulford found when he took over as Air Officer Commanding, Far East, must now be examined, at least as far as Malaya is concerned. It had been laid down that in the absence of a fleet the task of defending Malaya fell primarily on the RAF, and that for this purpose a force of 336 first-line aircraft with a normal proportion of reserves was to be available by the end of 1941, although the previous Air Officer Commanding, Far East, had reckoned that he required 566 aircraft. But in April 1941 it did not seem to Pulford that even the figure of 336 would be met. He could count for reconnaissance on one squadron of three flying-boats and two squadrons of Hudson aircraft; for offensive operations he had only two squadrons of Blenheim bombers (one of which had an endurance of less than a thousand miles), two completely obsolete squadrons of torpedo-bombers and one squadron of Blenheim night-bombers; and he was in the process of forming four squadrons of

[1] One Chinese labour company was raised locally after the outbreak of war in December 1941 and two more in January 1942.

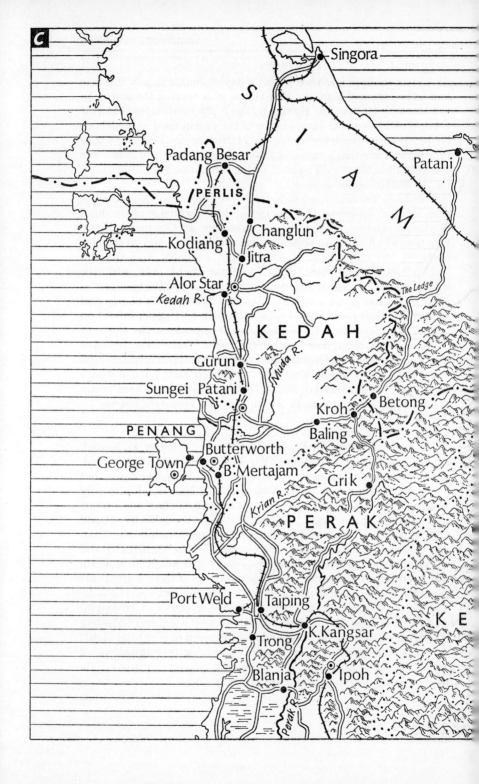

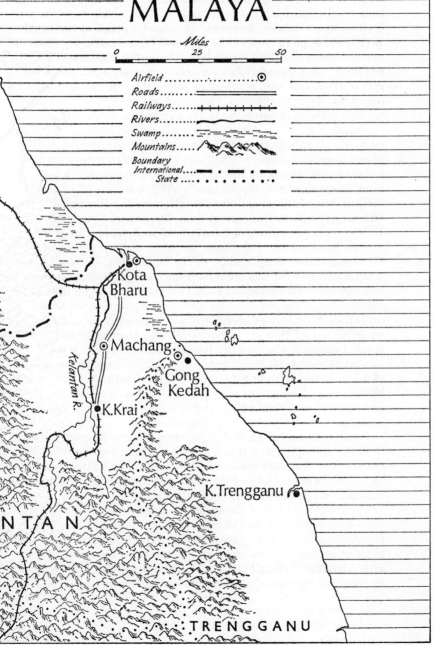

C

NORTHERN
MALAYA

Miles

0   25   50

Airfield .... ⊙
Roads ....
Railways .... +—+—+—+—+—+—+
Rivers ....
Swamp ....
Mountains .....
Boundary
International ....
State .....

Kota
Bharu

⊙ Machang

⊙ Gong
Kedah

Kelantan R.

● K.Krai

K.Trengganu ●

N T A N

T R E N G G A N U

Buffalo fighters manned by Australians and New Zealanders. In addition he had a large number of RAF personnel sent in advance from the United Kingdom to form additional squadrons as the aircraft became available. But it was by offensive action alone that the RAF could hope to prevent the Japanese from establishing bases in southern Siam and northern Malaya. The Buffalo fighters, of American design and manufacture, were comparatively slow, had a poor rate of climb and were not very manœuvrable; though said to be a match for Japanese fighters, they were to prove to be very much inferior to them, in particular to the Japanese navy Zero fighter.

Most, but not all, of the airfields available had been developed as civil airfields and, located to suit civil requirements, were unsuitably placed from the military point of view. In northern Malaya the main airfield on the west coast was at Alor Star in Kedah, which lay only some thirty miles from the Siamese frontier; behind it there were airfields at Sungei Patani and Butterworth (opposite Penang), and two airfields in Perak at Taiping and Ipoh. On the east coast of northern Malaya there was a group of three airfields in Kelantan: Kota Bharu, located less than two miles from the coast and ten miles from the Siamese frontier, Gong Kedah, thirty miles south-south-east from Kota Bharu and only six miles from the coast, and Machang, which was not ready for operational use, twenty-five miles south of Kota Bharu. These three airfields were all dependent for their maintenance on a single-line metre-gauge railway and were not connected by road with the rest of Malaya. In central Malaya there were airfields at Kuala Lumpur in the west and Kuantan in the east, the latter being located only six miles from the coast. In Johore there was an airfield at Kluang, and a landing ground at Kahang, on the road between Kluang and Mersing. On Singapore Island there were three RAF airfields (Seletar, Sembawang and Tengah) and a civil airport at Kallang.

There was a reasonable warning system covering Singapore Island from the north, but no warning system had been developed to cover the northern and most vital airfields, partly owing to their nearness to the Siamese frontier and the coast and partly because of lack of communication facilities, especially in Kelantan.

The ground defence of the airfields located close to the coast was almost impossible. It was obvious that the Japanese, should they invade Malaya, would as their first objective take action to seize airfields in or near Malaya. Alor Star was beyond their reach except after a landing in Siam, but Kota Bharu, Gong Kedah, and Kuantan were so near the coast that successful landings would include them in the initial beachhead. Looking at the problem from the Japanese point of view, their first task on invading Malaya was to seize a conveniently located airfield in southern Siam such as Singora and/or to make a landing to secure the Kelantan airfields or possibly, but less likely, Kuantan. The fact that airfields had been built in areas where it was almost impossible to defend them set Percival and Pulford an extremely difficult problem.

11

Preparations for the Defence of Malaya

May–December 1941   *Map B, p. 12, and Map C, pp. 100–1*

In May 1941 General Percival started to reorganize the anti-aircraft defences of Malaya. As the original defence scheme had covered only Singapore Island and part of southern Johore, the War Office had provided only sufficient equipment for that purpose. With the extension of the defence scheme to cover the whole of Malaya and the decision to rely on the RAF, it became necessary for the anti-aircraft defences to be extended to cover the airfields in north Malaya and certain key areas such as Penang, Ipoh, Taiping and Kuala Lumpur. As early as 1936 the War Office had approved the provision of anti-aircraft defences for Penang, but had taken no action to approve additional equipment to cover the other vital areas in Malaya. No equipment for Penang had been sent to Malaya by May 1941, and all that General Percival and Air Marshal Pulford could count on was the approved defences for Singapore (three heavy and one light anti-aircraft regiments and a searchlight regiment), which were reinforced during 1941 by a newly raised and partially trained heavy anti-aircraft regiment from India. There was therefore little they could do to defend airfields and vulnerable points in Malaya against air attack. Percival, by reducing the scale of defences at Singapore, with Pulford's agreement, made one battery of heavy anti-aircraft guns and one mobile battery of light anti-aircraft guns available to III Corps. He also took over command of the anti-aircraft defences of Singapore from the Fortress Commander, since it was essential, now that fighter aircraft were becoming available, that a co-ordinated fighter-cum-gun defence scheme was instituted. Additionally, he arranged that a Group-Captain, RAF, who had had experience of the air defence of Britain and whom Pulford had put in charge of the fighter defence of Singapore Island, should issue orders direct to the anti-aircraft artillery headquarters if the island were attacked.

With inadequate anti-aircraft defences, the existence of an adequate warning system was of vital importance. In the absence of radar equipment, which could not be spared by Britain, reliance had to be placed on observers. But the efficiency of an observer system depended on the keenness and aptitude of the personnel and on an efficient system of communication. In Malaya the provision of both observers and communications at short notice was very difficult. A warning system covering Singapore Island existed, but there was none in the north. A scheme was quickly drawn up with the civil government for the extension and improvement of the system of communications in northern Malaya, but little could be done in the few months left before war broke out, since there was insufficient time to find and train suitable personnel, and most of the material and equipment had to come from overseas. Although ordered, none of it had arrived by December 1941. The blame for the lack of a warning system in the north must be shared by Air Marshal Babington and General Bond.

Shortly after assuming command General Percival had been instructed to make another review of the forces required to defend Malaya, and before submitting his views to the Chiefs of Staff early in August he made an exhaustive survey of the probable battle area in northern Malaya. His requirements were much greater than those asked for by Bond in 1940. He wanted an additional division and a tank regiment to act as a reserve for III Corps, some extra corps troops, another brigade for 9th Division in eastern Malaya to bring it up to a full division, a machine-gun battalion to reinforce the weak 8th Australian Division, and the garrison of Singapore Island, which would also act as a reserve for Johore, to be brought up to the strength of a division by the addition of an infantry brigade and a battalion, and a second tank regiment. He thus wanted a force of forty-eight battalions and two tank regiments as against the thirty-one battalions which he could foresee having by the end of 1941. He also asked for two heavy anti-aircraft regiments for the defence of airfields in Malaya, and an accretion of strength for the anti-aircraft defences allotted to Singapore Island and southern Johore. Percival's only omission was a request for a pool of twenty per cent reinforcements for all units in the garrison and the staff to form proper training camps and schools.

Major-General Gordon Bennett had for some time been dissatisfied with the role allotted to 8th Australian Division and, as soon therefore as he knew that a second Australian brigade was being sent, he asked Percival to give the Australian force a definite task. After the arrival of 27th Australian Brigade in mid-August, Percival therefore gave 8th Australian Division the responsibility for the defence of Malacca and Johore. Gordon Bennett moved his headquarters to Johore Bahru at the end of the month, 22nd Australian Brigade relieved 12th Indian Brigade in the Endau–Mersing area and 27th Australian Brigade was deployed in central and north-western Johore. This change of role satisfied Gordon Bennett's desire to have some definite responsibility for the defence of Malaya, and also made it more likely that the Australian formation would be able to operate as a complete formation under its own commander, a point on which the Australian government laid great stress. As a result of the alterations in the general dispositions, 12th Indian Brigade became Percival's general reserve and moved to the Port Dickson area on the west coast. In September 28th Indian Brigade arrived to replace the brigade of 9th Indian Division sent to Iraq in the spring, and was sent to the Ipoh area to become the reserve to Heath's III Corps. Since no other formations reached Singapore before the war broke out in December, the time has arrived to consider the dispositions which Brooke-Popham (the Commander-in-Chief, Far East) and Percival adopted to meet the anticipated invasion (*see chapter 9*).

*

There was now no doubt that, having occupied southern Indo-China, Japan's next step, if she decided to go to war, would be to invade northern Malaya by way of southern Siam with the intention of advancing on Singapore down the west coast of Malaya, which offered excellent rail and road communications. The situation therefore existed which had been envisaged by General Sir Theodore Fraser in 1924–5, and by General Sir William Dobbie and Percival in 1937. With virtual command of the sea, the Japanese were free to invade the east coast of Malaya, to capture the airfields which had conveniently been built for them almost on the coastline in Kelantan as well as at Kuantan in Pahang, or alternatively to take a short cut by landing in the Endau–Mersing area so as to make a short-range attack on Singapore. A landing in that area was unlikely, except in conjunction with an advance from Siam down the west coast, as there was no airfield conveniently placed near to Mersing and it was within easy range of the British airfields at Kluang and on Singapore Island. The possibility of a direct attack on Singapore Island could, however, be discounted, for it ran counter to the general trend of Japanese military thought, and she was unlikely to commit her fleet to an attack on the island, which was well defended against a sea-borne invasion.

At this point we must again take a look at maps B and C on pages 12 and 100. Malaya is divided down the centre by a ridge of mountains running from north to south and petering out in Johore. To the east the country is mainly covered with jungle. Except for the single-line railway from Gemas to Kota Bharu and Siam it was in 1941 poorly served with communications. The only main road of importance was that from Kuantan across the central range to Raub. The coastline consisted largely of sandy beaches with a few patches of mangrove, and there was a rough track following the coastline and connecting the villages.

The western coastal strip was highly developed, with a good system of trunk roads running from Johore Bahru to the Siamese border and fed by innumerable secondary and estate roads. The main railway from Singapore crossed the causeway into Johore and thence ran northwards to the Siamese border and on to Bangkok; there were spurs from it to the ports of Malacca, Port Dickson, Port Swettenham, Telok Anson, Port Weld and Butterworth. The country was highly cultivated, with only a few areas of jungle. The two northern States contained the rice-growing areas, while the remainder contained most of the large rubber estates, tin mines, oil-palm groves and pineapple plantations. The west coast was heavily fringed with mangrove, and there were few beaches suitable for landings. The State of Johore had only one east–west road, that from Batu Pahat through Kluang and Jemaluang to Mersing. On the eastern side there was a direct road from Endau and Mersing to Johore Bahru.

Although the Japanese were firmly established in southern Indo-China and had airfields from which the whole of Malaya and Singapore Island was within range of their bomber aircraft, it was obvious that, to support an advance down the western side of Malaya, they would in the first instance require airfields in southern Siam and northern Malaya. There were Siamese airfields at Singora and Patani, within fifty miles of the Malayan frontier, and three British airfields in Kelantan, the one at Kota Bharu being, as we have said, less than two miles from the coast and that at Gong Kedah six miles from the coast. It was evident both to the Japanese and British planners that these would be the first objectives of any invading force. It was also obvious that, when they had captured Singora and Patani, the Japanese would advance as rapidly as possible southwards along the Singora–Alor Star–Kuala Kangsar and the Patani–Kroh roads in a double-pronged advance which would make the defence of Perlis and Kedah, the rice-producing area and granary of Malaya, extremely difficult. Any force detailed to defend this area was liable to be enveloped, for its communications could be cut once the enemy force advancing from Patani had reached Kroh, from where there was a direct road leading westwards to Sungei Patani. On the other hand a successful landing by the Japanese at Kota Bharu, though it would give them the use of the group of three airfields in Kelantan, would not be likely to have such serious consequences.

It was because of the difficulty of defending Perlis and Kedah that first General Bond, and later Air Chief Marshal Brooke-Popham, suggested to the Chiefs of Staff that British forces should cross the Siamese frontier and seize Singora and Patani as soon as it was evident that Japan intended to attack. Both said that such action would only be possible if Malaya were allotted extra formations over and above those estimated to be required for the defence of the country.

Shortly after his arrival in Malaya General Percival considered this idea with a view to carrying it out without the additional troops which both Bond and Brooke-Popham had said were essential for the purpose. If it were to be carried out, 11th Indian Division would have alternative roles—to advance into Siam or to occupy a defensive position covering Alor Star. As Brigadier General Staff I Corps in France early in 1940, Percival knew the plan whereby the BEF was either to stand on the defensive on the left of the French army, or to abandon its defensive positions and advance into Belgium should the German army enter that country and involve her in the war. Thus it was perhaps natural that he would consider using a similar strategy in Malaya. The situation to be faced was, however, entirely different from that which had obtained in the European theatre. In the Far East, Siam had been under the general control of Japan since January 1941 (*see page 62*), and could not afford to offer Britain any facilities or come to an agreement with her in the event of war. In order to retain even a semblance of freedom and to avoid total occupation by Japanese forces, she would be more likely to offer resistance to any British advance into her territory. Furthermore, realizing the utmost importance of ensuring the active support of the United States, Britain could not take the risk of appearing to be the aggressor by moving into Siamese territory before it was absolutely certain that she was being attacked by Japan or that Siamese neutrality was being violated.

Despite these grave disadvantages, which would probably in the end render the whole idea nugatory (as in fact proved to be the case), Brooke-Popham and Percival pursued it. A careful examination of the whole problem was instituted, from which it transpired that the forces available were insufficient to occupy both Singora and Patani, that an advance and occupation of Singora was possible, provided the operation could take place between October and March (that is, during the north-east monsoon when the state of the ground would confine Japanese armoured formations to the roads) and that the operation could begin at least twenty-four hours before the Japanese had attempted a landing at Singora.

This plan, however, left Patani free to the Japanese, and a force landed there could advance without opposition down the Kroh road thus threatening the communications of the forces at Singora and giving the Japanese access to the entirely undefended states of Perlis, Kedah and Perak. To counteract this difficulty, Percival proposed to occupy a defensive position on this road at a point known as The Ledge, where the road traversed a steep ridge some thirty-five miles inside Siamese territory. This meant that both the forces allotted for the occupation of Singora and the Ledge position would have to invade Siamese territory and be prepared to meet not only opposition from Siamese troops or border guards, but also possible demolition on roads and railways, which might delay them. The success of the operation depended therefore almost entirely on its being undertaken well in advance of any possible Japanese landings. Under any circumstances it was a gamble, for there were many unknown factors involved, any of which could result in the disastrous failure of the operation.

Early in August, with Percival's agreement, Brooke-Popham told the Chiefs of Staff that he was considering the possibility of occupying Singora, for which operation, to be known as Matador, he would require three brigade groups supported by four bomber and two fighter squadrons. The operation, he said, could not be undertaken before the arrival in September of 28th Brigade from India and then only if the Dutch, in accordance with the ADB Agreement, sent air reinforcements to Malaya. About the same time officers in plain clothes were sent into Siam to carry out a reconnaissance of the Singora area, where they found Japanese officers doing exactly the same thing. Although they were unable to get a sight of the important airfield, they reported that a force of three brigade groups would suffice for the operation in the wet season, though a fourth brigade would be necessary in the dry season.

The Chiefs of Staff, clearly doubtful about the feasibility of Matador, asked Brooke-Popham if he thought it were a practicable proposition. He told them that it was feasible and that sufficient forces would be available from 1 October onwards. In the middle of September the Chiefs of Staff said that, as their policy was to avoid war with Japan, they had no intention of violating Siamese territory before the Japanese, but asked what was the minimum period of warning required to enable the operation to be launched. At the same time they warned Brooke-Popham that, though they agreed with Percival's August estimate of the forces required for the defence of Malaya, they would be unable to meet it in the foreseeable future.

They added that the need to reinforce the army garrison would gradually diminish as the British naval and air strength increased. It is almost incredible that the Chiefs of Staff could have made such a statement, bearing in mind the many warnings which had been received both in London and Washington that Japan was about to strike; for they knew very well that, with the drain on their resources caused by the Middle East campaign and by the flow of aircraft to Russia, they would not be able to keep their promise to bring the RAF garrison up to the agreed strength of 336 first-line aircraft by the end of 1941, and that the Eastern Fleet could not be an effective fighting force until the late spring of 1942.

Brooke-Popham replied that Matador could be put into motion in thirty-six hours from the time that permission to act had been received from London. As the plan then stood, troops could not reach Singora or the Ledge position in under sixty hours from the receipt of permission from London and, if the Siamese were to offer any resistance or to blow up bridges and culverts, this time might easily be extended by another thirty-six or forty-eight hours. To be safe, therefore, a minimum of, say, four days' start would be necessary to ensure success. In view of the policy of the British government, it should have appeared evident that Matador could never be launched in sufficient time to have a real chance of success. It was at this point that the whole idea should have been dropped, unless Percival's demand for a reserve division for III Corps could have been met at once and the RAF could have been brought up to the agreed strength in 1941.

But, far from being dropped, every effort was made to press ahead with the plan. The effect of the retention of Matador and thus of the alternative role for 11th Division was very serious. The alternative roles were in no way compatible, since the one demanded a rapid move by road and rail for which very complex administrative arrangements, involving adjustments in the organization of units, had to be made, while the other required the occupation of a defensive position whose preparation was far from complete. The alternative roles might have been tackled by fully trained troops, but it must be remembered that the troops available in Malaya were only partially trained even for a defensive role, and Matador required special training. Furthermore, with the staff involved in making the many administrative arrangements for the complicated rush forward into Siam, while at the same time keeping an eye fixed on the state of the defences to be occupied if Matador did not take place, training tended to suffer. Yet it was the training of troops which ought to have had first priority.[1] In addition, the third brigade required for Matador (28th) was not even placed under the command of 11th Division but was retained in corps reserve at Ipoh, some 120 miles to the south.

Let us now consider Percival's plan for the defence of Malaya, drawn up on the assumption that circumstances might make it impossible for Matador to be carried out. From 1940 onwards both the Chiefs of Staff and the commanders in Malaya had looked on the primary task of the army garrison as being the defence of the airfields from which the RAF were to operate to keep the Japanese invading forces at a distance. Although by August 1941 it was quite evident that the RAF would not have the strength to carry out its task efficiently, the plan was still based on the defence of airfields in northern Malaya. The defence of the airfields at Alor Star and Sungei Patani on the western side of the range offered a problem to which there was no really satisfactory solution, because the existence of the Patani–Kroh road made it possible for the airfields and the troops allotted for their defence to be enveloped. Since the main Japanese advance had to follow the main north–south communications, the enemy had to be held on the frontier or at some point well north of Alor Star if the airfield at that place was to remain usable, but, to make the defence of Kedah possible, the Patani–Kroh road had to be blocked and this, as has already been shown when considering Matador, meant an advance of some thirty-five miles into Siamese territory to seize the only really satisfactory defensive position, The Ledge. If this could not be accomplished, Kedah and the airfields at Alor Star and probably Sungei Patani were lost.

The 11th Division, allotted the task of defending Kedah, had only two brigades (six battalions), a battalion close to the frontier at Kroh and another located on Penang Island. The plan, originated during Bond's tenure of command and accepted by Percival and Heath, was for 11th Division to hold a prepared defensive position covering Jitra, only some twelve miles north of the Alor Star airfield. There it was hoped to hold the main Japanese thrust.[2] In addition,

---

[1] The administrative arrangements were highly complicated owing to the need for great speed. Generally the infantry had to be moved by rail and all mechanized transport by road. In addition large quantities of bridging material had to be carried for it was known that many road bridges were under reconstruction or might well be demolished. There was also the possibility that Siamese resistance might have to be overcome on the frontier, which meant that some infantry units had to be in a position to fight long before Singora was reached.

[2] A position on the frontier further north was ruled out since the only possible defensive position lay in a highly malarial area.

the battalion at Kroh, followed as quickly as possible by the battalion from Penang, was to thrust aside any Siamese resistance on the frontier and move forward rapidly to seize and hold the Ledge position. Assuming 11th Division could hold the main Japanese thrust, everything depended on the ability of the troops known as Krohcol, who were allotted to the Patani–Kroh road to seize and hold The Ledge, for once that position was lost there was no suitable position for defences until Kroh itself was reached. There a defensive position had been partly prepared west of Kroh covering the Kroh–Sungei Patani road, but not the road running south from Kroh through Grik to Kuala Kangsar, which had been erroneously reported as unsuitable for the movement of troops. Thus, whether Matador was or was not put into operation, the defence of Kedah and the northern airfields depended on whether the Ledge position could be reached and put into a state of defence before the Japanese reached it, and this turned once again on how soon before the Japanese landed Malaya Command would be permitted to move troops into Siamese territory.

On the east coast the defence of Kelantan was almost as difficult as that of Kedah. The beaches from Kota Bharu southwards were everywhere suitable for landings, certainly until the north-east monsoon reached its maximum in January. A brigade group of 9th Division, consisting of four battalions, was allotted to its defence and ordered to meet the invader on the beaches with the purpose of preventing a landing. Although history shows that an invader has seldom been stopped on the beaches, this policy was accepted by Malaya Command, because the airfields which the army had been asked to protect were too close to the beaches themselves. The most likely point of attack was immediately north-east of the Kota Bharu airfield, for at this point a landing would be as close as possible to its objective. One battalion was given a nine-mile stretch of beach to cover in this area, and a second battalion was given a twenty-six-mile stretch of beach to its right which stretched as far as the mouth of the river near the Gong Kedah airfield. The other two battalions were retained in reserve. The defences, consisting of pill boxes and a few paltry obstacles, were built by the troops themselves to the detriment of their training and, owing to the enormous length of the front to be held, many of the pill boxes could not be manned and were merely dummies. No attempt was ever made to test the defences by trial landings from the sea, though this course was advocated by the Chief Engineer. There was little chance of holding the Kota Bharu airfield, and only a very faint hope for Gong Kedah.

112

The defence of the areas in northern Malaya, considered to be vital because of the position of the airfields, was entrusted to eight battalions on the western side of the range and four on the eastern side; there were also three battalions in immediate reserve which, owing to their distant position, could only really be used effectively in the west, making a total of fifteen battalions—slightly less than half the available force. Of the balance of sixteen battalions, two were guarding the airfield at Kuantan, eleven holding Johore and Singapore and three were in general reserve.

Was there any other way in which Malaya could have been defended with any hope of holding the invaders so far north that time would be given for reinforcing formations and aircraft to reach Singapore? It is submitted that, had the task of the army in Malaya not been the protection of the RAF airfields, and had Brooke-Popham, Bond and Percival heeded the ideas given in the Indian Army training directives there was another method of defending Malaya which had a greater chance of success even with the existing understrength garrison.

There were four main factors affecting the issue, namely: that in the close country of Malaya infantry was the predominating arm and, provided it was properly trained, equipped and supplied, should have been considered to be the mobile arm; that the terrain favoured the attacker rather than the defender, and thus that the bulk of the infantry formations ought to have been employed as far as possible in an offensive role; that, to succeed, the Japanese had to secure the use of the north–south communications on the western side of the Malay peninsula; and that vital points on these communications, particularly at bottlenecks, would have to be strongly defended so as to make troops available for the offensive, to bring the invaders temporarily to a halt and thus to provide opportunities for mobile infantry columns to act offensively against their communications.

Before considering how a defence plan based on these factors could have been developed, it is advisable to deal with the problem of the northern airfields, on the assumption that their defence was no longer the army's primary task. It has already been shown that the defence of the three Kelantan airfields was wellnigh impossible, but was it really necessary to make the attempt? The task of the RAF was to locate the enemy convoys while at sea and then inflict on them so much damage that either the ships would turn back or the invasion would be carried out by a greatly reduced force. For this purpose the available short-range strike aircraft required forward airfields such

I

as Kota Bharu, but if the RAF were to fail to carry out its task, and it was quite clear by August 1941 that its strength and composition made this highly probable, the airfields were of no value to the defence, especially as they were bound to fall to the first enemy onslaught. Thus it was a waste of effort to deploy a brigade of four battalions in Kelantan: all that was necessary was, say, an Indian State battalion for the local security of an engineer detachment which would have the task of firing pre-laid demolition charges to make the airfields unusable for as long a period as possible, and then withdrawing down the railway, destroying all the bridges and culverts as far south as Kuala Lipis. The same plan could have been applied at Kuantan and to the trunk road running west from it. Such a plan would have freed 9th Division with its two brigades for use west of the central range and the Japanese would have gained very little more than they did under the plan that was adopted.

The defence of Kedah and the airfields of Alor Star and Sungei Patani offered many difficulties. The airfield at Alor Star had some importance, since it was a staging point on the air reinforcement route from India, being approximately 275 miles from the airfield at Victoria Point. It was, however, only 40 miles north of Butterworth, which was within the range of reinforcing fighters staging at Victoria Point. There was also the probability that, as part of their plan to invade Malaya, the Japanese would take steps to sever the air reinforcement route by occupying the airfields at Tavoy, Mergui and Victoria Point in Burma, all easily reached from Siamese territory, and thus making it necessary for all short-range aircraft to be brought to Singapore by sea or to be flown off aircraft-carriers. For these reasons the airfields at Alor Star and Sungei Patani could have been treated in the same way as suggested for those in Kelantan—used while they could be used, but with no steps taken to try to defend them. With Alor Star, Sungei Patani, Kuantan and the Kelantan airfields dealt with in this way, the army would have been free to work out a plan of defence without being tied to the apron-strings of the RAF.

What could the army have done to slow down the Japanese once they had obtained a suitable base in southern Siam and had occupied Kota Bharu? The only solution was to ensure that the Japanese were denied the use of the north–south rail and road communications. This could have been done with strong defended areas prepared and garrisoned at points where the Japanese would have to reduce them in order to make use of the communications, such as at points where the road or railway systems ran close together. At the same time highly mobile infantry formations, trained to move across country and be independent of roads, would have had to be located in positions from which they could rapidly counter-attack the Japanese endeavouring to reduce these defensive positions. Without detailed reconnaissance on the ground it is not possible to select exact positions, but there are certain obvious areas where such defences might have been prepared.

The retention of Penang was of the greatest importance for, once in Japanese hands, it would provide them with a base from which to launch amphibious attacks anywhere along the west coast and so outflank the defenders. The first object therefore should have been to deny the use of Penang harbour to the Japanese, which meant holding the island as well as an area in Province Wellesley, including Prai and Butterworth. To accomplish this, Perlis and Kedah would have had to be abandoned and defended areas prepared to cover this area. It seems fairly evident that the places which should have been held were Gurun on the main road and railway, which offered a good defensive position, and a point on the Siamese frontier north-east of Kroh. Had defensive positions been prepared in these areas and garrisoned, say by two brigade groups at Gurun and one at Kroh with a fully mobile infantry division close up in reserve ready to counter-attack, the Japanese might have been held for a considerable time and the RAF would have had the use of Butterworth airfield, for which fighter and anti-aircraft defences could have been provided by reducing the scale of the Singapore defences. It goes without saying that efficient anti-tank obstacles would have had to be erected on all roads or possible lines of approach for tanks, and covered by carefully sited minefields and anti-tank guns, of which the garrison had a reasonable number.

Once Penang was lost there was a danger that any defences built further south could be outflanked by enemy landings on the west coast. Nevertheless there were a number of possible places where defences could have been built, such as in the Taiping–Kuala Kangsar area, the Kuala Kubu and the Kuala Selangor area (provided the passes over the central range were rendered unusable), and the Tampin bottleneck on the northern borders of Johore. If defended areas had been prepared at some of these points and stocked with supplies for a lengthy period, they could have been expected to hold out even if enveloped by amphibious landings in their rear, and thus they would have denied the Japanese the use of the communications for some time. Finally there were possible areas in southern Johore, but as the whole object of this type of defence was to gain time for

115

reinforcing formations to arrive, it could have been hoped that the
defences in Johore would not have to be manned, except of course
those covering the Mersing–Jemaluang road, in case of a landing in
the Endau–Mersing area.

Since Britain did not have command of the sea around Malaya, the
position of the country was almost that of a besieged fortress. But
not quite, as the sea communications to Singapore were likely to
remain usable at least for some weeks. Throughout history the most
important man in a fortress after the fortress commander has been
the chief engineer. This fact was recognized in London; for it happened that, in the usual course of events, the Chief Engineer,
Malaya, was due for relief in August 1941. Brigadier I. Simson, the
officer selected to replace him, was chosen because of his experience
of military defensive works and of some of the civil defence organizations in Great Britain, which during 1940 had been in a very similar
position to that which might occur in Malaya in 1941–2.

Before Simson left for Singapore, the Director of Fortifications and
Works (DFW) at the War Office briefed him. He told him that there
had been some friction between his predecessor and General Bond
(both were engineer officers) and that, in view of the possibility of
war with Japan, it was up to him to work for close co-operation with
General Percival and to use his influence as Chief Engineer to arrange
for anti-tank obstacles and rearward defended areas to be constructed, so that if the garrison was forced to withdraw from north
Malaya they would have *pointes d'appui* on which to fall back. Since
Simson, as Chief Engineer, would find it difficult to oppose the policy
of the General Staff in Malaya, the DFW told Simson that he would
ask the Chief of the Imperial General Staff (CIGS) to write to General
Percival requesting him to consider as a matter of urgency the construction of such defences, pointing out that Simson was well qualified to advise them on the subject. Although specifically asked to do
so, the DFW gave Simson no written instructions. No letter to this
effect was ever sent by the CIGS, and it would appear that the
General Staff in the War Office was not prepared to order the construction of defences.

On arrival at Singapore in August 1941 Simson carried out a
reconnaissance of northern Malaya and Johore, so that on the receipt
of the expected letter from the CIGS he would be in a position to
advise Percival on the location and type of defences needed. By mid-
October no letter had been received and Simson was in an awkward
position. He sought an interview with Percival and his Chief of
Staff and urged them to consider the need for defences, basing his

arguments on experience gained in France in 1940, and in Britain after Dunkirk when invasion was possible. He explained that he was in a position to provide adequate supervision of civil labour and the necessary technical assistance, but that, once war broke out, it would be difficult to find either supervisors or labour. He suggested the provision of anti-tank defences in depth at many natural defiles on the north–south railways and roads coupled with the preparation of demolition chambers for major bridges, the construction of a ring of permanent and field defences in southern Johore to cover all approaches to Johore Bahru (developed from the defensive line which Dobbie had begun in 1938 with War Office approval—*see page 32*) and the preparation of field and permanent defences, underwater obstacles, fire traps and minefields on the northern coast of Singapore Island and at the mouths of rivers on the west coast of Malaya where the Japanese might make landings to outflank the defence. Simson was clearly thinking at the time on lines similar to those which have been suggested above as an alternative way of defending Malaya.

Percival refused point blank to consider these proposals. He cannot be held entirely to blame for his refusal at a time when both Brooke-Popham and the Governor held the view that the danger of war with Japan was remote or even had passed. (*See page 75.*) He was clearly committed to a defence plan approved by the War Office; he had great difficulty in getting financial approval for any expenditure, the wholesale construction of defences would have needed War Office policy and financial approval, and labour was in short supply. He knew that the civil administration would offer every objection to the construction of defences, both because they would be bound to encroach on private property, and on the grounds that his proposals were a sign that the army did not intend to fight for northern Malaya, the old cry that had bedevilled the deliberations of the War Committee throughout 1940.

During his visits to formations, Simson had found that they had not received the instructions in pamphlet form which he knew had been issued by the War Office on how best to deal with enemy tank attacks. Towards the end of November he discovered that stocks of these pamphlets, all neatly tied in bundles as they had arrived from London, were stored in the General Staff Offices in Fort Canning. Since most of the troops (British, Australian, Indian and Malay) forming the garrison had never seen a tank and knew little of its capabilities or how to destroy it, he took the matter up with Percival and suggested that he should prepare an illustrated booklet for issue to formations and units, based on the War Office pamphlets. Percival agreed, and Simson accordingly prepared a booklet of some forty pages including illustrations. This was ready for issue by 6 December but reached the fighting formations too late to be of use. This oversight on the part of the training staff at Headquarters Malaya Command was to result in 11th Indian Division having to withstand attack by Japanese tanks without having any training in how best to combat them or how to prepare suitable anti-tank defences.

*

At the end of June 1941 the British Ambassador to China, Sir Archibald Clark-Kerr, proposed to the British government that an appropriate civil organization, headed by a man of considerable standing, should be set up in the Far East to prepare a policy and institute a programme for the co-ordination of civil activities throughout the Far East, in case communications between the various civil authorities and London were interrupted. On 18 July the Rt Hon. Alfred Duff Cooper, then the Chancellor of the Duchy of Lancaster, was chosen by the War Cabinet to go to the Far East to investigate Clark-Kerr's proposal. It is indicative of the general *laissez-faire* attitude in London towards the Far East that, although Duff Cooper received his terms of reference on 19 July, it was not till some seven weeks later that he reached Singapore. In this seven weeks the general situation in the Far East had rapidly deteriorated.

After discussing matters with the civil and military authorities in Malaya, the British Ambassador to China and the British Minister to Siam, and visiting the Netherlands East Indies and Burma, Duff Cooper called a conference at Singapore on 29 September, attended by Sir Shenton Thomas, Air Chief Marshal Sir Robert Brooke-Popham, Vice-Admiral Sir Geoffrey Layton, Sir Archibald Clark-Kerr, Sir Josiah Crosby (Minister to Siam) and Sir Earle Page (special Australian envoy to the British War Cabinet). The conference came to the conclusion that, as Japan was concentrating considerable forces for war against Russia and it could be assumed that she was well aware of the danger of being involved at the same time with Britain, the United States and the Netherlands, it was improbable that she was contemplating war in the south Pacific at any rate for the time being. Moreover, since it was unlikely that Japan would undertake a landing on the east coast of Malaya during the north-east monsoon (due to begin towards the end of October) the possibility of war for a number of months could be discounted.

It is almost unbelievable that a conference consisting of men of

118

such standing could come to this conclusion, for it ran counter to all the available evidence. It must have been due to their being supplied with information by the intelligence services that the Japanese were preparing for war with Russia. (*See chapter 9.*) For the Commander-in-Chief, Far East, to have allowed the conference to think for one minute that the Japanese could not land on the east coast of Malaya in the north-east monsoon is extraordinary, for it had been proved by experiment in 1937 to be possible, and this was well known to General Percival, who had been General Dobbie's chief staff officer at the time.

The conference gave it as their opinion that the only deterrent to Japanese aggression was the presence of a British fleet at Singapore and, aware of the impossibility of finding such a fleet within a reasonable time, expressed the view (already held by the Prime Minister but not by the Admiralty) that the presence of even one or two capital ships at Singapore would have immense propaganda value. They proposed that an announcement should be made that an agreed plan of action existed between the British, American and Dutch governments and would be put into action in the event of a Japanese threat to their territories in the Far East. This latter proposal could not be put into practice because of the unwillingness of the United States to commit herself. It can be said quite fairly that the conference accomplished little and had the effect of lulling the authorities in the Far East into slumber.

It was not till a month later that Duff Cooper submitted his report to the War Cabinet in London. In it he recommended that there should be a Commissioner-General for the Far East at Singapore, who would prepare the way for the formation of a War Council, should that be necessary, take over a number of political and diplomatic functions then carried out by the Commander-in-Chief, Far East, and act as a liaison link between the War Cabinet in London and the civil and military authorities in all territories in the Far East. Although this report was sent off on 29 October, it did not reach London till 24 November and no action on it had been taken by the time Japan entered the war.

*

The replacement of Brooke-Popham by a younger man with up-to-date experience of war had been under consideration in London since August 1941, and on 1 November Lieutenant-General Sir Henry Pownall was selected to take over the appointment of Commander-in-Chief, Far East. Pownall was an able and forthright man, who

119

had been Chief of Staff to the Commander of the British Expeditionary Force in France and therefore had firsthand experience of modern war. There was however to be a delay in his taking up the appointment, because early in November an argument arose on the subject whether the form of command should be that of one supreme Commander-in-Chief or of three equal heads, one from each Service, holding joint command. It was not till 25 November that the Chiefs of Staff agreed to having one man in supreme control. No change in command had therefore been made by the time war broke out. Unwilling now to swap horses in mid-stream, the Chiefs of Staff decided to leave Brooke-Popham in command and changed their minds only when Duff Cooper brought pressure to bear on the War Cabinet. Pownall was then ordered to take over as soon as he could reach Singapore. A situation thus existed in which a man who knew that he was to be superseded was left in charge at the most critical moment. On him depended the vital decisions to be taken in the days preceding the Japanese attack; decisions on which the outcome of the campaign might well depend.

12

War Comes to Malaya

December 1941   *Map C, pp. 100–1*

At the end of September 1941, Sir Robert Brooke-Popham estimated
that it was highly improbable that Japan was contemplating going
to war with Britain for some months; almost simultaneously Admiral
Layton expressed a similar view. During the following month
Brooke-Popham paid a second visit to Australia, where he told the
Australian War Council that he believed Japan had temporarily
diverted her attention to Manchuria and that she could not undertake a large-scale attack in the south for at least three months. He
also told the Council that, although the aircraft that Japan could
bring to bear on Malaya would outnumber the British aircraft there,
they were of inferior quality—a statement which was soon to be
proved quite untrue.

In the latter half of November reports reaching Malaya suggested
that the Japanese air strength in southern Indo-China had been
nearly doubled, that landing-craft had been loaded into ships at
Shanghai which were moving south, that Japanese naval forces in
the South China Sea had been reinforced, and that a convoy had
arrived at Hainan Island, where it was thought that a Japanese
division was under training. By the third week of November all the
signs that the Japanese were likely to launch an attack southwards
from their bases in southern Indo-China were present, and in Malaya
General Percival ordered precautionary measures which included the
protection of vulnerable points to be taken.

In view of this information, Brooke-Popham asked the Chiefs of
Staff to define the circumstances in which they would authorize the
launching of Matador. At the same time he reminded them that the
success of the operation was dependent on the fact that it must forestall the Japanese at Singora. Next day he not only instructed
General Percival to be ready to launch Matador at short notice and
to warn the troops on the east coast of Malaya to be ready for action,
but also ordered some of the RAF squadrons to move to their war
stations. The Chiefs of Staff replied to his telegram on 25 November
to the effect that it was not feasible for the British government to
commit itself in advance, and that a decision on Matador would
reach Singapore within thirty-six hours of knowledge reaching
London that the Japanese were on the move. Two days later Brooke-
Popham learned that the American consul at Hanoi had reported

that the Japanese were likely to attack the Kra Isthmus and northern Malaya without a declaration of war about 1 December. He therefore again reminded the Chiefs of Staff that Matador was designed to forestall the Japanese at Singora, pointing out that not only could Japanese troops begin disembarking at Singora some thirty-three hours after sailing from Saigon, but that even if they were to defer the sailing of a convoy till after they had crossed the Siamese border elsewhere, their troops could be at Singora within the period of thirty-six hours which would elapse before he would receive permission to act.

On 28 November the Admiralty ordered Admiral Phillips, who had just arrived in the *Prince of Wales* at Colombo, to fly to Singapore and then on to Manila to discuss with the Americans and Dutch the co-ordination of the naval plans in the Far East. At the same time they permitted the *Prince of Wales* and *Repulse* to sail for Singapore. Meanwhile Admiral Layton, then at Singapore, had taken all the precautions he could, including arrangements for the RAF to undertake air reconnaissance of an area within an arc of some 180 miles from Kota Bharu; but lack of aircraft made it impossible to cover the whole of the Gulf of Siam. He also asked the Dutch to send submarines to watch the Siamese coast in the vicinity of Singora and the Americans to reconnoitre the Manila–Camranh Bay area from Manila.

Having considered the views submitted by Brooke-Popham, the Chiefs of Staff came to the conclusion that the presence of Japanese ships off the coast of Siam did not constitute an act of war, and that to move into Siam on this pretext would put Britain into the position of violating its neutrality. On 29 November they told him that they were not prepared to acede to his request until they were able to obtain from the United States an assurance that she would enter into a war with Japan as Britain's ally.

Meanwhile, Percival, who was also responsible for the defence of Sarawak, which had a garrison of only one battalion, had gone to Kuching to examine the defence scheme with the local commander. On 30 November, when he embarked to return to Singapore, Percival was told by the captain of the destroyer that he had just received orders to get back to the naval base at the maximum possible speed. On his arrival there on 1 December Percival learnt that the American–Japanese negotiations in Washington had broken down, that Japan might invade Siam, the Philippines and the Netherlands East Indies at any time, and that the British Government had asked Washington for an assurance that she would provide armed support if action were taken to forestall Japan at Singora. Percival immediately arranged for the Volunteer Forces to be mobilized and for the whole garrison to be brought up to the second degree of readiness, and asked the RAF to intensify the air reconnaissance over the South China Sea. The need for these measures was proved the next day, when it became known that certain members of the Siamese Government had suggested that Japan should land troops at Kota Bharu; this they said would result in British troops violating Siamese territory and, since Britain would therefore appear to be the aggressor, Siam could declare war on Britain. On 2 December Brooke-Popham asked the Chiefs of Staff for authority to launch Matador should such circumstances arise, pointing out that, as a result of a Japanese landing at Kota Bharu, war between Britain and Japan would have already broken out. He received no reply to this request till the morning of the 8th.

On 5 December, having at long last received assurance from the United States that she would enter the war should Japan attack British territory, the Netherlands East Indies, or on Matador being undertaken either in reply to the violation of Siamese territory or to forestall a Japanese landing on the Kra Isthmus, the Chiefs of Staff told Brooke-Popham that he could order Matador to be launched without reference to London if the Japanese violated any part of Siam or if he had information that a Japanese expedition was advancing with the apparent intention of landing on the Kra Isthmus. Provided Brooke-Popham acted swiftly, it would now be possible for the Japanese to be forestalled at Singora, and the Ledge position to be occupied; this came as a great relief to Percival, who had set great store on the Matador operation.

Throughout December 1941 there was heavy cloud over the South China Sea for long periods, and only a few clear days. In northern Malaya there was both heavy cloud and heavy rain on the day the Japanese had selected for the invasion. Fortunately, about midday on 6 December a Hudson aircraft on reconnaissance at the extreme limits of its range reported seeing through gaps in the cloud a convoy of three transports with a cruiser escort south of Cape Cambodia, steaming north-west, and shortly afterwards another convoy of some twenty transports with an escort of cruisers and destroyers, well astern of the first convoy and roughly some one hundred miles south-east of Cape Cambodia, steering due west. Both convoys were south of latitude 6° North and some 250–260 sea miles from the coasts of southern Siam and northern Malaya; they were therefore well within range of the point where it had long been expected the Japanese would make their initial landing. On the same day the Far East

123

Combined Intelligence Bureau had received warning of the deparure of these convoys and of the actual points of attack. Information was also received that Siamese frontier guards were erecting road blocks near the frontier on both the Singora and the Kroh–Patani roads.

General Percival was at III Corps Headquarters at Kuala Lumpur when he heard the news that these convoys had been sighted. He expected that the Commander-in-Chief would order Matador to be launched immediately, and instructed General Heath to arrange for 11th Division to be ready to move off at short notice. At the same time he asked the Federated Malay States Railways to arrange for the trains required for the move to be held ready at the agreed entraining point. But on his return to Singapore that evening he was surprised to find that Matador had not been ordered. Apparently Sir Robert Brooke-Popham, after consulting Admiral Layton and Admiral Phillips's Chief of Staff, had come to the conclusion that when abreast of Cape Cambodia the second convoy would turn north-west, following the first convoy, and that both might have been routed to Bangkok rather than to Singora. Bearing in mind that British policy was to avoid war with Japan and that the Japanese–American conversations had been (momentarily) resumed, he took counsel with his fears. Thus, at the moment when bold action was essential Brooke-Popham hesitated, and the one and only opportunity to reach Singora before the Japanese was lost. His action is even more surprising in the light of the ADA Conference in February 1941 (*see pages 67–8*), and the ADB Conference of April 1941 (*see pages 68–9*), in both of which, under his chairmanship, it was recommended that the movement of any Japanese naval vessels south of latitude 6° North should be considered as constituting an act of war. It is also surprising that no notice was taken of the last-minute information provided by the Intelligence Bureau which gave Singora and Kota Bharu as the points of attack. There is no proof, however, that it ever reached Brooke-Popham.

Efforts to locate the Japanese ships by air reconnaissance were intensified, but heavy cloud cover prevailed and no further contacts were made during 6 December or during the night of the 6th/7th. Since it was considered that the convoys had been moving north-west, a Catalina flying-boat was sent at dawn on the 7th to try to locate them in the Gulf of Siam, but it failed either to report or to return. Not until about 6 p.m. on the 7th were reports received from some of the Hudson reconnaissance aircraft flying low that Japanese vessels had been sighted about one hundred miles north-east of Singora steering south-west towards that port, that others were steaming south parallel with the coast near Patani, and that a Hudson had been fired on by a Japanese cruiser.

After an interview with the Siamese Foreign Minister on 7 December the British Minister in Bangkok, Sir Josiah Crosby, sent a telegram to Brooke-Popham urging that British forces should not be allowed to cross into Siamese territory unless Japan had struck the first blow. He said that Siam was sympathetic to Britain and in opposition to Japan but, if Britain violated Siamese neutrality, the situation could be drastically altered. It seems that Crosby did not know that the Siamese Cabinet were divided and was not aware of the information which the Far East Intelligence Bureau had received from clandestine sources on 2 December.

As soon as Percival heard the news of the Hudson reconnaissance, he realized that Matador was no longer a feasible operation for, even if it were ordered at once, there was not enough time left to forestall the Japanese at Singora, which was clearly the Japanese objective. He therefore told Brooke-Popham that to launch it that evening would be unsound. Later he accompanied Sir Robert to a conference with Admiral Phillips, who had just returned from Manila. Still fearing, in view of the information received on 2 December and Sir Josiah's telegram of the 7th, that the Japanese were trying to force Britain to be the first to violate Siamese territory, and aware of Percival's views that the operation was no longer feasible, Brooke-Popham decided about 10.30 p.m. not to order Matador to be launched that night. He thought, surprisingly, that circumstances might still make the operation a feasible one, and so about midnight Heath was instructed to keep the troops standing by.

The decision taken on the evening of the 7th not to launch Matador did not, however, affect the issue, for the Japanese convoys arrived off Singora and Patani during the early hours of 8 December and their troops started landing before dawn; furthermore, it became known in Singapore shortly after 1 a.m. on the 8th that Japanese troops were attempting to land at Kota Bharu. At about 4 a.m. Japanese aircraft bombed Singapore itself. Thus war, which till mid-November no one in authority in Malaya believed would come until March 1942 at the earliest, came to a country which was almost completely unprepared for it.

*

Let us now examine the Japanese plan for the invasion of Malaya. The Japanese *25th Army*, commanded by Lieutenant-General T. Yamashita, known as the Lion of Manchuria, had been given the task of capturing Singapore, while *15th Army*, commanded by Lieutenant-General S. Iida, was, after *25th Army* had occupied Bangkok, to prepare a base in Siam for the invasion of Burma. The *25th Army* consisted of *Imperial Guards, 5th* and *18th Divisions* with *56th Division* in reserve (*see appendix*). Yamashita's plan was for *Imperial Guards Division*, moving overland from southern Indo-China, to seize and occupy Bangkok in order to bring Siam under complete control; it was then to prepare to move south by rail into Malaya to support the army's operations for the capture of Singapore. The *5th Division* was to land two regiments at Singora and one at Patani, move swiftly southwards to occupy Perlis and Kedah and then advance southwards along the western side of Malaya. One regiment of *18th Division* was to land at Kota Bharu, seize the Kelantan airfields and then move southwards along the east coast towards Kuantan. It was to be followed up by a second regiment. This left *25th Army* with one regiment of *5th Division* and *18th Division*, less its regiments allotted to the Kota Bharu area, in immediate reserve, to be landed as soon as possible at Singora; and *56th Division* in Japan, as an additional reserve.[1]

Simultaneously with the landings at Singora, Patani and Kota Bharu, a regiment of *55th Division* (part of *15th Army*) was to be landed at four points along the Kra Isthmus, between 100 and 300 miles north of Singora, to secure the railway line running from Bangkok to Singora and to seize a group of three airfields which lay between 100 and 225 miles north of Singora. Well aware that the British were contemplating a move northwards to try to forestall them at Singora, the Japanese had a plan ready to meet this eventality. If it were to occur, *5th Division* was to assist the regiment of *55th Division* to gain complete control of the group of airfields along the Kra Isthmus and to postpone its landings at Singora and Patani until air superiority over southern Siam had been secured.

The three regiments of *5th Division* and the one of *18th Division* sailed from Hainan Island in a convoy of nineteen transports at 5.30 a.m. on 4 December (this being the second of the convoys spotted by air reconnaissance). The regiment of *55th Division* sailed in a convoy of seven transports at 1.50 p.m. on 5 December (this being the first of the convoys spotted). Both convoys were given naval escorts. Close naval cover was provided by *7th Cruiser Squadron* (four cruisers with 8-inch guns and a division of destroyers) and distant naval cover by *Southern Force* (two battleships, two cruisers

---

[1] The success of *25th Army* was such that Yamashita had no reason to call on *56th Division*.

and a number of destroyers). At the same time a screen of submarines was deployed across the route which any British naval forces would use in an attempt to attack the convoys, and a minefield was laid between Pulau Tioman and the Anamba Islands off the east coast of Malaya. It will be seen that these naval forces, supported as they were by an air fleet based in southern Indo-China, were quite adequate to deal with a threat from such British naval forces as were in the Far East.

So that they could be covered by fighter aircraft operating from airfields in southern Indo-China, the convoys were routed close to the coast. After passing Cape Cambodia they were to move west-north-west to a rendezvous in the Gulf of Siam which was 100 miles from the nearest airfield on Phu Quoc Island (off the west coast of Indo-China), some 185 miles north of Kota Bharu and 170 miles north-east of Singora; they were to reach this rendezvous at 9 a.m. on 7 December. There they were to be joined by two transports carrying the ground personnel of the squadrons of *3rd Air Division*, already concentrated in the vicinity of Phu Quoc Island, which were to fly into Singora as soon as the airfield there had been secured. The rendezvous had been carefully worked out to ensure that the times selected for the landings could be kept, to give credence to rumours which had been allowed to circulate that Japan had embarked on a sea-borne invasion of Bangkok, and to ensure that once past Cape Cambodia the convoys would be as far as possible outside the range of British reconnaissance aircraft but still under their own fighter protection during the 7th.

Once the whole force of twenty-eight transports and their immediate escorts had assembled at the rendezvous, they were, provided the British had not by then occupied Singora, to split into their various component parts and move as rapidly as possible to their several destinations. The convoys destined for Singora and Patani were to arrive there at 3.30 a.m. on the 8th and the convoy for Kota Bharu was to arrive at 12.45 a.m.

It is evident that the Japanese had left nothing to chance. Although the convoys were likely to be sighted in clear weather while moving westwards along the south coast of Indo-China, they passed out of range of British land-based reconnaissance aircraft after passing Cape Cambodia and could only be spotted by flying-boats, of which there were few. The convoys were under close air protection by day throughout the journey and made their approach to their destinations under cover of darkness.

*

The Commander-in-Chief, Far East, did not, of course, have at his disposal the information given in the preceding paragraphs, but he did know that sizeable Japanese convoys were south of latitude 10° North moving towards the Gulf of Siam. Their destination was clearly Siam, and their objectives would obviously include the Kra Isthmus with its important airfields. Brooke-Popham had therefore complete freedom to launch Matador without reference to London. As has been shown he hesitated and lost the opportunity that existed. Had he ordered the operation on the afternoon of 6 December, 11th Division, even allowing for some resistance by Siamese frontier guards, would probably have reached Singora late on the 7th. It is now clear that the Japanese would have had news of the advance as soon as the British troops had crossed the Siamese border; in all probability they would have adopted their alternative plan, and the defence would have gained precious time. That Brooke-Popham hesitated can be understood, but it is surprising that neither he nor Percival realized that the occupation of the Ledge position was necessary whether Matador was or was not launched. Although by the 7th Matador was no longer feasible, it is difficult to understand why, in the circumstances, orders were not issued that evening for Krohcol to move into Siam and for 11th Division to be told to cancel Matador and take up its alternative defensive role. Had such action been taken a valuable twenty-four hours would have been gained. The blame for the lack of action must be laid mainly on the Commander-in-Chief's shoulders, but Percival could and should have pressed him on 7 December for 11th Division to be released from Matador and for Krohcol to be allowed to start its move to gain the Ledge position.

13

The Commanders in Malaya

Before dealing with the short and disastrous campaign in Malaya, let us have a look at some of the men who were to be in charge of it: Percival and Heath (the General Officer Commanding, Malaya, and the commander of III Corps), Gordon Bennett (8th Australian Division), Barstow (9th Indian Division), Murray-Lyon (11th Indian Division) and their brigadiers (*see appendix*).

Lieutenant-General A. E. Percival served throughout the First World War with distinction, and not only rose to command a battalion but for a short time also held the temporary command of a brigade. After a period of service in Africa, he qualified at both the Army and Naval Staff Colleges and in 1932 was promoted Colonel. From then on, with the exception of a year as a student at the Imperial Defence College, he served in various staff appointments until early in 1940, when he relinquished his appointment as Brigadier General Staff I Corps, then forming part of the British Expeditionary Force in France. He then commanded 43rd Division in the United Kingdom for two and a half months and, after a period of three months in the War Office as Assistant CIGS, was given command of 44th Division, also in the United Kingdom. After holding this appointment for nine months he became General Officer Commanding, Malaya, at the age of fifty-four. It will be seen therefore that from 1932 to 1941 he spent nine years as a staff officer, just under a year as the commander of a formation and, with the exception of his service as a young officer in the First World War, had had no experience of command in war. He proved from all accounts to be a brilliant staff officer, but was, however, quite untried as a commander and had neither the drive nor the ruthlessness which was needed by the commander who was to succeed General Bond in Malaya in 1941. His appointment to command the equivalent of an army in Singapore was probably due to the influence of Field-Marshal Sir John Dill, under whom he had served.

On arrival in Malaya Percival had two difficulties to face, both of which sprang from his having been Dobbie's staff officer in Malaya in 1936–8. One was that, having had the experience of drawing up the brilliant appreciation submitted by Dobbie in 1937, he had to guard against taking a preconceived view of the problem of the defence of Malaya and to approach it afresh in the light of conditions in 1941. The other was his relationship with the Governor, Sir Shenton Thomas. When he was on Dobbie's staff he was frequently in contact with Sir Shenton; in 1941 he returned as General Officer Commanding and as a member of the legislative assembly, and the relationship between the two men was on quite a different footing. Both men probably found it difficult to adjust themselves to the new circumstances which, in the event of war, would necessitate Percival taking the responsibility more and more from the Governor's hands.

Lieutenant-General Sir Lewis Heath, an officer of the Indian Army, was some two years older than Percival and, until the latter was appointed as General Officer Commanding, Malaya, was senior to him. His career was almost the complete opposite to that of Percival. With the exception of two years as an instructor at the Senior Officers' School in India, he had been with troops, often on active service in the North-West Frontier of India, and had commanded a brigade on that frontier for three years. He also had had experience of active operations in 1940–1, when he commanded 5th Indian Division in the Middle East. He was therefore an excellent choice for the command of a corps. Unfortunately, relations between Percival and Heath were not harmonious. Percival had never had any direct contact with the Indian Army, which he tended to consider second rate, and therefore did not always see eye to eye with Heath on tactical and strategical matters. This lack of harmony did not, however, affect their professional co-operation before and during the early stages of the campaign. But it did play its part later when III Corps was forced to withdraw from northern Malaya and Heath advocated a long withdrawal straight to the Johore border. The proposal was sound in itself, but it resulted in Percival losing confidence in a man with whom he had never been on the best of terms.

Both Major-General D. M. Murray-Lyon, a British service officer who had transferred to the Indian Army, and Major-General A. E. Barstow of the Indian Army were competent and well qualified to command divisions. Neither man had had any experience of active command as a divisional commander nor, owing to the conditions in Malaya, had either had any opportunity of training his divisions and formations with all their supporting arms. Furthermore they were both commanding troops who were not fully trained. Thus, compared with their Japanese opposite numbers, they both began the campaign at a considerable disadvantage. The same applies to the commanders of the brigades which had been sent from India, with the sole exception of Brigadier A. C. M. Paris commanding 12th Indian Infantry Brigade, who had had the opportunity of training his brigade with most of its supporting arms for a considerable period (*see chapter 10*); a factor which was to show itself very clearly during the campaign.

Major-General H. Gordon Bennett, the commander of 8th Australian Division, born the same year as Percival, was not a professional soldier. At the age of twenty-one he had been given a commission in an infantry regiment of the Australian Militia. When compulsory service was introduced into Australia in 1912, Bennett was promoted to the rank of major. He went overseas with the Australian Imperial Force as second-in-command of a battalion in 2nd Australian Brigade in 1914 and saw service both in Gallipoli and in France. In the former theatre he showed great bravery and a sense of leadership and was soon in command of his battalion. In France at the end of 1916 he was promoted to the rank of Brigadier-General and given command of 3rd Australian Infantry Brigade which, with the exception of two short periods in 1917 when he was temporarily in command of 1st Australian Division, he commanded till the end of the First World War. He returned to Australia with a considerable reputation and re-entered civilian life. But he kept his commission and interest in the militia and soldiering. In 1921 he was given command of 9th Australian Infantry Brigade and in 1926 of 2nd Australian Division, the highest command available to a militia soldier. In 1930 at the age of forty-three he was promoted substantive Major-General, thereby becoming the youngest general in the Australian military hierarchy.

In 1937 he wrote a series of articles to the newspapers in which he alleged that senior militia officers were being excluded from the command of divisions and that preference was being given to officers of the Permanent Staff Corps, who were trained mainly as staff officers and were therefore not fit for command in war. He also alleged that as a result of poor training programmes the militia were inefficient, and that senior militia officers were not being trained to fit them for high command in war. When the Second World War broke out, Bennett was not recommended for the command of the 6th, 7th or 9th Australian Divisions, which were formed and sent to the Middle East. Bennett, galled by this treatment, made determined efforts to vindicate himself, but the Military Board, while recognizing his qualities, felt that he was a controversial figure whose temperament disqualified him for active command overseas. Thus, when 8th Australian Division was formed, the command was given to Major-General V. A. H. Sturdee, an officer of the Permanent Staff Corps.

At this point fate stepped in. The Australian Chief of the General Staff and three Australian Ministers, including the Army Minister, were all killed in an air crash at Canberra. As a result Sturdee was appointed Chief of the General Staff, and at Sturdee's request Bennett, now fifty-three, was appointed to command 8th Australian Division, which was then destined for service in the Middle East but which was eventually sent to Malaya. An ambitious man, Bennett made every effort not only to get his division concentrated in Malaya but also to get himself appointed as the General Officer Commanding Australian Imperial Force, Malaya, in lieu of his appointment as General Officer Commanding 8th Australian Division. He succeeded in this effort on 30 October 1941. Since he was an extravert, impetuous in all his actions, and resented criticism, he was not an easy man for someone of Percival's character to have as a subordinate.

Nor was all well within the Australian division in Malaya. In March 1941, during a training exercise in which 22nd Australian Brigade commanded by Brigadier H. B. Taylor had to move from the Port Dickson area to support 12th Indian Brigade, Bennett, who had only one brigade to control, was unable to restrain himself from interfering with the handling of Taylor's brigade, and serious friction resulted. Although the difference between the two men was patched up it left its mark; Taylor, an excellent brigadier, lost confidence in his divisional general and thereafter kept himself aloof from divisional headquarters and as far as he could went his own way. Since Bennett was a man who believed in control from the rear, assisted by liaison officers, and never went forward in action to see for himself and to discuss matters with his brigadiers, the coolness between the two men was never cured.

When it was decided to send 27th Australian Brigade to Malaya, Bennett demanded the right, already accorded to the commander of 1st Australian Corps in the Middle East, to make his own promotions to fill vacancies from within his division. This right was ceded by the Military Board but, when the commander of 27th Brigade relinquished his command because of ill health, Bennett selected one of his junior battalion commanders, Lieutenant-Colonel D. S. Maxwell, a doctor by profession and a militia soldier, to be promoted to the command of the Brigade. Although he had served with distinction in the First World War, Maxwell was not up to the standard of many others suitable for the post. This lack of experience as a commander resulted in his leaning on Bennett for help and advice. Thus, throughout the campaign, he always located his headquarters as close as he could to divisional headquarters. As a result he was frequently out of touch with events on the front which he was supposed to be controlling and was unable to exercise proper command over his brigade; a fact which was to make itself felt during the latter portion of the campaign.

14

The Disastrous First Four Days of the Campaign

8–12 December 1941 *Map C, pp. 100–1, and Map D, p. 145*

As soon as it was known that Japan had begun hostilities, General Percival and Air Marshal Pulford made three decisions: to send a dawn air reconnaissance to Singora, to send the Blenheim bomber squadrons located at Alor Star and Sungei Patani to attack the Japanese transports off Kota Bharu at first light, and to order a battalion from 12th Brigade at Port Dickson to move to Kuala Krai, where it would reinforce 8th Brigade. As this battalion could not reach Kuala Krai until the morning of 9 December, by which time it was probable that the Kota Bharu airfield would either be useless or in enemy hands, the wisdom of the last order is questionable.

No sooner had these decisions been taken than about 3.30 a.m. warning was received at Singapore that unidentified aircraft were approaching Singapore from the north-east. Warnings were immediately sent to all Service establishments, and the anti-aircraft defences were prepared. Attempts were also made to alert the civil Air Raids Precautions organization, but without any results. Despite the anxieties of the previous week the civil authorities were still so sure 'that it could not happen to us' that, it being a weekend, the staff of the headquarters of the ARP organization were sleeping peacefully in their own beds and the headquarters was unmanned. Thus the Japanese bombers, arriving over the island about 4 a.m., found all the street lights ablaze. Bombs were dropped on the Seletar and Tengah airfields without causing much damage, but some fell in the centre of the city, causing heavy casualties amongst the Asian population. The British could not use night fighters for fear that their presence in the skies would confuse the inexperienced anti-aircraft gunners. Anti-aircraft fire failed to obtain any hits on the Japanese aircraft, which withdrew unscathed. All in all, the attack was a rude awakening for the population of Singapore, who had always been told by the civil authorities that war was unlikely and that the defences were strong enough to secure them from any attack by land, sea or air.

At Kota Bharu, despite artillery fire and attacks on the transport and landing-craft by the Hudson aircraft of the Australian squadron stationed at the airfield, the Japanese succeeded during the night in landing three waves of troops near the airfield. Only one transport was hit and some landing-craft were damaged. The defenders at the point of attack resisted until they were all killed, but gradually during the night the Japanese extended their original beachhead by infiltrating through the widely spaced defences; by dawn they had three battalions ashore and a bridgehead of reasonable size. At first light the bombers from Kedah arrived to find that the Japanese transports had disappeared; they therefore went on to Patani but failed to hit any of the transports lying off that port and returned to their bases without having achieved anything. While they were refuelling and rearming, both airfields were attacked by Japanese aircraft, and a number of the bombers were destroyed or damaged on the ground. The RAF's only offensive weapon thus received a serious blow. Shortly after dawn Brigadier B. W. Key, commanding 8th Brigade, issued orders for his two reserve battalions to counter-attack the Japanese beachhead, one from the west and one from the east. His plan was sound, but the terrain over which it was to be launched was intersected by creeks, and the troops had had insufficient training in mobile operations. Both battalions lost direction and cohesion, and as a result the attack failed completely.

About 4 p.m. on 8 December a rumour spread among the RAAF personnel on the airfield that the Japanese had reached its perimeter. The passage of stray bullets across the airfield gave credence to the rumour. There was no truth in it; nevertheless a semi-panic set in, and somebody telephoned Air Headquarters in Singapore saying that the airfield was under attack. In view of this information and since aircraft had been damaged on the ground during the day by Japanese air attacks, Pulford ordered the squadron to withdraw to Kuantan. The aircraft flew off and the ground personnel of the squadron, having set fire to the operations room and some of the stores, hurriedly set off in lorries for Kuala Krai. The squadron made no attempt to damage the runways, to destroy petrol stocks or to blow up the reserves of bombs and ammunition, and it was left to Key to destroy the oil storage tanks by gunfire that evening.

While these events had been taking place on the airfield, the civil authorities had also evacuated the Sultan of Kelantan, his entourage and most of the civil population of the town of Kota Bharu to Kuala Krai, which was the provincial administrative headquarters. This made Key's task easier. With three of his battalions disorganized and the fourth holding the long stretch of beach down to Gong Kedah in the south, he realized that he would be wise to abandon the defence of the already useless airfield and to concentrate his forces between it and the town, with his left flank secured by the Kelantan River. When the Japanese transports reappeared off the beaches at about 7 p.m. on 8 December, he sought permission from General Barstow (11th Division) to withdraw to the new position. This was granted, and by dawn on the 9th he had occupied it, though all three battalions had suffered further disorganization as a result of a night withdrawal in heavy rain and pitch darkness over difficult country.

The Japanese quickly attacked Key's new position. Realizing that there was no longer any advantage in holding the town which had already been evacuated, and that his position was not suitable for prolonged defence, Key disengaged and by nightfall on 9 December had retired to a new position some twenty miles further south. He covered this withdrawal with the Hyderabad battalion which Percival had sent up by rail from his reserve and which had arrived that morning. The Japanese did not follow up, and the 10th passed quietly, many of the troops cut off or lost during the operations of the 8th and 9th rejoining their units. That evening there were rumours that the Japanese had made further landings in the vicinity of the Gong Kedah airfield. Since a landing in this area threatened his communications and the RAF no longer required the use of any of the Kelantan airfields, Key wisely decided to withdraw his whole force to Machang during the 11th. Barstow, however, seeing that there was no longer any strategical advantage in holding on to Kelantan, asked General Heath to agree to the concentration of 8th Brigade at Kuala Lipis. Heath agreed to this but Percival refused to countenance such an early and long withdrawal.

Shortly after 9 a.m. on 8 December an aircraft which had carried out a reconnaissance landed very badly damaged at Kota Bharu. The pilot reported that the Japanese had landed both at Singora and Patani and that Japanese aircraft were already operating from the Singora airfield. Brooke-Popham then decided to release 11th Division from Matador and to allow Percival to send Krohcol into Siam to occupy the Ledge position. For some reason these orders failed to reach Heath till 1 p.m. At 1.30 p.m. Heath placed 28th Brigade at the disposal of 11th Division, ordering it to move forward to Alor Star, released the division from standing by for Matador, instructed its commander, Major-General Murray-Lyon, to occupy the Jitra position and to send Krohcol across the border into Siam, and ordered the previously reconnoited position at Gurun to be prepared for defence. The delay of some twelve hours from the opening of hostilities was to prove fatal, for it gave the Japanese who had landed at Singora and Patani some ten hours' start, of which they made full use, as will be shown. The onus for the greater part of the delay must lie with Brooke-Popham.

*

Early on the morning of 8 December Admiral Phillips, Commander-in-Chief, Eastern Fleet, heard that the Japanese were landing troops at Singora, Patani and Kota Bharu. He had made clear in his discussions with the Americans at Manila that in the event of war his squadron could not remain at Singapore with any degree of safety and had suggested making a rendezvous with the US Asiatic Fleet somewhere among the islands forming the Netherlands East Indies. Now, however, he concluded that his small but powerful squadron should sail into the Gulf of Siam, where it could attack the Japanese transports. Clearly he considered that his small squadron would not be in danger from air attack moving up the east coast of Malaya but only when it actually entered the Gulf of Siam.

About noon Phillips called a conference of all his senior officers on board the *Prince of Wales* and announced his intention of taking the squadron into the Gulf of Siam. He said that from the information available to him the Japanese transports were covered by one battleship, five cruisers and some twenty destroyers. He admitted, however, that he had no reliable information on the strength, disposition or efficiency of the Japanese air forces in southern Indo-China. After some discussion it was agreed that his plan for a surprise raid, although hazardous, should be adopted; and Phillips decided to sail from the naval base about 5.30 p.m. that evening.

Just before the fleet sailed Air Marshal Pulford told Phillips that it was very doubtful whether he could provide fighter protection off Singora on 10 December. This rendered the operation more hazardous, and Phillips would have been wiser to have called it off and to have taken his squadron southwards out of danger of air attack to join the Dutch fleet in the Java Sea, or to have gone to Ceylon. However, leaving his Chief of Staff, Rear-Admiral A. F. E. Palliser, behind in Singapore to keep in touch with Pulford, Phillips sailed. In the early hours of the 9th Palliser informed him that, although the air reconnaissance for which he had asked on the 9th and 10th could be provided, fighter cover off Singora on the 10th was definitely not possible. In the same message Palliser told him that it was known that the Japanese had large bomber forces in southern Indo-China and probably in Siam, that Kota Bharu airfield had been abandoned and that it was probable the RAF could not operate from any of the

137

northern Malayan airfields. At this time Phillips and his squadron were still south of the Anamba Islands and, for the second time, he had information which indicated that it would have been prudent to have called off the operation. Nevertheless, with no protection other than the anti-aircraft guns of his two capital ships and his four destroyers, he decided to carry on. It seems evident that he discounted the danger of air attack, and had absorbed the view that the Japanese air force was inefficient. Even if he escaped detection on the 9th and sailed into the Gulf of Siam during the night of the 9th/10th, his chances of escaping destruction were negligible.

During the evening of the 10th three enemy aircraft were seen from his flagship, and it was evident that the Japanese knew of his position. Only then did Phillips realize that the risk he was taking was unjustified and shortly after dark, when some 275 miles from Singapore, he turned about and made for Singapore at high speed. He did not, however, know that he had been sighted by a patrolling submarine just before 2 p.m. on the 9th, that Japanese naval air flotillas were already searching for him and that whatever course he took on his return journey to Singapore he was likely to have to withstand heavy air attack.

Meanwhile, an unfortunate incident occurred at Kuantan. The troops manning the beach defences, having been warned that a ship had been seen towing barges in the vicinity of that area, thought that they sighted some boats offshore after dark. They immediately assumed that the Japanese were attempting a landing and opened fire. A report that the enemy was attempting to land at Kuantan was sent to Singapore and Palliser duly passed this on to Phillips. At about 1 a.m. on the 10th Phillips altered course to close in on Kuantan, where he hoped to create havoc among the Japanese transports he expected to find there. An hour later he was spotted by another enemy submarine.

When Phillips arrived off Kuantan at 8 a.m. and found that the reports of a landing were false, he re-set his course east of the Anamba Islands to return to Singapore. Meanwhile, before dawn the Japanese had sent out twelve reconnaissance aircraft to search for the British squadron in the area where, from the 2 a.m. report from the submarine, it was likely to be, and at dawn thirty-four bombers and fifty-one torpedo-bombers took off from Saigon. About 10 a.m. Phillips's squadron was located by a Japanese reconnaissance aircraft, which directed the attacking force towards it. The result is well known. The *Repulse*, hit by five torpedoes, sank at 12.33 p.m., and the *Prince of Wales*, hit by five torpedoes and one bomb, sank at

1.20 p.m. The only news of the attack which reached Singapore was a laconic wireless message from the *Repulse*, sent just before noon, saying 'Enemy aircraft bombing', but the message gave no position. Not until one hour after the spotter aircraft from the *Prince of Wales* landed at Penang at 11.30 a.m., did Air Headquarters at Singapore learn where the squadron was located. Seven minutes later eleven fighter aircraft took off but they arrived at the scene of action as the *Prince of Wales* sank and the Japanese aircraft were disappearing over the horizon. Thus Phillips's sortie ended in utter disaster; the only redeeming feature being that 2,081 officers and ratings out of a total of 2,921 from the two ships were saved.

The events of 10 December 1941 gave the Japanese complete command of the South China Sea, the Java Sea and a great part of the Indian Ocean. This action had a disastrous effect on British morale throughout the world and enhanced that of the Japanese. Few in Britain, or elsewhere, who heard of the loss of the two capital ships will ever forget the dismay that struck their hearts, a dismay which remained with them till the American naval victories at the battles of the Coral Sea and in particular Midway in the summer of 1942.

On 10 December, before the news of the loss of the British capital ships was known, the Prime Minister appointed Duff Cooper, who was already at Singapore, to be Resident Minister for Eastern Affairs at Singapore. His terms of reference made it clear that his appointment was not to impair the existing responsibilities of the Commanders-in-Chief or Britain's representatives in the Far East, or their official relationship with their respective departments in London. He was to give the Commanders-in-Chief political guidance and relieve them, as far as was possible, of extraneous responsibilities so they could give their full attention to the conduct of the campaign. He was, however, given the power to settle emergency matters on the spot when there was no time to refer them to London, and was also authorized to give, at his own discretion, overriding authority to departmental officers to incur expenditure when he was satisfied that urgent action was necessary and there was no time to refer back to London. There was, however, a proviso that expenditure normally remained the responsibility of the appropriate ministries in London, and the view was expressed that the Resident Minister would rarely have to take action where large financial commitments were involved. Since from 8 December there was a constant state of emergency in Malaya, these terms of reference gave Duff Cooper immense powers, which, if used to the full, would have been of great value in the month to come but, if used without tact, could produce only friction in the already cumbersome government machinery in Malaya and Singapore.

The Resident Minister was also to preside over a War Council consisting of the Governor (Sir Shenton Thomas), the Commander-in-Chief, Far East (Air Chief Marshal Sir Robert Brooke-Popham; after 23 December Lieutenant-General Sir Henry Pownall), the Commander-in-Chief, Eastern Fleet (Admiral Phillips; after his death, Admiral Layton), the General Officer Commanding, Malaya (Lieutenant-General Percival), the Air Officer Commanding, Far East (Air Vice-Marshal Pulford) and Mr V. G. Bowden (representing the Australian government). It was also agreed that Major-General Gordon Bennett (8th Australian Division) should attend the council's meetings, if he so wished and his military duties permitted.

*

In northern Malaya, meanwhile, the Japanese army air force, which had quickly established itself on airfields in southern Siam, set to work on 8 December to destroy the British air forces based in northern Malaya and thereby to gain air supremacy. Owing to the weakness of the RAF, the very limited anti-aircraft protection provided for its airfields, the lack of any proper warning system and a numerical superiority of some four to one, the Japanese had little difficulty in achieving their object. On the east coast, in Kelantan State, the airfields at Kota Bharu, Gong Kedah and Machang had been evacuated during the afternoon of the 8th and the squadrons withdrawn to Kuantan; while on the west coast, in Kedah State, squadrons were withdrawn from Alor Star and Sungei Patani to Butterworth (on the mainland, immediately east of Penang). Moreover, of the 110 British aircraft located in northern Malaya on the morning of the 8th only 50 were left fit for operations by the evening.

On 9 December Air Vice-Marshal Pulford sent six Blenheim bombers from Singapore to attack the Singora airfield. They were to be joined by an escort of Buffalo fighters from Butterworth, but the few available fighters there were fully engaged in providing cover for that airfield, and so the Blenheims went on to Singora unescorted. Despite heavy anti-aircraft fire and attacks by numbers of Japanese fighters, they managed to drop their bombs in the target area, but three of them were shot down. A second attack with the remaining Blenheims was planned for the afternoon, but just as they were about to take off from Butterworth the Japanese attacked the airfield with bombers and low-flying fighters. All the Blenheims were destroyed or damaged except one which, flown by the Squadron-Leader, A. S. K. Scarf, was airborne at the time of the attack. All alone Scarf flew on to Singora, dropped his bombs in the target area despite the same fierce opposition as had been met in the morning and returned to Malaya. He was, however, mortally wounded but before he died he managed to land his aircraft at Alor Star. For this gallant effort he was awarded a posthumous VC. This ended the RAF's attempts to counter-attack, for there were few bombers left and without fighter escort they could accomplish little. In fact Pulford decided then and there that he would have to confine his attacks to night bombing.

Meanwhile, Pulford had ordered all but two of the squadrons now concentrated at Kuantan to return to Singapore. He was only just in time, for shortly after noon Japanese aircraft attacked Kuantan, which was entirely without anti-aircraft defences, and destroyed seven aircraft of the squadron left there. The remaining aircraft were then hurriedly flown to Singapore, and the ground personnel, as at Kota Bharu (*see page 135*), abandoned the airfield on 10 December in considerable disorder. By the evening of the 9th, the RAF had been forced to evacuate the three airfields in Kelantan State (Kota Bharu, Gong Kedah and Machang), the single one in Pahang State (Kuantan), and the two in Kedah State (Alor Star and Sungei Patani), and in northern Malaya had only a combined fighter and bomber force of ten aircraft at Butterworth. The Japanese had in two days gained complete air superiority in northern Malaya.

On 10 December, at the same time as the abandonment of Kuantan, the RAF withdrew their ground staffs from Alor Star and Sungei Patani. Bombs which could not be moved, petrol stocks and control buildings were destroyed at Alor Star, but the runways were not put out of action. At Sungei Patani, as at Kuantan, the withdrawal of the ground staff was unnecessarily hurried, and there was considerable disorder similar to that which had occurred at the Kota Bharu airfield, with stocks of petrol, oil and important stores being left behind for the benefit of the Japanese.

*

The 11th Division, with its two brigades organized for their proposed dash forward to Singora, had been standing by for some forty-eight hours in atrociously wet weather alongside their entraining stations or at the starting points for the road parties. Morale was high and all ranks were eager to start, but, as time passed and the expected orders did not come, morale began to sink. The order received at 1.30 p.m. on 8 December to return to the practically abandoned and mostly waterlogged defences at Jitra, coupled with the need to reorganize themselves for a defensive battle, reduced their morale even lower. They marched back dispiritedly and began the task of pumping water out of their defence posts, repairing them and re-laying the signal communications and barbed-wire entanglements pulled up for Matador. With weary and dispirited troops this was to be a long business, and the division could not be ready for some time to meet the Japanese onslaught, which was to come much more swiftly than anyone had imagined.

Despite the fact that III Corps had been placed at the first degree of readiness on the 6th, Krohcol, which had the vital task of reaching and holding the Ledge position and so protecting the communications of 11th Division, had not even been concentrated at Kroh ready to cross the frontier. It had been planned that it should consist of two battalions, the light battery of the Federated Malay States Volunteers, a company of engineers and a field ambulance. But at 1.30 p.m. on the 8th, when it received its orders to advance into Siam, Lieutenant-Colonel H. D. Moorhead, the column commander, had only his own battalion available, for the second one had not arrived from Penang and the FMS Volunteer battery had not completed its mobilization. Moorhead crossed the frontier at 3 p.m. on the 8th and immediately met with opposition from Siamese frontier guards. By nightfall he had advanced only three miles. Next day the advance proceeded extremely slowly and it was not until late in the afternoon, when opposition suddenly ceased, that Betong, a village only five miles from the frontier, was occupied.

Early on the morning of 10 December, with his battalion carried in the lorries of an Australian transport company, Moorhead set off for The Ledge. Six miles short of the objective, however, he came under fire from Japanese troops who, thanks to Brooke-Popham's continued hesitations and the dilatory way in which the Siamese opposition had been dealt with, had been allowed to win the race for this vital position. A Japanese regiment, supported by light tanks and light artillery, had landed at Patani at about 3 a.m. on the 8th and by the afternoon of the 10th, some sixty hours later, had covered the seventy-five miles to the vital Ledge. The encounter battle that followed was disastrous. Japanese tanks quickly overran the leading company, and on the 12th, with his battalion reduced to about half its strength, Moorhead withdrew to a defensive position astride the road from Kroh to Sungei Patani. The 11th Division's line of communication was now threatened and, whatever happened when the Japanese attacked at Jitra, its position and the defence of Kedah was in jeopardy. The cost of the original delay, with the failure to concentrate Krohcol when III Corps was placed at the first degree of readiness, was to prove high.

It must be noted here that the Headquarters of III Corps was located near Headquarters 9th Division at Kuala Lumpur, about 250 from Jitra. The control of both 11th Division and Krohcol was delegated to General Murray-Lyon, the divisional commander. Furthermore, on the night of the 11th/12th General Heath went on an apparently unnecessary journey by train to Singapore. He was thus out of touch with the situation at the vital point, while too heavy a load was placed on Murray-Lyon.

The plan for the defence of Kedah, failing the launching of Matador, was to hold the pre-selected Jitra position with 11th Division (which would be allotted its third brigade), to send one battalion forward on the main road to Singora, to meet and delay the Japanese advance in the vicinity of the frontier, and to send forward an armoured train with a detachment of infantry along the railway line through Perlis for the same purpose. While his two brigades were reorganizing the Jitra position, Murray-Lyon carried out this plan. The Punjabi battalion (the reserve battalion of 15th Infantry Brigade allotted to the right sector of the Jitra position) moved up the main road and penetrated some ten miles into Siam, where it awaited developments, while the armoured train with a detachment from a battalion of 6th Infantry Brigade (allotted to the left sector of the Jitra position) moved up the railway, blew a railway bridge in Siam and withdrew gradually towards Jitra, destroying bridges as it went.

At 9.30 p.m. on 9 December the advance guard of the Japanese *5th Division*, consisting of two battalions, a light battery, a tank company and some engineers, led by the tanks moved down the main road with their headlights blazing. The two leading tanks were hit by anti-tank fire and stopped. The Japanese columns then came to a halt; but the Punjabi battalion, as its orders were purely to delay the enemy, withdrew during the night to Changlun (some six miles south of the frontier), having destroyed a number of culverts on the roads. On arrival there it occupied a defensive position astride the road behind a destroyed bridge over a stream. The original plan was for the battalion, having checked the Japanese force in the vicinity of Changlun, to retire later to the main outpost position some eight miles further south at Asun.

143

Because of the delay in occupying the Jitra position, and the time required to prepare it, Murray-Lyon realized that he would not be ready to meet a Japanese attack before 12 December. In consequence he ordered Brigadier K. A. Garrett, commanding 15th Brigade, to go forward with a Gurkha battalion from the reserve (28th) brigade and delay the Japanese till the 12th. On arrival at Asun about midday on the 10th, Garrett ordered the Gurkhas to take over the Asun outpost position and the Punjabis to concentrate forward at Changlun. Early on the morning of the 11th the Japanese attacked the Punjabis and drove them a short distance back from the destroyed bridge over the stream; in doing so they captured two anti-tank guns.

Late in the afternoon the Punjabis began to move back in heavy rain. The Japanese, who had quickly repaired the road bridge they had captured early that morning, resumed their move south about 4 p.m. Thus it was that a Japanese column headed by tanks followed by lorried infantry suddenly appeared out of the gloom and murk. Driving right through the Punjabis' rearguard, it overran a section of anti-tank guns and then drove across the bridge in front of the Asun outpost position, which had not been blown. It was well into the Gurkhas' position before the leading tank was brought to a halt by a well-directed shot from an anti-tank rifle. The Japanese infantry, leaving their lorries, quickly attacked the Gurkhas, who were already thrown into confusion by the sudden appearance of a Japanese column, including tanks, in their midst, and cleared the road. The column, still led by the tanks, then drove on until it reached the outskirts of the Jitra position, where it was brought to a halt by a well-sited anti-tank battery. Thus, by the end of the 11th, this sudden Japanese thrust had advanced some ten miles, scattered two battalions and inflicted heavy casualties. Garrett himself was cut off, but with a few hundred men managed to get back to Jitra the next day, as did other small parties. But many were taken prisoners and the remnant of both units were quite unfitted to take part in the battle for Jitra.

To the west the armoured train with its detachment of infantry withdrew into the Jitra position on 11 December. But again disaster struck. As the infantry and guns approached down the road into the Jitra position, the officer responsible for blowing up the bridge did so, thinking that the column was Japanese. Since there was no material at hand to repair the bridge quickly, seven anti-tank guns, four mountain guns and a number of tracked carriers and other vehicles had to be abandoned.

The Jitra position was not a good one. It stretched from the jungle-

144

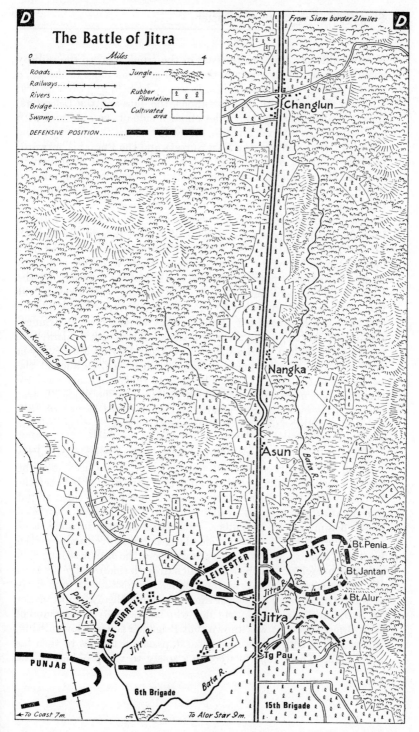

The Battle of Jitra

Miles
0 _____ 4

Roads.....
Railways...
Rivers.....
Bridge.....
Swamp.....

Jungle.....
Rubber Plantation
Cultivated area

DEFENSIVE POSITION.........

From Siam border 21 miles

Changlun

From Kodiang 5m.

Nangka

Asun

Bata R.

LEICESTER

JATS

▲Bt. Penia

Bt. Jantan

▲Bt. Alur

EAST SURREY

Perlis R.

Jitra R.

Jitra R.

Jitra

Jitra R.

Bata R.

PUNJAB

Tg Pau

6th Brigade

15th Brigade

←To Coast 7m.

To Alor Star 9m.

L

covered hills two miles to the east of the trunk road to the railway some four miles to its west and thence for some six miles to the sea, a total width of some twelve miles. It was to be held by two brigades: 15th, on the right with two battalions, the Jats and the Leicesters, forward, covering some two miles on each side of the road and with one battalion in reserve; and 6th, on the left across the railway to the sea with two battalions, the East Surreys and the Punjabis, forward, covering a front of some eight miles and with one battalion in reserve. The position was nowhere more than one and a half miles in depth. Much of the front was protected by swamps, and the most likely line of attack was just east of the main road, since it offered the easiest line of approach. It was here, however, that there was the least depth of the position—about half a mile. Behind the forward post of 15th Brigade lay the Jitra and Bata Rivers, each with only one bridge and that on the trunk road. There were no road communications from the trunk road to the left of the position. By the time the battle was joined the reserve battalion of 15th Brigade, cut up at Changlun, had ceased to exist; of the reserve brigade (28th), one battalion had been left in the vicinity of Alor Star and Sungei Patani airfields to protect them against possible attack by parachute troops and one had been destroyed at Asun, leaving Murray-Lyon with a reserve of only one battalion, which he had to allot at the beginning of the battle to 15th Brigade to replace its lost unit. He therefore had no reserve with which to influence the battle. It was evident that everything depended on the forward troops of 15th Brigade standing fast, assisted by counter-attacks by the brigade reserve.

With their tanks checked on the main road in front of the Jitra position, the Japanese sent out patrols to probe the extent of the position east of the main road. Finding that gaps existed between the defended localities, the advanced guard commander decided to put in a night attack with his available infantry. This attack, launched about 3 a.m. on 12 December, penetrated slightly into the area astride the road held by the Leicesters, but was eventually driven back by a counter-attack. Just as dawn broke the Japanese launched a further attack east of the road, which drove a small wedge between the Leicesters and the Jats on their right, but this time an immediate counter-attack failed to recover the lost ground. Meanwhile Brigadier W. St J. Carpendale (28th Brigade), who had been given command of 15th Brigade when it was known that Brigadier Garrett was missing, was receiving continuous reports of Japanese attempts to turn his right flank. These reports were due solely to the probings of the

Japanese patrols east of the road. The inexperienced junior commanders and troops, however, exaggerated the situation to such an extent that Carpendale came to the conclusion that the real threat was that of an enveloping movement around his right flank. He therefore deployed his reserve Gurkha battalion astride the road on the line of the Bata River and appealed to Brigadier W. O. Lay (6th Brigade) for help. Lay sent him two companies from his left (Punjabi) battalion and two more from his reserve (Punjabi) battalion. Carpendale used the two former to strengthen the Jats' right flank, one of the latter to extend the right of the Gurkhas' position on the Bata River and kept one in reserve. All these movements took place during the night without General Murray-Lyon being informed.

When the Jats failed to drive out the dawn Japanese attack by an immediate counter-attack, Carpendale again asked Lay for help and was given the remainder of his reserve (Punjabi) battalion. This left Lay with one battalion (East Surreys) in their original position on the left of the Leicesters but with no troops west of the railway and no reserves. Carpendale then ordered Lay's reserve Punjabi battalion to launch a counter-attack supported by artillery to regain the lost ground in the centre of the position. Unfortunately the Jats on the right and the Punjabis who were undertaking the counter-attack mistook each other for Japanese and opened fire. Although this error was soon brought under control, it caused sufficient delay for the artillery-support programme to have finished by the time that the battalion actually moved into the attack. The result was obvious: the counter-attack failed, with serious casualties.

About 9 a.m. on 12 December Murray-Lyon heard of the night's events. Carpendale, who was convinced that the Japanese were about to envelop his right flank, had committed to defensive positions all his reserves and the troops he had borrowed from 6th Brigade, except the battalion about to undertake the counter-attack. When this failed Murray-Lyon, with no troops left in reserve with which to influence the battle, was faced with a crucial decision. He was aware that the RAF had already abandoned Alor Star airfield, that Krohcol was in retreat in face of a superior force, that there was therefore a threat to his line of communication, and that he had been ordered by General Heath to take no risks, since his formation was the only one available to defend northern Malaya. He also realized that the morale of his troops had deteriorated and that they were no match for the Japanese. To stand and fight might well mean the complete destruction of his division; for he knew the Japanese were bound to launch a full-scale attack on Jitra with their main body within the next twenty-four hours.[1] His chances of defeating such an attack were small, since he had no reserves. Even if he managed to hold the main Japanese attack, he would soon have to abandon Kedah and withdraw behind the Muda River some fifty miles to the south to prevent his line of communication being cut behind him. Consequently, he decided that his best course was to disengage and withdraw behind the Kedah River to the reconnoitred, but not prepared, positions at Gurun.

He telephoned III Corps to explain the position and to obtain Heath's agreement to his proposed action; unfortunately, Heath was in Singapore (*see page 143*) and the request was therefore passed to General Percival. Neither Heath nor Percival back in Singapore had any idea of the true position and the danger in which 11th Division stood. It seemed to them that an early withdrawal so soon after the opening of the campaign would have a devastating effect on the morale of the civil population as well as on the whole garrison. Quite unaware of the tactical considerations which had prompted Murray-Lyon's request, they felt they could not allow him to withdraw, and he was therefore told to stay and fight the battle at Jitra.

No sooner had Murray-Lyon received this decision than the Japanese again attacked in the gap already existing between the Jats and the Leicesters. This time they drove in the left of the Jats and penetrated as far south as the Bata River held by the Gurkhas. As a result the Leicesters' right flank and the Jats' left flank were dangerously exposed. Brigadier Carpendale then decided to withdraw the Jats so as to prolong the Bata River position to the east and to concentrate the Leicesters west of the main road so that they could counter-attack eastwards at dawn on 13 December, and asked Brigadier Lay to counter-attack with his remaining battalion (East Surreys), which had not up to now been engaged, across the main road to the north of the Leicesters. Murray-Lyon approved the main points of this plan, but ordered the East Surreys to withdraw into reserve around Alor Star. In this he was correct, for he had to re-create a reserve and there was little danger in the area held by 6th Brigade.

Unfortunately Carpendale, having obtained approval for his plan, suddenly changed his mind. He ordered the Leicesters to withdraw to

[1] It is now known that the Japanese *5th Division* had planned to launch a night attack at about 3 a.m. on 13 December with two regiments (six battalions), one on each side of the road with the maximum artillery and tank support. It is highly probable that this attack would have penetrated the front held by the Jats and the Leicesters and possibly even that of the Gurkhas on the Bata River.

a new defensive position running north-west from the bridge at Tanjong Pau on the main road over the Bata River. The Leicesters, who had suffered only thirty casualties in the action since midnight on the 11th/12th, objected to leaving their prepared defences for an unreconnoitred position in ricefields. But Carpendale was adamant, and the withdrawal to the new position was completed by 7 p.m. Carpendale's decision to change his plan caused a great deal of confusion, especially around Tanjong Pau and the bridge over the Bata River on the trunk road.

Murray-Lyon happened to see this on his way back to his head-quarters. When he reached it, he found a number of reports awaiting him, all of which in fact were false, but which stated that the Leicesters were withdrawing as the result of a further Japanese attack, that the Jats had been overwhelmed and that the Japanese were attacking the right flank of the Bata River position held by the Gurkhas. Everything in 15th Brigade's area must have seemed to him to have been in utter confusion. Simultaneously he heard that Lieutenant-Colonel Moorhead's battalion had reached Kroh reduced to less than half its original strength. If the information he had was correct, then he had no hope of withstanding the expected Japanese attack on 13 December without courting complete disaster. He therefore decided that a withdrawal behind a tank obstacle, such as the Kedah River, was now an absolute necessity. For the second time he asked Heath's permission to withdraw, and once again his request was sent on to Singapore. This time he was told that his task was to fight for north Kedah, to hold up the Japanese tanks on good obstacles and to dispose his force in depth along the trunk road; he was also told that reserves were being sent for use in the divisional area.[1] He was in addition given discretion to withdraw from the Jitra position and told that Krohcol would cease to be under his command from midnight of the 12th/13th. Murray-Lyon had by this time no alternative but to withdraw if he could. At 10 p.m. he therefore ordered his division to disengage at midnight and get behind the Kedah River as best it could. This ended the battle of Jitra. The Japanese advance guard, without support from their main body, had forced 11th Division from a prepared defensive position which it had been hoped would be held for a considerable time.[2]

[1] The 12th Infantry Brigade (less its battalion which had already been sent to Kelantan).

[2] Some officers taken prisoner told the Japanese that it was expected that the Jitra position would be held for some three months—a very optimistic view but one not out of line with the very erroneous view held in Malaya about the efficiency of the Japanese army.

The decision to disengage and withdraw, although it was the only possible course, could not have been worse timed. It was pitch dark and pouring with rain, the units of both brigades were inextricably mixed up and in confusion, and with all units except the Gurkhas on the Bata River line having moved, communication did not exist except by runner. As a result the order for the withdrawal did not reach many of the units located furthest from the trunk road. There was no time to backload the many tons of supplies and ammunition in and around the defensive position, and many of the guns and vehicles could not be got back on the trunk road because of the mud. Nevertheless the division, less those units which never received their orders, disengaged and withdrew in good order about 4.30 a.m. on 13 December. Losses in men and equipment were extremely heavy: 15th Brigade was reduced to a quarter and 6th Brigade to about half its original strength. The 28th Brigade was better off, because only two of its battalions had been engaged; one of these had suffered only a hundred casualties, but the other, which had been overrun in the Asun outpost position, had only sufficient men to form one company. Since there was no pool of trained reinforcements available to fill the gaps and reserves of equipment were very small, the situation facing Murray-Lyon on the morning of the 13th was more than gloomy.

One must ask how was it that a small Japanese advance guard supported by a company of tanks was able so easily to defeat a British–Indian division and drive it from a well-prepared position within twenty-four hours?

The failure to prepare Malaya properly against invasion, the faulty dispositions based on a theoretical assumption of planned strength rather than on the actual strength of the existing army and air garrisons, the poor state of training of the troops, the inexperience of many of the leaders, the existence of alternative plans for the formation entrusted with the defence of Kedah and the lack of decision over Matador by the Commander-in-Chief, Far East, all played their part. The poor training of the unblooded troops, the inexperience of the brigade, battalion and the junior commanders and the fact that the division had never carried out combined training with all arms was undoubtedly the main cause.

There were a number of subsidiary causes, such as the surprise caused by the presence of enemy tanks (which none of the Indian troops had ever seen), the bad handling of the available anti-tank guns, and the speed and efficiency of the Japanese attacks. The fact that the Matador plan existed and that 11th Division had alternative roles resulted in its not being properly prepared for either also had its effect. This, coupled with the unnecessary and overlong hesitation before the division was told to occupy the Jitra position, played its part; for the division was not ready to meet an attack before 12 December and this resulted in its reserve being used in a delaying role (which it was not fit to undertake) and in its loss. The situation was in fact nearly out of control when the Japanese made their first contact with the Jitra position in the evening of 11 December. Furthermore it was also utterly unsound for Murray-Lyon to have been given command of the operations on the Kroh road, a task which was that of the corps commander.

The whole strategy for the opening of the campaign was faulty. The obsession, which had existed for so long, that the role of the army was to defend the airfields required by the RAF forced the army command to deploy the only division it had available for the defence of Kedah north of Alor Star, where the only possible position was at Jitra; that position would in any case have had to be abandoned, however stout the defence, unless the Kroh road were firmly held, and the chances of that were small from the beginning owing to the fact that Krohcol was neither ready nor allowed to cross the border into Siam for some twenty-four hours after war actually broke out.

One can sum up by saying that those responsible for the conduct of the land campaign in Malaya committed every conceivable blunder. They underrated their enemy, they paid insufficient attention to the training of their troops, and they delayed taking urgent decisions even after the Japanese had landed on Malayan soil. Singapore and the naval base were lost between 8 and 12 December. Once the broken 11th Division was forced to withdraw from Jitra, the Japanese onrush could only have been delayed by brilliant generalship and a rapid redeployment of the troops available. However well the remnants of 11th Division fought, they had little hope of holding the Japanese, for there was no means by which their ranks could be filled with trained men and there were no positions already prepared on which they could fall back.

15

The First Phase of the Campaign: The Retreat to the Perak River

13–23 December 1941   *Map C, pp. 100–1*

At midnight on 12/13 December Krohcol came under direct command of III Corps, and General Percival placed his command reserve, 12th Brigade, commanded by Brigadier Paris, at General Heath's disposal. Brigade Headquarters and one battalion (2nd Argyll and Sutherland Highlanders) were to reach Ipoh by rail during the afternoon of the 13th, and the second (Punjabi) battalion on the 14th; the third (Hyderabad) battalion was still with 8th Brigade in Kelantan (*see page 134*). During the 13th, Krohcol drew back across the frontier and occupied the previously prepared position west of Kroh. This position protected the Kroh–Sungei Patani road, but not the unmetalled track which ran over the pass to Grik where it joined the metalled road running south to Kuala Kangsar. Neither Heath nor any of his senior staff officers had ever seen this track, and in selecting the position west of Kroh Heath had relied on reports from junior officers that it was impassable for infantry with transport. It was indeed a very poor road, especially in the rains of the north-east monsoon, and any British or Indian battalion with its mechanized transport would have found it wellnigh impassable. But it did lead straight to Kuala Kangsar and therefore had considerable strategical value, since a force passing down it would be in a position to cut the line of communication of the defenders of Kedah and northern Perak.

The Japanese pre-war espionage system had supplied Tokyo with full details of all the communications in Malaya, so that they were well aware of the state of the track and considered it to be usable. The regiment which had landed at Patani had therefore been ordered to move by way of Kroh and Grik to seize the crossings over the Perak river near Kuala Kangsar, which was *5th Division*'s first objective. The neglect of this track in pre-war planning was to prove disastrous. By this time aware of the danger presented by the track, Heath ordered the Argylls on arrival at Ipoh to send one company, with some armoured cars under command, to Grik and the rest of the battalion to Baling to support Krohcol. The next day (14 December) he placed Krohcol under command of 12th Brigade and gave Paris the task of protecting 11th Division's communications from any attempt by the Japanese to cut them off by advancing along the Kroh–Baling road to Sungei Patani.

While this defence was being prepared, further north 11th Division had been undertaking a difficult night withdrawal from Jitra. By dawn on 13 December this tired and disorganized formation was disposed in depth, south of the Kedah River, with two more or less intact Gurkha battalions of 28th Brigade acting as rearguard on the line of the river,[1] 6th Brigade holding a position astride the main road some five miles further south and the very depleted 15th Brigade, now only some six hundred strong, in reserve further south. All units spent the day reorganizing, feeding and resting, and were rejoined by many of their men cut off or lost during the sudden night withdrawal.

The bridges over the Kedah River had not been prepared for demolition, since no one had anticipated such a sudden withdrawal, but the necessary explosives had been placed close at hand; these were hurriedly put into position shortly before dawn. Two incidents then occurred: General Murray-Lyon and his Commander, Royal Engineers, were standing by the road bridge early on the 13th watching the last of the retreating troops crossing it, when two motor cyclists approached at high speed. It was not until they were on the bridge that it was realized they were Japanese. Both were killed, but Murray-Lyon, fearing that they might be followed by tanks, ordered both the road and railway bridges to be blown up, although not all the divisional transport had crossed to the south bank of the river. The road bridge was successfully demolished, but although the girders of the railway bridge sagged and the rails were cut it failed to fall. The premature demolition of the bridges cut off the armoured train and a number of armoured carriers. Orders were however given to the crew of the train to start it on its way south and then to abandon it, with the idea that under its extra weight the bridge would collapse, or that the train would be wrecked on the bridge and thereby block it. But the unexpected happened; the driverless train trundled across the bridge without being derailed and proceeded on its way south till it ran out of steam. If the weight of a heavy armoured train could not bring the bridge down, it should have been evident that it could carry light decking and tanks crossing one at a time, but through lack of explosives no further attempt was made during the day to complete its demolition.

But for the unblown railway bridge Murray-Lyon was now behind

[1] The third battalion of this brigade had been lost at Asun and the survivors of that débâcle were sufficient to form only one company. See page 150.

153

a good tank obstacle. He had therefore complied with the orders he had received the previous night and was in a position to dispute the passage of the river. Japanese infantry, which had closed up to the river during the morning, made a determined effort to cross it and to gain a bridgehead south of the road bridge in the afternoon. Some of them gained a foothold on the south bank, but they were soon forced back by the Gurkhas. Nevertheless, considering that his troops were in no condition to withstand a determined attack by the Japanese main body, Murray-Lyon decided to make a second night withdrawal of some twenty miles, again in pouring rain, but this time without being under pressure, to the position at Gurun, which was, as we have said, reconnoitred but unprepared. Once again orders went astray, and it was therefore not until midday on 14 December that the last of the weary troops reached Gurun.

It will be remembered that on 8 December General Heath had given instructions that this position should be put into a state of defence, but for various reasons no work had been done. Nevertheless, the unprepared position was much better than that at Jitra, as the only possible line of attack was on a narrow front astride the main road and railway. Murray-Lyon gave 6th Brigade (Brigadier Lay) the task of holding this vital area and deployed 28th Brigade, commanded by Brigadier Carpendale, on its right, keeping 15th Brigade, under command of Brigadier Garrett again, in reserve. No sooner were the last of the troops in position about 2 p.m. than Japanese tanks and infantry appeared and began to probe the defences. Anti-tank guns scored a hit on one tank, whereupon the others withdrew, but Lay had to organize a counter-attack to stop enemy infiltration.

During the afternoon of the 14th Heath paid his first visit to Murray-Lyon; the latter explained that his troops were by then unfit to undertake constant short withdrawals and to fight a succession of rearguard actions. He gave as his opinion that the whole Corps should be concentrated much further south and that 11th Division should move back to the selected concentration area direct by rail or by a series of long bounds. To stay and try to fight the Japanese at Gurun or elsewhere in Kedah or even north Perak was, he said, dangerous and of little value, for the Japanese could advance from Kroh by way of Grik to Kuala Kangsar and thus force the division to retreat. The concentration area for the Corps (which meant the withdrawal of 9th Division from its position east of the main range) would have to be well south of Kuala Kangsar. Heath accepted Murray-Lyon's views in principle but told him that his immediate task was to stop the enemy at Gurun; Heath himself was going to use 12th Brigade to protect the division's right flank on the Grik–Kuala Kangsar road.

On his return to his headquarters that evening Heath expressed similar views on the telephone to General Percival. He said that in his opinion it was entirely wrong to fight at Gurun and that 11th Division should now be withdrawn to the Perak River, delaying the Japanese by demolition and by making a temporary stand on the line of the Muda River to allow for the evacuation of Penang. Such a long withdrawal at this stage in the campaign was from a political point of view extremely difficult to accept, and Percival ordered Heath to cover Penang and not to withdraw south of the Muda River without his permission.

There is no need to go into any detail of the fighting at Gurun. The Japanese, using the same tactics as at Jitra, attacked straight down the main road about 1.30 a.m. on 15 December and broke into 6th Brigade's area, overwhelming the headquarters both of the East Surreys and of 6th Brigade and killing all the staff at both, except the brigadier, who happened to be away from his headquarters at the moment it was attacked. The situation was saved by Brigadier Carpendale, who with units of his own and of 15th Brigade checked the Japanese at Gurun village, some two miles behind the original forward defences. It was a matter of exhausted and inexperienced troops surprised by a sudden attack by fresh Japanese troops. Early on 15 December, when he realized the sad state of affairs, Murray-Lyon ordered an immediate withdrawal to a temporary position some seven miles to the south and then during the night of the 15th/16th to the Muda River line. By the morning of the 16th the division was behind the tank obstacle provided by the river, but this withdrawal exposed the rear of 12th Brigade and made a decision on the future of Penang very urgent. Realizing his danger, Brigadier Paris had already withdrawn 12th Brigade from Baling and on 15 December had positioned his Punjab battalion at the point where the road crosses the Muda River some ten miles east of Sungei Patani, with the Argylls some five miles behind it to provide the necessary depth to the position.

Before the war broke out it had been decided that, in the event of a withdrawal, two battalions would be left as a garrison on Penang island. While the events described in the previous chapter were taking place, the Japanese had bombed George Town on the island both on the 11th and 12th. These raids were unopposed, for there were no anti-aircraft defences and no fighters at Butterworth.

The attacks set half the town on fire, extensively damaged the dock installations and caused very heavy civilian casualties. On the 12th the Resident Councillor and the Fortress Commander at Penang decided to evacuate during the night of the 13th all European military and civilian women and children, together with the wounded and sick who could be moved. On the 13th a fighter squadron with eight Buffalo aircraft was sent from Singapore to Butterworth. It was therefore able to intercept the next Japanese attack, shooting down five of the attackers for the loss of one Buffalo.

On the morning of 14 December the policy to be adopted towards Penang was discussed by the Far East War Council. Admiral Layton, who had succeeded Phillips as Commander-in-Chief, Eastern Fleet, pointed out that the anchorage at Penang was at that time of no value to the Royal Navy. General Percival said that the security of Penang depended entirely on the outcome of the battle in Kedah, that it would be unwise to weaken III Corps by putting a garrison on to the island, and that, if 11th Division were forced back, military necessity would make it advisable to evacuate Penang despite the effect that this action would have on the civilian morale in Malaya. The War Council accepted these views, and General Heath was told that he could order the evacuation of Penang if the Japanese advance could not be stopped, but that all essential installations and stores of use to the enemy should be destroyed. The Governor issued similar instructions to the Resident Councillor. The decision when to act now lay with Heath.

Meanwhile, the situation in Penang had deteriorated to such an extent that the Municipal Commissioners of George Town told the Fortress Commander on the 14th that the civil administration had entirely broken down and that as a result there was a danger of epidemics breaking out. This was the position when Heath, with 11th Division about to withdraw behind the Muda River, issued on 15 December orders for the evacuation of the island by the night of the 16th/17th. No detailed plan for the removal or demolition of stores and installations had been drawn up, but events had moved so rapidly that the inside of two days gave insufficient time for the depleted staff without civilian labour to organize the evacuation in an orderly manner. The civil airport, the power station, some of the machinery and plant in factories and the fixed defences were destroyed, but much that should have been done was left undone. Some three thousand tons of tin in the form of ingots or alloys—one of the raw materials of which Japan was very short—were left intact. The broadcasting station was not destroyed, with the result that the

Japanese were shortly using it to pour out anti-British propaganda. A large number of self-propelled craft, barges and junks, which had been deserted by their crews, were left at their moorings instead of being sunk, thus presenting the Japanese with a fleet of coastal vessels which could be used to ferry their troops down the west coast of Malaya and so outflank the defence. After the evacuation had been completed, attempts were made to mine the exits of the harbour and to destroy some of these craft before they fell into Japanese hands, but all these efforts failed. Since the available shipping was insufficient to carry more than the essential military personnel (even though some five hundred Asians of the Volunteer Forces decided to remain behind with their families) most of the Malay and Chinese community on the island was left to face a Japanese occupation.

*

The 11th Division, now behind the Muda River, was far from secure, since its right flank was liable to be turned if the Japanese advanced west from Kroh. Moreover, its communications would be threatened if the Japanese decided to advance through Grik towards Kuala Kangsar. Furthermore, if the Japanese were to force a crossing of the river, they would benefit from the country immediately to its south, which was very suitable for the use of tanks. On 16 December Heath therefore placed 12th Brigade under Murray-Lyon's command and ordered him to fall back another twenty-five miles and occupy on the 17th a position behind the Krian River, which with its extensive swamps formed a reasonable tank obstacle. At the same time he ordered both 6th and 15th Brigade to be sent back to Taiping to be reorganized and re-equipped and Krohcol to be disbanded, its units being absorbed into 11th Division.

The next day Heath realized that the small force he had sent to protect the Grik Road would not be able to hold the Japanese should they decide to advance along it. On the 18th, therefore, he once again took 12th Brigade under his own command and moved it to Kuala Kangsar to meet this threat. The same day, knowing that the Perak River, which ran from north to south, did not offer a satisfactory position on which to hold the Japanese forces despite its width and the fact that it was bridged in few places, Heath foresaw that in the near future he would have to withdraw 11th Division east of the river and then go back some thirty-five miles to Kampar, where there was a bottleneck on the north–south communications and where he had some hope of stopping the Japanese advance.

By 16 December the initial disasters in Kedah made it necessary for General Percival to reconsider the strategy of the campaign. He thought that the Japanese had landed one division at Singora, a second at Patani and a third at Kota Bharu and had a fourth in Siam which was already moving south in support of the Japanese *5th Division*. Although this was an over-estimate it indicated what a desperate situation he was facing. With the complete command of the sea and air the enemy were free to land troops anywhere on the east coast of Malaya. He considered therefore that he could not denude the defences of Mersing or Singapore Island. His task was the security of the naval base and to accomplish it he decided that he must hold the Japanese as far north in Malaya as possible to give time for reinforcements to arrive, which he knew could not be before mid-January at the earliest. Heath had suggested a withdrawal to Johore, where the whole of the available forces could be concentrated. But Percival felt that such a withdrawal would give the Japanese the use of airfields in central Malaya, from where they would be in a position to attack convoys bringing reinforcements to Singapore. He came to the conclusion that he would have to do his best to hold the Japanese in northern Malaya with 11th Division and to husband his remaining air strength carefully, using it only for general reconnaissance and the protection of convoys and of the naval base.[1] The already exhausted 11th Division would therefore have to fight on without any close air support or further reinforcement. By the 17th he had decided that Heath would have to withdraw 11th Division behind the Perak River and thereafter attempt to prevent the Japanese from crossing it for as long as possible. When Heath telephoned him on the 17th to express his anxiety about the possible results of the unfavourable developments on the Grik Road, he approved a withdrawal behind the river but only when Heath considered it to be absolutely necessary.

On 18 December there were two events of importance. A conference, attended by Commonwealth and Dutch representatives, was held at Singapore under the chairmanship of Duff Cooper. This conference came to the conclusion that the only possible course of action was to try to hold the Japanese as far north as possible in order to prevent them having the use of airfields in central Malaya, from

[1] Including reinforcing aircraft flown in from the Netherlands East Indies, the total strength was then about one hundred aircraft. With the reinforcement route now cut, air reinforcements could come only by way of Sabang in Sumatra (for long-range aircraft), while fighters could only arrive by sea or be flown from Australia by way of the Netherlands East Indies. His air strength could not therefore be built up quickly.

where they could attack convoys bringing reinforcements to Singapore. Thus they endorsed the views on strategy already expressed by Percival the previous day. They reported that the situation was very grave and asked the Chiefs of Staff to send as quickly as possible reinforcements consisting of one infantry division, one brigade group, men to replace losses in 9th and 11th Divisions, five anti-aircraft regiments, an anti-tank regiment, fifty light tanks and further supplies of ammunition and equipment. For the RAF they asked for four fighter and four bomber squadrons; they warned that more reinforcements might be required later.

The same day Percival met Heath at Ipoh and discussed the situation, which at that moment seemed slightly better, since Murray-Lyon was not being pressed on the Krian River and it seemed that 12th Brigade (now brought up to full strength by the return of the Hyderabad battalion from Kelantan) might check the Japanese on the Grik Road. Percival confirmed his instruction of the 17th, giving Heath the authority to withdraw behind the Perak River when necessary, and instructed him to prepare defensive positions in depth between Ipoh and Tanjong Malim in order to impose the greatest possible delay on the Japanese. Percival decided, however, that 9th Division (General Barstow) should continue to remain in eastern Malaya to deny the Kuantan airfield. At the same time he asked the Perak flotilla (a destroyer and some light craft) to oppose any attempt by the Japanese to move by sea down the coast between the mouth of the Krian and Perak Rivers (thus threatening 11th Division's left flank) and a seaborne force (Roseforce) to raid the Japanese communications west of the Perak River. Since III Corps's plan now was to oppose the Japanese advance by brigade groups operating in depth on the single road south of Ipoh which provided a bottleneck in the north–south communications, steps were to be taken to rest and re-organize 11th Division. The 12th Brigade was allotted to the division, 6th and 15th Brigades were combined into one brigade (6th/15th), the East Surreys and the Leicesters were combined into what became known as the British Battalion, and several of the Punjabi battalions were also combined. At the same time all the brigadiers, who had become casualties for one reason or another, were replaced and on 24 December Paris, who had been in Malaya since 1939 and had greater experience of local conditions than Murray-Lyon, replaced him in command of 11th Division.

Percival's decision to keep 9th Division, consisting of two brigades, in eastern Malaya must, however, be questioned. The problem was to hold the Japanese as far north as possible, and it must have been clear that, if this were to be accomplished, the full strength of the garrison in Malaya would have to be deployed west of the main range. It would appear that Percival was still obsessed by the need to protect airfields, which had been his role before the war broke out. To leave one brigade at Kuantan without support in an attempt to hold, as he thought, a whole Japanese division was asking for its destruction or at least its being severely mauled, and he could not afford to waste his slender strength on detachments. There is little doubt that the decision to leave 9th Division east of the main range was a major error. The main battle had to be fought out on the western side of the peninsula, and the greatest possible strength should have been made available to III Corps. The complete demolition of the Kuantan airfield and its installations, and the withdrawal of the whole of 9th Division across the main ridge to support 11th Division in the main and decisive battle would have been a much sounder decision.

The next few days were to prove that General Heath's anxiety about the situation on the Grik road was justified. The whole of the Japanese regiment which had landed at Patani had turned south at Kroh, albeit without its tanks, and, despite all efforts of 12th Brigade to hold it, was, by using the river to outflank successive defensive positions on the road, making far too rapid a progress towards Kuala Kangsar. On 21 December Heath therefore placed all formations west of the Perak River under Murray-Lyon's command and told him he could withdraw across the river as and when it became necessary.

Since there was now a very distinct danger that the Japanese threat on the Grik road would sever 11th Division's communications, Murray-Lyon began a gradual withdrawal and, after observing the course of the action on the Grik road on 21 and 22 December, decided to withdraw all his forces across the river during the night of the 22nd/23rd, destroying both the permanent road and railway bridges north of Kuala Kangsar and the pontoon bridge which carried the road over the river at Blanja, fifteen miles south of the town and some twelve miles south-west of Ipoh.

On the same day that III Corps withdrew across the Perak River, Lieutenant-General Sir Henry Pownall relieved Sir Robert Brooke-Popham as Commander-in-Chief, Far East. This change came too late to have any significant effect on the conduct of the campaign and in any case, as will shortly be seen, Headquarters Far East was to be swallowed up in a new command.

Having captured the airfields at Alor Star, Sungei Patani and

Butterworth, the Japanese quickly repaired their cratered runways. In this they were helped by the stocks of material which before the war had been accumulated at each airfield for repairs of this nature—stocks which could neither be removed nor destroyed. They also impressed large numbers of local Malay and Chinese as labourers and set them to work round the clock to render the runways serviceable. By 20 December they were able to move their fighter and bomber squadrons forward from Singora and Patani to the abandoned RAF airfields. As soon as this move had been completed, they once again began their efforts to destroy the remaining RAF squadrons. On the 21st and 22nd they attacked the Kuala Lumpur airfield. This was defended by eighteen anti-aircraft guns of various calibres and by fifteen Buffalo fighters flown by Australian pilots. Air combats continued throughout both days, and by the end of the 22nd only three Buffalos were fit for action. There are no reliable records of the damage inflicted on the Japanese air force, but losses inflicted were thought to equal the losses of the defenders. With their vast numerical superiority the Japanese could accept losses with equanimity, but to Air Marshal Pulford the loss of twelve fighters was serious, for they could not be replaced until reinforcing aircraft reached Malaya some time in January. He therefore evacuated the airfield, withdrawing the remaining aircraft to Singapore, and thereafter adhered strictly to Percival's policy of husbanding all fighters for the protection of the base and of convoys bringing in reinforcements. The Japanese air force was now free to devote part of its strength to the direct support of *5th Division*.

Percival and Pulford had already realized that they could not hold Malaya unless they could somehow stop the Japanese thrust sufficiently far to the north of Singapore to make it possible for reinforcements to reach them. Let us therefore now see what action was being taken to send the necessary reinforcements. Those in charge in Malaya wasted no time in asking for them. Almost immediately after the outbreak of war on 8 December Brooke-Popham realized that, owing to his numerical inferiority in the air, the Japanese would quickly be able to gain air superiority. He therefore told the Chiefs of Staff that the outcome of the battle in northern Malaya would probably turn on the number of aircraft available and emphasized the need for large air reinforcements being sent without delay. On the 11th Admiral Layton asked for the dispatch of all destroyers, submarines, aircraft and minesweepers that could be spared from other theatres. On the 16th, after the disaster at Jitra and Kroh, Brooke-Popham asked for the dispatch from India as soon as practicable of

M   161 one brigade group and four hundred reinforcements for each of the fifteen battalions by then included in 11th Division. On the 18th the conference at Singapore also made specific requests for large army and air reinforcements which, if they arrived in time, might enable the naval base to be secured.

In London, although nothing could be done to provide the naval reinforcements for which Layton had asked, steps to send other reinforcements to the Far East began on 11 December. Presumably under the delusion that the weak garrison in Malaya could hold the Japanese thrust despite the loss of air superiority and command of the sea, only aircraft and some artillery units were to be sent to Singapore. The Prime Minister and the Chiefs of Staff cabled the Commander-in-Chief in India (General Sir Archibald Wavell) that day saying that Burma, hitherto under command of Brooke-Popham, was now placed under his command and that he was to resist any Japanese advance into Burma and try to take the offensive to cut the Japanese communications down the Malay peninsula. At the same time the Prime Minister told Wavell that he could retain 17th Indian Division—the first division of India's second expansion to be ready, which had been earmarked to be sent to Iraq in February 1942 for equipment and training as a fully mechanized formation—in India, and that 18th British Division, four fighter squadrons and a number of anti-aircraft and anti-tank units were being sent to him. Wavell was to marry these with his own forces to form an 'Eastern fighting front'. This message was followed up on 13 December by one from the Chiefs of Staff asking Wavell how he proposed to reinforce Burma. Wavell replied that Burma was not capable at that time of maintaining even one British brigade (let alone a division) and he was proposing to send an Indian brigade (45th) from 17th Division to Burma as soon as possible.

To meet Brooke-Popham's urgent request for reinforcing aircraft the Chiefs of Staff allotted him eight Hudsons then at Darwin in Australia, ordered eighteen Blenheims to be flown from Egypt to Singapore and made arrangements for another fifty-two Hudsons to be flown from the United Kingdom by way of the air-reinforcement route to Singapore. On 13 December, however, the key airfield on this route at Victoria Point had to be evacuated and two days later was occupied by the Japanese; fighters could thus not be sent by that route and could only be sent by sea or flown off aircraft-carriers, and bombers would have to be diverted to fly from India to Sabang at the north-west corner of Sumatra. On 17 December the Chiefs of Staff arranged that fifty-one Hurricane fighters in crates,

162

with twenty-four pilots, already loaded in a convoy then at the Cape should be diverted direct to Singapore. Thus within a few days from the outbreak of war some fifty-eight bombers and fifty-one fighters were allotted to Malaya, but it was to be a long time before any arrived. By 25 December only seven out of the eighteen Blenheims dispatched from the Middle East had reached Malaya by way of Sabang, the remainder having crashed or become unserviceable on the way. The eight Hudsons reached Singapore from Australia on 29 December. Of the fifty-two Hudsons only twenty-three had begun their long journey from Britain by 6 January 1942 and very few reached Singapore. The crated Hurricanes were not expected to arrive till the middle of January and they then had to be erected and tested before they could be available for operations. This sad story shows very clearly the fallacy of the theory, held for so long by the Air Ministry, that the mobility of aircraft made it possible for any threatened point to be quickly reinforced. (See pages 15 and 21.) Air Marshal Pulford therefore could not hope seriously to interfere with Japanese air activities till about the middle of January, and by that time it would probably be too late.

The disasters in the opening days of the campaign quickly changed the direction of the flow of army reinforcements from India to Malaya. By 17 December it had been agreed that two brigades of 17th Indian Division should be sent as quickly as possible from India to Singapore: 45th Brigade sailing on 22 December 1941, and 44th on 1 January 1942. All the reinforcements for 9th and 11th Divisions which could be found, though they were only semi-trained, were to sail on 8 January. In addition it had been agreed that the leading brigade of 18th Division (53rd), which was at sea, would be sent direct to Singapore, and that Australia would send a machine-gun battalion and reinforcements for 8th Australian Division. Malaya could thus expect to receive considerable reinforcements from early January onwards. Unfortunately the formations on arrival would not be fit for battle under Malayan conditions for some time, since such training as they had received had been directed towards mechanized warfare in desert country, and the British 53rd Brigade would be physically unfit for immediate operational duties after their long voyage.

The dispatch of further air reinforcements was essential; for if the approaches to Singapore were not covered, the convoys would be unable to reach the port. Thus on 26 December arrangements were made for the aircraft-carrier *Indomitable* to sail on the 31st from Durban to Port Sudan in the Red Sea, where she was to embark forty-eight Hurricane fighters with their pilots, proceed to Sumatra or Java and then fly the aircraft off to make their way to Singapore. But again these reinforcements could not be available till at the earliest the end of January.[1] At the same time it was arranged that the Middle East theatre would find an armoured brigade (headquarters and two regiments), equipped with American cruiser tanks, and fifty light tanks for dispatch to Singapore as soon as shipping was available. Three days later the Chiefs of Staff ordered three RAF squadrons and two anti-aircraft regiments, due to arrive at Durban on 8 January, to proceed to Singapore instead of to Suez as originally planned.

[1] These Hurricanes were flown off the *Indomitable* to airfields in Java on 26 January, too late to take part in the campaign for Malaya.

16

The Second Phase of the Campaign: The Loss of Central Malaya

24 December 1941–14 January 1942   *Map E, pp. 166–7, and Map F, p. 175*

With the withdrawal of III Corps across the Perak River the second phase of the campaign began. Thanks to the existence of the Kroh–Grik–Kuala Kangsar road the Japanese had been able to turn the right flank of the British forces defending Kedah. They had thus accompanied their direct thrust down the trunk road by a strong thrust along the Grik road which aimed at severing the British line of communication to Kedah. From Kuala Kangsar southwards, however, the trunk road and railway ran too close to the central range to make it possible for the right flank of the defenders to be turned. In their pre-war planning the Japanese had foreseen this, and had concluded that from Kuala Kangsar southwards they would be in a position to turn the British left flank by means of amphibious landings at suitable points on the west coast of Malaya. To make amphibious operations possible, they had brought assault landing-craft to Singora and had transported these by road and rail across the Kra Isthmus. The failure by the British forces to destroy a large number of self-propelled vessels of all types when Penang was evacuated gave the Japanese a large coastal fleet with which to operate along the west coast of Malaya. Since by the time the Japanese had occupied Penang they had attained complete air superiority over northern and central Malaya, they could undertake amphibious operations with little fear of interference. To ensure that they had sufficient fresh troops for each successive thrust down the trunk road and for their proposed amphibious operations, they brought the *Imperial Guards Division* by rail from Bangkok. From 24 December onwards therefore the Japanese action took the form of strong thrusts supported by tanks down the trunk road, accompanied by operations by sea and river to turn the British left flank.

During the short lull from 24 to 26 December, while the Japanese were concentrating their formations and bridging the Perak River, General Heath, with General Percival's agreement, organized the defence of the trunk road in depth with brigade groups; each brigade in succession was to check the Japanese and then to fall back behind another already in a semi-prepared position. Heath decided to occupy in succession two main positions: one at Kampar twenty miles to the

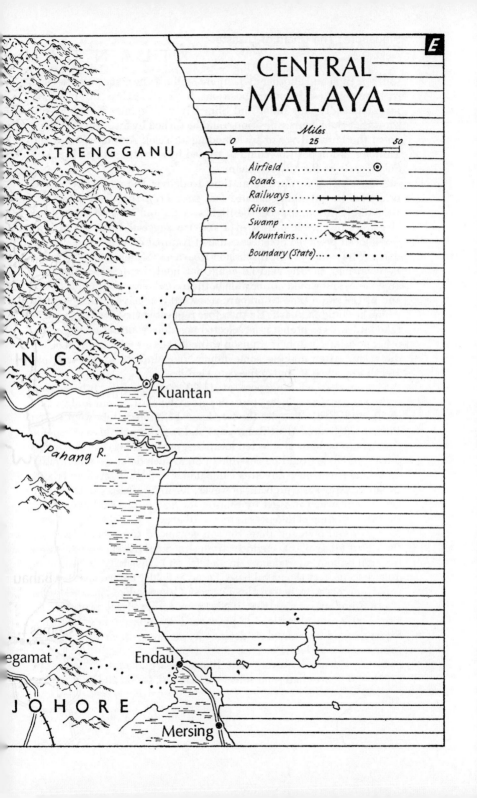

south of Ipoh and another at Tanjong Malim some sixty miles beyond it. Between these two main positions, he selected three intermediate positions at Tapah, Bidor and Slim River. A glance at map E will show that the Kampar position could be turned by an enemy advance down the Perak River or by a landing at Telok Anson and that the Tanjong Malim position could be turned by a landing either at Kuala Selangor or at Port Swettenham.

After visiting forward formations to deliver the pamphlet he had prepared on anti-tank defence (*see page 117*), the Chief Engineer, Brigadier Simson, stayed the nights of 22 and 23 December with Heath at his headquarters at Ipoh. He suggested that III Corps would need prepared defences south of Kampar on which it could fall back. After considerable discussion Heath gave Simson a message for Percival in which he said he could not hold the Japanese for long anywhere, and would not be able both to conduct a continuous battle and at the same time to prepare rearward defensive positions on to which he could fall back. He therefore requested that Percival should take measures to prepare the selected positions south of Kampar and other positions in Johore. Simson wrote down this message at Heath's dictation. After making some minor amendments in the wording Heath approved it, but refused to sign it.

Simson reached Singapore at 11.30 p.m. on the 26th, having visited the main engineer stores depots at Kuala Lumpur and Gemas on his way south. Despite the late hour, he immediately went to see Percival, delivered Heath's message and urged him to give orders for defences to be built at selected localities, pointing out that the period during which it would be possible to build such defences was rapidly vanishing since, once any area came under air attack, civilian labour would disappear. Percival, however, firmly refused to take any action, and when pressed by Simson for his reasons said eventually that the building of defences in rearward areas was bad for the morale of troops and civilians alike. Simson continued to press the case for the use of all available engineer troops to supervise the construction by civil labour of defences in defiles and especially in southern Johore to protect the naval base. Percival finally agreed that Simson could put his case before the Fortress Commander, Major-General Keith Simmons, saying that if Simmons accepted the proposals he would raise no objections. Approached by Simson next morning Simmons said he wanted no defence works undertaken and gave the same reasons as had Percival.

It is evident, however, that Simson's arguments in favour of building defences had some effect on Percival, for on 29 December he tried, without telling Simson, to organize Public Works Department (PWD) works groups. His idea was that the PWD would produce the necessary labour which, under instruction from III Corps engineers, would build any defences which the corps might require. Percival's ideas might have produced some results had 9th Division been able to take charge of the PWD parties. Unfortunately III Corps was far too involved to spare engineer officers and others to supervise the proposed work, and, as the retreat continued, the supply of labour diminished, so nothing was done. The only practical help given to III Corps came from Simson, who had arranged to construct moveable tank obstacles consisting of concrete blocks to be connected by heavy chains. These he now sent forward and dumped alongside the trunk road at likely defiles, such as Slim River, where the retreating troops might make a stand.

On 26 December 12th Brigade (now commanded by Brigadier I. M. Stewart), in position on the trunk road some eight miles north of Ipoh, was attacked by a regiment of *Imperial Guards Division*. At the cost of some two hundred casualties the brigade resisted until the evening of the 27th. But by then it was evident that 28th Brigade (now under Brigadier W. R. Selby) at Blanja was about to be attacked, and General Paris (commanding 11th Division) did not wish that brigade to be mauled, as he wanted it for the defence of the Kampar position. He therefore decided to break off the action and ordered 28th Brigade to move back to Kampar and 12th Brigade to occupy a covering position some five miles north of Kampar, south of the junction of the Ipoh and Blanja roads. By this means he hoped to gain several days' respite, but as usual the Japanese moved too quickly. A regiment of *5th Division* was passed through the *Imperial Guards Regiment* and made contact with 12th Brigade in its covering position during the afternoon of 28 December. By this time 12th Brigade, which had been continuously in action without relief, had nearly reached its limit of endurance, and to make matters worse the Japanese had begun to use some of their aircraft in support of their advancing troops. It is not surprising therefore that when attacked again north of Kampar on that same afternoon the troops put up somewhat less resistance than at Ipoh. By midday on the 29th, after some twenty-four hours of heavy fighting, the brigade had been forced back to within three miles of the Kampar position. Realizing that the situation was becoming desperate, Paris gave Stewart permission to withdraw through the Kampar position to Bidor. The withdrawal that evening nearly ended in disaster, since the bridge on the trunk road in front of Kampar was not ready for demolition when the troops passed through. Heroic action by the infantry of 28th Brigade and sappers of 3rd Field Company held off the Japanese till the bridge was destroyed, but only in the nick of time. For the first time since Jitra 11th Division was now in a prepared position.

Aware of the danger of amphibious landings, General Percival had arranged for the Royal Navy's Perak Flotilla to guard the coast, and to land raiding parties from 'Roseforce' at Trong on 28 December. Having landed successfully 'Roseforce' ambushed and destroyed some enemy staff cars and transport west of Perak River and was then re-embarked and taken back to Port Swettenham. This was the only raid attempted, for on 30 December the base ship for the flotilla was bombed and sunk together with five fast motor boats on their way from Singapore to join the flotilla. From that time on the Japanese coastal flotillas had complete freedom to move as and when they wished, and it was not long before the outflanking movements down the coast developed.

When occupying the Kampar position Paris had sent 1st Independent Infantry Company and 3rd Cavalry (equipped with trucks and armoured cars) to Telok Anson in case the Japanese should attempt a landing there or move troops down the Perak River to threaten his rear. He had anticipated the Japanese, for at about 7.30 p.m. on 1 January 1942 one and a half Japanese battalions, which had embarked at Port Weld in landing-craft and barges, towed by a number of coastal steamers, landed at the mouth of the Bernam River and shortly afterwards moved towards Telok Anson. On the morning of the 2nd a Japanese *Guards* battalion, which had been ferried down the Perak River, landed at Telok Anson, where the two forces (now amounting to two and a half battalions) joined up. News of the presence of enemy shipping off the coast near the mouth of the Bernam River had reached Paris on the 1st, and he had immediately ordered Stewart with his weary 12th Brigade to cover the road which led from the coast to Bidor. By the morning of the 2nd the brigade was deployed astride the road in some depth at a point some four miles east of Telok Anson.

Meanwhile, about dawn on 1 January, the Japanese *5th Division* had launched its attack on the Kampar position. One regiment moved straight down the trunk road supported by tanks, while another tried to envelop the British left flank. Fighting went on throughout the day with the Japanese making little impression on the defences. In view of the threat about to develop from Telok Anson, Paris asked Heath for permission to withdraw from Kampar when he deemed it necessary. Heath and Percival, who were both at

Kuala Lumpur that day, again considered the general strategic position. Percival was still intent on denying the Japanese the use of Kuantan airfield until the convoy carrying the first reinforcements for Malaya arrived, and hoped that it could be retained till 10 January. After that date he was willing, he said, to concentrate 9th Division in the Kuala Lipis–Jerantut area. He therefore told Heath that his task was to keep the Japanese north of Kuala Kubu (that is, to hold the selected position at Tanjong Malim) until 15 January. With this proviso, he agreed that Heath could give Paris the discretion to withdraw from Kampar when he thought fit.

Throughout the 2nd the Japanese continued their attacks down the trunk road, but again the defence stood firm. There now seemed to be every possibility that 6th/15th Brigade, reinforced as necessary by 28th Brigade, could hold the Japanese for several more days. But the threat to Paris's communications continued to grow, and he felt that the weary 12th Brigade would not be able to prevent the out-flanking force from reaching the vicinity of Bidor for long. He therefore decided on the night of the 2nd to disengage and to move back to the Slim River position. The withdrawal was accomplished successfully, and by 4 January 12th and 28th Brigades were in the Slim River area, covered by 6th/15th Brigade some fifteen miles to their north. It should be noted that both in the vicinity of Ipoh and again at Kampar the troops of 11th Division despite their weariness fought extremely well against fresh Japanese infantry and had taken the measure of the tank menace.

Despite its weakness, the RAF had not been idle between 24 December and 4 January. Daily reconnaissance patrols were flown from Malaya and Sumatra, and the one and only photographic reconnaissance aircraft flew frequently to Singora and Patani. On the 26th this plane took photographs of a convoy of thirty-five ships lying off Singora, and the next day of over one hundred aircraft crowded on the Sungei Patani airfield in Kedah. This target clearly warranted an attack by the remains of the striking force, and on the night of the 27th six Blenheim bombers attacked the airfield. Photographs taken on the 28th showed that twelve Japanese fighters and three bombers had been destroyed or damaged. The raid was therefore repeated the next night and further damage was caused.

During this second phase of the campaign, on the east coast of Malaya the regiment of the Japanese *18th Division*, which had landed at Kota Bharu on 8 December, had been instructed, after securing the Kelantan airfield, to move down the coastal track on the east coast with the object of capturing the airfield at Kuantan. Its southward progress was slow, for it relied entirely on horse transport, and most of the streams and estuaries on the east coast were unbridged. Not until 30 December therefore did the Japanese make contact with 22nd Indian Brigade (Brigadier G. W. A. Painter) in the vicinity of Kuantan. From the beginning of the war Painter had the task of defending the airfield located west of the Kuantan River and only six miles from the coast, and he had deployed one of his three battalions to hold eleven miles of beach defences north of Kuantan village, a second the line of the Kuantan River covering the airfield from the north and north-east, and had kept the third in reserve well to the west of the airfield.[1] The RAF had evacuated the airfield shortly after the outbreak of the war, and Painter's brigade was left to deny its use to the Japanese for as long as possible. There were considerable differences of opinion between Heath and Percival over the role of Painter's brigade. Heath wanted 9th Division concentrated as soon as possible, for use either to make a counter-stroke against the Japanese left flank in the vicinity of Tanjong Malim, or to secure the Kuala Selangor or Port Swettenham areas to protect his left flank while he held the Japanese at Tanjong Malim with 11th Division. Percival, on the other hand, was most anxious that the Kuantan airfield should be denied to the Japanese for as long as possible, so that they would not have it in use before 13 January, when the convoy bringing the British 53rd Brigade from India was due to reach Singapore. On 27 December Heath suggested to General Barstow (9th Division) that Painter should withdraw his troops behind the river (which meant the abandonment of the beach defences) as soon as any threat developed from the north. His object was to ensure that, if attacked, the brigade would not suffer losses of guns and transports which might be cut off east of the river. Unfortunately Painter objected to any change in his dispositions, and Barstow let him have his way. On the 29th Heath insisted that the brigade should be redeployed as he had suggested and said that both Percival and he were in entire agreement that the preservation of the brigade's entity was of greater importance than the imposition of two or three days' delay in the denial of the airfield. Heath's order was passed by Barstow to Painter, who ordered all the guns and transport east of the river to cross it by ferry on the night of 30 December and for his forward battalion to withdraw from the beach defences to an outpost position covering the river. This order came too late, for during the day the Japanese attacked the battalion's

---

[1] The third battalion, which had been with 8th Brigade at Kota Bharu, had rejoined at Kuantan about the middle of December.

northern flank and made repeated efforts to put the ferry out of action. Heavy fighting ensued, but during the night all the guns and transport were able to cross the river, although the battalion suffered casualties which amounted to more than half its strength.

In view of his latest orders Painter told Barstow on the 31st that he was withdrawing his brigade from the airfield on the night of 31 December/1 January. He was now told that, though it was of the utmost importance that his brigade should not be jeopardized, it was desirable that the airfield should be denied to the enemy, as reinforcements were shortly expected to reach Malaya and their safe arrival might be hampered if enemy aircraft had the use of the airfield. Percival's determination to hold on to the airfield for as long as possible had prevailed over Heath's views. Painter therefore withdrew all his troops west of the river and disposed them for the defence of the airfield. On 1 January 1942 Painter's instructions were once again altered, for he was then specifically told to hold the airfield till 5 January. By the 2nd it was clear that the Japanese were preparing to attack the airfield from the north, and that Painter would become heavily engaged if he were to try to hold it for another three days. Then came a final change in his orders. Owing to the need to withdraw 11th Division from Kampar on the night of the 2nd/3rd, it became imperative that 9th Division should be concentrated for use west of the main north–south ridge. Heath therefore told Barstow that the airfield was to be abandoned and the brigade withdrawn to Jerantut forthwith.

Then and then only were the buildings and installations at the airfield which had not been in use since 9 December demolished and plans put on foot to withdraw the brigade during the evening of 3 January. The expected Japanese attack came in before the rearguard of half a battalion was clear. It had to fight its way out, and only the commanding officer, Lieutenant-Colonel A. E. Cumming, who was awarded a VC for his gallantry in the action, and forty men managed to break out. The brigade, having lost a third of its strength, then withdrew as ordered to Jerantut.

While these events were happening in the east, on the west of the main range Heath had been told by Percival that, in view of the imminent arrival of reinforcements, he was to deny the use of his airfields at Kuala Lumpur and at Port Swettenham to the enemy until 14 January. As soon as he heard of the Japanese landing at Telok Anson on the 1st, Heath realized that, even were 11th Division able to hold the Japanese thrust on the Slim River and at Tanjong Malim, more Japanese landings in the Kuala Selangor and/or Port

Swettenham areas might force him to retire to the south of Kuala Lumpur before the 14th. Having no reserve formation immediately available, he therefore hastily formed a scratch force consisting of one battalion and a field battery from 8th Brigade, then at Kuala Lipis, two Federated Malay States Volunteer Force battalions and 3rd Cavalry, which was withdrawing down the coastal track from Telok Anson, and placed it under the orders of Brigadier R. G. Moir, the line of communications commander, to prevent the enemy landing at Kuala Selangor. Heath was only just in time, for attempts by a Japanese amphibious force to land there were frustrated on the 2nd and again early on the 3rd. This caused Heath to reinforce the scratch force with a battalion from the five then in 6th/15th Brigade, which was holding the outpost position north of the Slim River. On 4 January Heath told Paris to bring 6th/15th Brigade back to Tanjong Malim that night. The same day Japanese troops, advancing down the coastal road from Telok Anson, reached Kuala Selangor and closed up to the river for a distance of some twelve miles from its mouth, thereby threatening both bridges over the Selangor River.

By the morning of 5 January, III Corps was disposed with 11th Division on the trunk road, with two of its brigades (12th and 28th) north of the Slim River and one (6th/15th) at Tanjong Malim; a scratch force of two Indian and two FMSVF battalions and 3rd Cavalry facing the Japanese across the Selangor River; 8th Brigade (less a battalion) at Kuala Lipis; and the weakened 22nd Brigade at Jerantut. The increased threat to his left flank (it is now known that the Japanese force in that area consisted of four battalions) caused Heath to move 6th/15th Brigade from Tanjong Malim to Rawang on the 5th and to order Lieutenant-Colonel Moorhead to assume command of all the units in the scratch force and to take over responsibility for the whole area from Rawang to the mouth of the Selangor River. This resulted in General Paris (11th Division) being left with only two brigades to defend the trunk road, one of which (the 12th) had reached the point of utter exhaustion.

Realizing that III Corps would shortly be forced to withdraw back to Johore, Major-General Gordon Bennett asked Percival on 4 January to allow him to take control of all operations in Johore, or, if that were not possible, for his division to be made responsible for western Johore. On the 5th Percival met Heath and Gordon Bennett at Segamat. The three commanders concluded that it would be unwise to try to check the Japanese advance in the States of Selangor, Negri Sembilan and Malacca, where the network of roads gave the

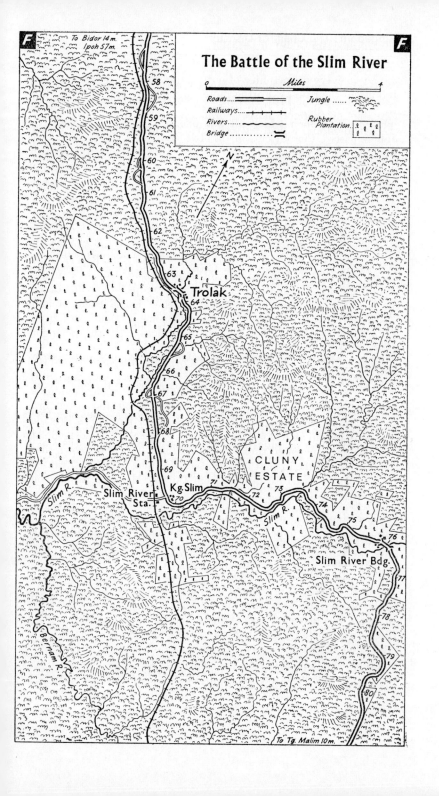

The Battle of the Slim River

Miles
0 ——————————————— 4

Roads............ ━━━━━
Railways......... ┼┼┼┼┼
Rivers.......... ～～～
Bridge........... ⊨

Jungle ...... 🌳
Rubber
Plantation. 🌴

To Bidor 14 m.
Ipoh 57 m.

58

59

N

60

61

62

63

Trolak
64

65

66

67

68

69

CLUNY
ESTATE

Slim R.

Slim River
Sta.

Kg. Slim
70

71

72

73

74

Slim R.

75

76

Slim River Bdg.
77

78

Bernam R.

79

80

To Tg. Malim 10 m.

Japanese every opportunity of outflanking the defence and making full use of their tanks. Furthermore, since they were free to land on the coasts of Malacca, they might well be able to seize the Tampin bottleneck through which all but one of the roads leading into Johore passed, thereby cutting off 11th Division. Realizing that 11th Division could not be expected to hold the Japanese unaided for much longer, Percival decided to place 45th Indian Brigade (newly arrived in Malaya) under Heath's command and instructed Heath once again to deny the airfields at Kuala Lumpur and Port Swettenham till 14 January and then to withdraw to Johore, where the main line of resistance would be Mersing–Segamat–Muar. He rejected Gordon Bennett's requests of 4 January, on the grounds that the move of the Australian division would cause administrative difficulties, and made Heath responsible for western and Bennett for eastern Johore. In consequence, Heath told Paris to conduct an orderly withdrawal, holding Kuala Kubu till 10 January and then moving slowly back in stages to reach Tampin by 24 January. Heath's instructions to Paris were not, however, to be put into force, for 11th Division was to be virtually destroyed on the Slim River on 7 January, and the withdrawal to Johore carried out much more quickly than had been anticipated.

At the point where the road and railway approach the Slim River, it runs from east to west; the railway crossing was at Kampong Slim and the road crossing at Slim River bridge some six miles further east. From Kampong Slim the road and railway run north-west side by side for some six miles through rubber plantations to the small village of Trolak. One mile north of Trolak both the road and railway enter into a thick belt of secondary jungle, which was deemed to be quite impassable for tanks and probably impassable even for the Japanese infantry. Both Percival and Heath had seen the area and realized that it lent itself to defence, since in the defile north of the rubber estate the only line of approach was the road and railway, which were nowhere more than half a mile apart and generally very much closer.

The 12th and 28th Brigades had reached the area on 3 January, and until the 5th were covered by 6th/15th Brigade. Thus they had at least three days to prepare their defensive positions. Paris decided to create two defended areas around Trolak and Slim River, giving the 12th Brigade (Brigadier Stewart) the former and 28th Brigade (Brigadier Selby) the latter. He allotted each forward brigade one troop of anti-tank guns and kept his anti-tank regiment less these small detachments in reserve at Tanjong Malim. Brigadier Stewart disposed his brigade in depth down the road and railway with two battalions in the defile: a Hyderabad battalion to hold an outpost position some two miles north of the rubber estate, and a Punjab battalion the main position behind it. He gave the Argylls the task of covering Trolak village and the exits from the jungle defile and retained his fourth battalion in reserve resting near Kampong Slim but ready to occupy a previously reconnoitred and prepared position one mile south of Trolak village. He allotted the troop of anti-tank guns and all the anti-tank mines at his disposal to the Punjab battalion in the main position, and the anti-tank obstacles to the Hyderabad battalion in the outpost position. Since he considered that there was little scope for field artillery in a normal role, he deployed only one battery and left the other two batteries in reserve in 28th Brigade's area some four miles east of Kampong Slim. Brigadier Selby decided to dispose a battalion astride the railway and another supported by his troop of anti-tank guns astride the road near Kampong Slim, with his artillery regiment in support of them, and kept his third battalion in reserve to occupy, if necessary, a lay-back position half-way between Kampong Slim and Slim River bridge. He was instructed by Paris not to occupy his selected positions until told to do so, in order to give his troops the greatest possible rest.

These dispositions in considerable depth might appear to have been sound, but in practice they were not. The great danger was that tanks would break through the defile north of Trolak, yet Paris allotted the almost completely exhausted 12th Brigade to defend this vital area, giving it only forty anti-tank mines (though he had some fourteen hundred at his disposal) and a mere troop of anti-tank guns. In the defile itself the trunk road had recently been realigned to cut out bends. The loops of the old road, though partially impeded by encroaching jungle, were quite passable. Two existed in the area defended by the Punjab battalion in the main position, but these were left without anti-tank defences.

The battalions given the task of holding the defile had been fighting or moving since their arrival at Ipoh on 12 December, that is, for over three weeks. On arrival in the Trolak area after a fifteen-mile night withdrawal, they had had to set to work digging positions and erecting obstacles under constant air attack by day. Their surroundings were depressing—a ribbon of road and thick jungle on both sides—and from 5 January, once 6th/15th Brigade had withdrawn through them, they got precious little rest at night. The result was that they were almost asleep on their feet, and both officers and men were incapable of seeing what ought to be done or of realizing what had been left undone. What was needed at the Slim River was a fresh formation; but owing to General Percival's insistence on keeping 9th Division east of the main range there was no formation available.

As usual the Japanese followed up 6th/15th Brigade without delay and made contact with the Hyderabads on the evening of the 5th. They immediately attempted to move down the railway but were thrown back with loss. The next day information was received that there was a considerable concentration of Japanese tanks on the trunk road, and Stewart warned the Hyderabads that they were to withdraw from the outpost position early on the 7th. Before they could withdraw, however, a column of Japanese tanks and lorried infantry attacked straight down the road. The attackers cleared the first road block, overran the leading Hyderabad company and, by use of one of the loop roads, surrounded the companies of the battalion on the road, forcing them to withdraw to and retreat down the railway. Having thus disposed of the outpost battalion, the Japanese now faced the Punjabis in the main position. Although a number of tanks were destroyed by mines and anti-tank fire, others, finding and using the unprotected loop roads, surrounded the forward defended localities. They then moved on until checked by mines in front of the reserve Punjabi company. By using the same tactics they also surrounded and overwhelmed this position, and by first light at about 6.30 a.m. the tanks were through the area defended by anti-tank guns, mines and obstacles and debouching into the rubber estate. Since all telephone lines were out of action by 5 a.m., Stewart had little idea of the situation. However, he ordered the Argylls to put up road blocks north of Trolak and his reserve battalion to move into its prepared position south of the village. These temporary road blocks were quickly swept aside, and by 7 a.m. the enemy tanks were in Trolak. There the Japanese column paused to reorganize.

Meanwhile, back at Tanjong Malim, Paris had heard that there had been a partial break-through north of Trolak and at 7 a.m. he ordered Selby (28th Brigade) to occupy the prepared position in the vicinity of Kampong Slim. Having issued the necessary orders, Selby went to see Stewart to find out what the situation in front of him actually was. The Japanese tank column moving southwards passed through the undefended position south of Trolak and at about 7.30 a.m. ran headlong into 12th Brigade's reserve battalion moving up the road in column of fours. The troops on the road were scattered and the troop of anti-tank guns loaned by 28th Brigade, which had been sent forward to help the battalion hold the reserve position, was destroyed. The tanks then drove past the Gurkha battalion of 28th Brigade, which was in the process of occupying the position near Kampong Slim, at about 8 a.m. and about five minutes later ran into the rear of another Gurkha battalion moving east to take up its position covering the Slim River bridge. This battalion was also scattered with heavy casualties. Having passed for a few moments to shoot up Stewart's two field batteries parked in the rubber on the side of the road, the tanks reached the undefended Slim River bridge at 8.40 a.m., just over five hours from the launching of the attack some twelve miles further north. A gallant attempt made by a light anti-aircraft detachment equipped with Bofors guns failed to save the bridge, and the tanks swept on, leaving behind a detachment to guard it. They were finally brought to a halt at 9.30 a.m. by a field regiment at a point about two miles south of the bridge.

All was chaos in the area north of the Slim River when Japanese infantry followed up the tanks. By 11 a.m. Stewart and Selby, who were by that time at Kampong Slim, realized that 12th Brigade and a battalion of 28th Brigade had ceased to exist as fighting formations. They decided to hold on at Kampong Slim until nightfall in order to collect stragglers from the forward area and then, having destroyed their remaining transport, to retire down the railway to Tanjong Malim. Since the railway bridge had already been destroyed and the engineers could provide only planks across the gap, the survivors had considerable difficulty crossing the river. Nevertheless by dawn many of them had reached Tanjong Malim, twelve miles to the south. Of 12th Brigade only fourteen officers and some four hundred men reached that village, and of 28th Brigade some seven hundred and fifty all ranks.[1]

Any attempt to hold the Tanjong Malim position and the Selangor River area was now out of the question. General Heath could only break contact and withdraw the remnants of his available forces well to the south to reorganize. On 8 January, therefore, he ordered General Paris to try to hold Kuala Lumpur till midnight on the 10th/11th and then fall back to Seremban over thirty miles to the south. This was accomplished with difficulty, and on the evening of the 11th, having made a further landing at Port Swettenham,

[1] The Japanese claim to have taken some twelve hundred prisoners, many of whom were wounded, and in the week that followed rounded up another two thousand cut off and mostly starving. They also captured a large number of field guns, a few anti-tank and anti-aircraft guns and a very large quantity of transport,

the Japanese *25th Army* occupied Kuala Lumpur, the capital of Malaya.

And so the second phase of the campaign ended, as it was bound to do, with the loss of central Malaya; for after its defeat at Jitra 11th Division, though reinforced by 12th Brigade, had no hope of holding fresh Japanese formations on the trunk road while at the same time trying to stave off landings on the west coast designed to turn its left flank. Too much was asked of one tired and weary formation. It had fought well north of Ipoh and at Kampar, but the disaster at Slim River bridge was the inevitable consequence of asking more of it than was humanly possible. Throughout 11th Division's retreat of some two hundred and twenty miles (as the crow flies) from Jitra to Kuala Lumpur in twenty-nine days, 9th Division had been kept idle in Pahang except for the futile and unnecessary effort to hold the Kuantan airfield. The 9th Division should have been brought to the west of the main range to relieve 11th Division at least by the end of December. The 8th Brigade had reached Kuala Lipis on 22 December. It would have been possible for 22nd Brigade to have joined it there about the same date. The whole division could then have been moved without difficulty to the Slim River–Tanjong Malim area by the end of the month.

Kuala Lumpur was the main base for the formations allotted to the defence of northern and eastern Malaya, since from it the main road ran to Kuala Lipis and Kuantan, and it was served by rail from Port Swettenham. When III Corps retreated across the Perak River on 23 December, General Percival began to backload much of the accumulated supplies and reserves from the city, some to a base at Segamat and some to Johore Bahru and Singapore. Although a large part of the reserves was moved back by road and rail, the sudden collapse of 11th Division at Slim River and the forced evacuation of Kuala Lumpur ten days before it was expected resulted in the task being left uncompleted, and much of value fell into Japanese hands. The withdrawal from Kedah, Perak and Selangor had caused considerable congestion on the single-track railway line, which had passing places only at the main centres. Rolling-stock evacuated from the north became an embarrassment as the retreat continued, and the backloading of reserves became extremely and increasingly difficult, so much so that thirteen trains loaded with valuable equipment (including a consignment of maps of southern Johore and Singapore especially printed in Kuala Lumpur) had to be temporarily parked on the branch line to Malacca. Congestion at Gemas junction was so bad that they had not been moved by the

180

time that III Corps passed through Tampin on 13 January, and they fell into enemy hands. Throughout the retreat the FMS Railway and the Post and Telegraph services functioned most efficiently, despite the fact that some personnel near the forward areas deserted and engineer and signal troops had to be used to help in keeping these vital services going.

17

The Formation of ABDA Command and Plans for the Defence of Johore

January 1942   *Map G, p. 183, and Map E, pp. 166–7*

While the events described in the previous three chapters were taking place, the Japanese had crippled the United States Pacific Fleet at Pearl Harbor, had captured Hong Kong, had occupied most of Luzon and Mindanao in the Philippines and were in a position to threaten Australia, the Netherlands East Indies, Borneo and Burma. The Prime Minister had meanwhile crossed the Atlantic to discuss the war situation with his new ally. During the voyage he telegraphed the Chiefs of Staff saying, 'Beware lest [that] the troops required for the ultimate defence of Singapore Island and the fortress are not used up or cut off in Malay peninsula. Nothing compares in importance with the fortress.'[1] This and his previous statements regarding the importance of the defence of the 'fortress' (*see pages 64–5, 70*), should have alerted the Chiefs of Staff to the fact that he had a completely false picture of the strategic situation in Malaya.

At a conference in Washington attended by the Prime Minister, the President and their Chiefs of Staff, the Americans proposed that there should be some co-ordinating authority in the area from Australia westwards to the Bay of Bengal and northwards to Formosa. After considerable discussion it was agreed that an American–British–Dutch–Australian (ABDA) Command should be formed, and Roosevelt proposed that General Sir Archibald Wavell (then Commander-in-Chief in India) should be appointed Supreme Commander of the newly created command. On 29 December Wavell provisionally accepted the appointment, and on 15 January 1942 an ABDA Command headquarters was established at Bandoeng in Java.

Meanwhile, the Chiefs of Staff had agreed on the scale of reinforcements required for the Far East. These were: for Malaya, two divisions, one armoured brigade and eight light-bomber, two torpedo-bomber and eight fighter squadrons; for the Netherlands East Indies, two divisions; and for Burma, two divisions, a light-tank squadron and six light-bomber and six fighter squadrons. To implement this decision it was decided to send the remainder of 18th British Division to Singapore, and 1st Australian Corps (6th and 7th Australian

---

[1] Churchill, *The Second World War*, Vol. III, p. 565.

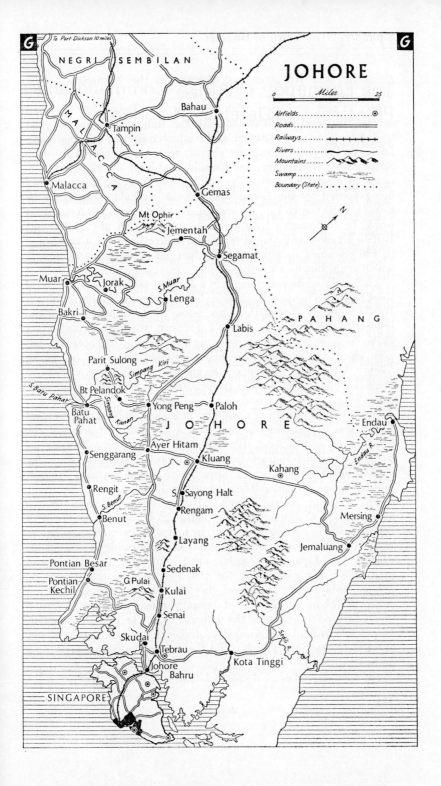

Divisions) and 7th Armoured Brigade to the Netherlands East Indies. Between 3 and 31 January, therefore, General Percival could expect to receive 18th British Division, two Indian brigades and several thousand reinforcements for the Indian divisions, an Australian machine-gun battalion, and reinforcements for 8th Australian Division. Fifty-one Hurricane aircraft were also expected to reach Singapore on 13 January, but it would be at least a week before they could be ready for active operations, and forty-eight Hurricanes being carried by the *Indomitable* from Port Sudan would not be available till the end of the month. In effect these reinforcements would be best summed up as the equivalent of a physically unfit British division, two almost untrained Indian brigades, a number of partially trained Indian and Australian reinforcements and aircraft which could but be a wasting asset.

After the Segamat conference of 5 January (*see page 174*), Percival went back to Singapore to consider how best he could defend Johore. By the morning of the 7th he had come to the conclusion that the critical period would be from 24 January, when he expected III Corps to reach the Tampin area, until the middle of February. His plan was that one Australian brigade should be moved over from eastern Johore and come under command of III Corps for offensive operations, being replaced in eastern Johore by two battalions, one from Singapore Island and one from III Corps. General Gordon Bennett was to remain in command in eastern Johore, and General Heath was to command in the west of the State. This meant the breaking up of 8th Australian Division, which Percival wanted to avoid and to which Bennett had always objected. However, the latter agreed, albeit grudgingly, to the move of 27th Australian Brigade, and to its coming under Heath's command.

That evening General Wavell arrived in Singapore, on his way to set up ABDA Command in Java. Although he was not *au fait* with the situation in his new command, he had already concluded that he was faced with a race against time. Everything depended on his holding the Japanese offensive until reinforcing formations and aircraft already earmarked for the Far East could arrive. As far as Malaya was concerned, he wanted the Japanese delayed north of Johore till the end of January, after which 18th Division could be used to reinforce the defence. Later, he thought, it might be possible to land two Australian divisions at Singapore to relieve the Indian divisions, which could then go to the Netherlands East Indies.

On 8 January, before flying to Kuala Lumpur to see some of the troops of 11th Division,[1] Wavell met Bennett at Johore Bahru and found a great contrast between Heath and him. He was impressed by Bennett's vigorous approach to the defence of Johore and by his desire to take the offensive with his Australian formations, and it seems that he did not realize either Bennett's limitations as a commander or the internal strains that existed in the Australian division. Then in Kuala Lumpur he was immediately struck by the fact that Heath and his staff were extremely weary, a fact which was scarcely to be wondered at. He also realized that the fighting value of 11th Division was at a very low ebb. Clearly what III Corps needed was to be withdrawn and reorganized; to effect this he decided that Bennett should be entrusted with the defence of north-west Johore.

That evening Wavell summoned Percival to the house which had been placed at his disposal and kept him waiting in an ante-room for a considerable time. Finally he called Percival in and without any discussion handed him a plan which he had written out in full and gave instructions that it was to be put into effect forthwith. Since the plan was almost exactly the opposite to the one which Percival had proposed, and somewhat similar to the one Percival had already turned down, Wavell's action came as a shock. Presumably Wavell had lost confidence in Percival the previous evening, and was impressed by Bennett's enthusiasm. Wavell's plan was that Bennett should be given responsibility for the defence of north-west Johore, and should fight a defensive battle on the general line Segamat–Mount Ophir–Muar. For this purpose Bennett was to have 8th Australian Division (temporarily less 22nd Australian Brigade, which was to remain at Mersing until relieved by troops from Singapore after the arrival of 53rd Brigade on 13 January), 9th Indian Division (its two brigades being brought up to strength by the freshest troops from 11th Division) and the semi-trained 45th Indian Brigade (recently arrived in Malaya and located at Malacca). When this was done, III Corps less those formations and units transferred to Bennett was to be withdrawn by rail and road to southern Johore, where it was to reorganize.

Whereas Percival's plan divided Johore into two parts so that each force could be disposed in depth and could, if necessary, fall back along its own communications, Wavell's plan would undoubtedly make command in case of a withdrawal much more difficult. Furthermore the general line of defensive positions selected by Wavell was forty miles wide and offered the Japanese two lines of advance as

[1] During Wavell's flight northwards and back again practically the whole of the available fighters in Malaya were employed as escorts.

well as the opportunity of landing in the rear of the defence. It also abandoned the Tampin gap, which had a width of only fifteen miles where the trunk and coastal roads ran close together. The position in the Tampin bottleneck was one of those where the Japanese advance might have been held for some time, had it been properly prepared, stocked with supplies and adequately garrisoned, and provided that a mobile force had been held behind it in readiness to take the counter-offensive against any exposed enemy flank (*see page 115*).

Having given these explicit orders Wavell flew on 9 January to Java to set up Headquarters ABDA Command. He took with him as a nucleus of the staff for the new command Lieutenant-General Sir Henry Pownall, the recently appointed Commander-in-Chief, Far East, as his Chief of Staff, and the staff of Headquarters Far Eastern Command.

On 9 January Percival issued the orders to put Wavell's plan into effect, and the following day he held another conference at Segamat with Heath and Bennett to organize the handover between III Corps and the Australians. It was then agreed that the force under Bennett's command should be known as Westforce. Moving by road and rail 9th Division reached Tampin on 12 January, and came under command of Westforce the following day. When the rest of III Corps withdrew through Westforce to the Kluang area, the second phase of the campaign could be considered to be over. The Japanese were now in control of all northern and central Malaya.

When III Corps had withdrawn through Westforce, Heath asked that an Indian Army officer, who understood Indian troops, should be placed in command of 11th Division in place of Paris, in order to restore the morale of that formation. He made it clear, however, that Paris had in no way failed as a divisional commander, but that exceptional circumstances caused the request. Percival agreed. Brigadier Key (8th Brigade) assumed command of 11th Division from 14 January and Paris went back to Singapore to reform his old 12th Brigade.

Air Vice-Marshal Pulford was also in a difficult situation. At the turn of the year, having gained air superiority in northern Malaya and having forced the RAF to evacuate the Kuala Lumpur airfield, the Japanese began to use part of their air force to attack 11th Division and the communications serving III Corps.

With the evacuation of the Kuala Lumpur and the loss of the Kuantan airfields, the RAF could use only the four airfields on Singapore Island, the one at Kluang and the landing-grounds at Kahang, Batu Pahat and Johore Bahru. All these were within close

range of the superior Japanese air force and any of them might have
to be evacuated at short notice, because the RAF could not afford to
lose any aircraft on the ground. Great hope was placed on the
expected arrival of the fifty-one Hurricanes, for it was felt that these
aircraft might enable the RAF to maintain air superiority at least
over southern Johore and Singapore. These crated aircraft had to
be erected and tested before they could be used operationally, and to
undertake these tasks on the existing airfields would have been taking a great risk of their destruction before they were ready for operations. To allow for dispersion of the existing squadrons and to ensure
the safety of the Hurricanes, Percival arranged to give Pulford a
priority call on all available labour to construct new airstrips in
southern Johore and on Singapore Island and to repair damage to
existing airfields. Use of the available labour in this way soon brought
about a general shortage for other tasks.

At the beginning of the second week in January, the Japanese
started to intensify their daylight bombing attacks on the airfields
and dock areas in Singapore. The defence was handicapped by the
lack of warning, for both the observer and radar warning systems
were now entirely inadequate, owing to the fact that it took the
Buffalo fighters about half an hour to reach an altitude of twenty-
four thousand feet (the height at which the Japanese bombers
usually flew) and because one-third of the anti-aircraft guns defending the island were the old 3-inch guns with a ceiling of barely
eighteen thousand feet. The defending fighter force consisted of four
British squadrons and one Dutch, with a total of some fifty-six
serviceable aircraft. Nevertheless on 12 January three enemy attacks
on Tengah airfield were intercepted and, for the loss of five Buffalos,
about six enemy fighters were destroyed. Unfortunately, as the
Japanese always provided their bombers with heavy fighter escorts,
the defending fighters were not able to get among the attacking
bombers. On the 13th an attack was made by eighty-one bombers
covered by fighters just as the convoy bringing 53rd Brigade of 18th
Division, two anti-aircraft regiments, one anti-tank regiment and the
fifty-one Hurricanes reached the port. Owing to a low cloud ceiling
the convoy escaped detection.

18

The Civil Administration in Malaya under War Conditions

The sudden and unexpected collapse in northern Malaya had its effect on the civil administration. So far the civil servants had completely failed to grasp the fact that if war broke out northern Malaya might well fall into enemy hands. This attitude is typified by the opposition put up by the Acting Governor and the Secretary for Defence in 1940 to the distribution of rice stocks throughout the country. As it had been decided to defend northern Malaya, they maintained it was quite safe to hold all the reserves of rice at Alor Star. Thus no plans had been made to cope with the loss of any Malayan territory. Nor had much thought been given to the probability that essential labour would desert under threat of bombing and that many of those in the voluntary civil-defence services would leave their posts in order to look after their families. Nor had serious thought been given to the problem of the evacuation of areas threatened by the enemy; for example, were Europeans and Asians to be treated on a basis of equality, where could those evacuated be housed and how could they be fed? It was the inherent capability of the British to improvise that resulted in many of the problems arising from invasion being solved locally by District Commissioners and officers of the PWD, the FMS Railways, and the Post and Telegraph services. These men deserve the greatest praise for the way they kept the civil administration in being in the various States of Malaya under circumstances of the greatest difficulty.

The lack of pre-war plans for the evacuation of the civil population from areas likely to be overrun by the Japanese soon made itself felt. On 17 December General Heath issued an order that all European women and children should be evacuated from Perak. As soon as Jones, the Colonial Secretary, heard of this he told the Governor that the evacuation of European women and children from Penang had already had a bad effect on the Asian population of Singapore. Sir Shenton Thomas thereupon prepared a statement to the effect that Heath's order was unauthorized and not only was no evacuation to be permitted but that trains carrying evacuees were to be turned back, first-class carriages removed from trains to deter Europeans from travelling, petrol was not to be supplied to private motorists, and cars travelling south were to be turned back. When this announcement was made at the War Council meeting on 18 December, Duff Cooper, the chairman, pointed out that, if this order were issued, it would be the first time in British history that fighting troops would evacuate an area leaving British women and children at the mercy of the enemy, and in this case a particularly cruel Asian enemy. He went on to say that it was not in order for the War Council or the Governor to countermand an order given by an officer in charge of operations, who might have well issued it so that the care of women and children would not hamper the movement of his troops. The Council agreed and the Governor cancelled the draft order. Naturally the stand made by Duff Cooper on this matter did not improve relations between himself and the Governor.

About the middle of December instructions were received from London that an unrestricted scorched-earth policy was to be applied throughout Malaya and Singapore. From a purely military point of view this may have been right, but it was hardly feasible for a colonial power to apply it to the detriment of the indigenous Asian population. To do so would have deprived them of many of the necessities of life. If Malaya and Singapore Island were completely overrun by the Japanese, it was taken for granted that the territory would sooner or later be wrested back from them. The majority of commercial undertakings, rubber estates, tin mines, iron and coal mines, and so on, were owned by European firms, but there were many that were the property of indigenous Asians, and the War Council concluded that the rigid application of a scorched-earth policy would be most unwise. After considerable exchange of telegrams between London and Singapore, it was decided that public utilities such as power plants and water supplies and food stuffs would not be touched. Nor would businesses, estates and mines owned by Asians unless these were of particular value to the Japanese. The speed of the retreat in Malaya was such, however, that it became almost impossible to apply the scorched-earth policy except in a few specific cases. Since no plans had been prepared to this effect before the outbreak of war, authority to destroy installations had in general to be delegated to the commander in the field. In the case of large installations, such as the coal mines in Selangor, whose destruction would take time, the decision was taken at governmental level in Singapore, but the work of demolition was left to the owners to carry out, helped as necessary by officers sent to aid in the preparation of plans and to ensure the supply of explosives. European and Asian owners were naturally reluctant to demolish their plant, and all too often action was taken too late to be effective.

The sudden decision to evacuate Penang forced upon the authorities by the military situation showed up the comparative inefficiency of the civil defence and auxiliary fire organizations. Despite their gallant work they had failed, because their numbers and equipment were entirely inadequate to deal with even one severe air attack. And as the débâcle at Penang was likely to happen elsewhere, unofficial members of the Legislative Council, led by Mr F. D. Bisseker, its senior member, and the Press demanded that civil defence throughout Malaya should be strengthened.

On 15 December with the full agreement of the War Council Duff Cooper had set up an advisory committee on civil defence. This consisted of himself as chairman, the Inspector General of the Police, Major-General Keith Simmons (Singapore Fortress Commander) and two officers of the Malayan Civil Service, one of whom, Mr (later Sir Alexander) Newboult, was secretary. The committee examined the structure of the civil-defence organization on Singapore Island in the light of the evidence of events in Penang. The following facts emerged: the Colonial Secretary, Jones, who on behalf of the Governor had been in charge of all passive civil-defence measures before the outbreak of war, had always refused to provide air-raid shelters for the population of the city on the grounds that it was an impossible task to provide for over half a million people. He had, however, built two evacuation camps outside the city capable of housing and feeding some 300,000 individuals at a cost of one million Straits dollars. These camps could cater for only about two-thirds of the pre-war population, and this had, after 8 December, been greatly augmented by the arrival of evacuees from Malaya. The auxiliary fire services had been neither properly integrated nor equipped. The Singapore Harbour Board had its own very efficient fire-fighting service. The Printing Department had its own private fire-engine and staff. The City Fire Services were understaffed and ill-equipped, with much of their inadequate lengths of hose old and unserviceable. No attempt had been made to consider the problem of providing secondary water supplies for feeding the fire-engines in case the water mains were cut. Insufficient thought had been given to the water problem should the island be closely invested and the supply of water from the reservoir in Johore cut off. Furthermore the personnel of the various civil-defence organizations were ill-supplied with steel helmets and respirators.

The man who had been head of the fire services in Penang, which had suffered from similar defects, reported after a three-day survey of conditions in Singapore that the city's fire services (except in the Harbour Board area) had no hope of coping with heavy air raids. The committee also noted that no steps had been taken to register the population, an essential step in preparation for food rationing which might become necessary, that no arrangements had been made to earmark alternative accommodation for government departments, and that no plans had been made to provide for alternative power stations and pumping stations should they be put out of action and water supplies cut off.

On 27 December, on the motion of adjournment of a special meeting of the Legislative Council, Bisseker spoke on the need for action in connection with civil defence and urged the appointment of someone with plenary powers to organize it. Jones replied that a body consisting of himself, the Brigadier in charge of Administration, Malaya Command, and the President of the Municipality was the authority empowered to take action in respect of civil defence. Duff Cooper was not satisfied that this body could deal with the situation as it then existed. He therefore decided that it would be necessary to appoint a Director General of Civil Defence (DGCD) and invest him with plenary powers to enable him to cut quickly through red tape and take effective action. Having reached this decision he asked Percival whether he would make his Chief Engineer, Brigadier Simson, available for the post. Because there was now a possibility that Singapore Island might be invested, General Percival was loath to lose the services of his Chief Engineer, who might have to undertake a role of major importance. He therefore at first opposed Duff Cooper's suggestion, but finally agreed, provided that Simson retained his appointment as Chief Engineer, Malaya Command. However when he was offered the appointment Simson refused to accept, on the grounds that his main task as Chief Engineer was to organize the defence of the island. In the event he was then ordered to take up the appointment and hand over his duties as Chief Engineer to his deputy.

On 31 December Duff Cooper told the War Council that it was necessary to ensure that there would be no breakdown in the civil-defence organization and that he proposed to appoint Simson DGCD with plenary powers under the War Council on all matters pertaining to civil defence in Singapore Island and Johore. Mr Bisseker would be Simson's deputy and also director of Labour and Transport. The Council agreed unanimously to the proposal, but decided that Jones should report the decision to the Governor and that the proposed terms of reference for the DGCD should be discussed next day.

That afternoon Duff Cooper sent a letter to Simson and Bisseker appointing them and giving them plenary powers, and added that all protective works around buildings and other places ordered by Simson should be completed immediately by and at the cost of the organization which owned them, the cost being charged to a suspense account for later adjustment by the Government. Copies of this letter were sent to the Governor, all Service Chiefs, to Jones the Colonial Secretary, the Secretary of Defence, the Inspector General of Police, the Manpower Bureau, the Food Controller, the Director of Civil Air Defence, the Public Works Department, the Singapore Municipality, the FMS Railways, the Singapore Harbour Board, the Singapore Traction Company, the Chinese Chamber of Commerce, the General Adviser and State Engineer in Johore and to all large engineering firms in the city; its terms were also published in the English and vernacular daily papers. Duff Cooper told Simson personally that he was to organize without delay physical protection for all public utility services and workshops employed on work for the government and the Services, and to make arrangements to provide labour and transport to meet the growing and sometimes conflicting demands from the Services, the Municipality, the Harbour Board and the civil-defence organizations.

That night the Governor was told of Duff Cooper's plans by Jones, and next morning at the War Council he opposed them, taking the line that only he, the Governor, could make such an appointment and give such powers. For some unknown reason Duff Cooper now agreed that Sir Shenton Thomas should make the appointments, and on 1 January the latter issued a communiqué to the Colonial Secretary and to a few government departments stating that Simson was appointed DGCD. This communiqué gave Simson much more limited terms of reference and conferred on him full powers on civil-defence matters in Singapore Island only, subject to existing laws and to the fact that he was solely responsible to the Governor. The effects of this change were to abolish the plenary powers given by Duff Cooper and to force Simson to work through the ordinary channels of government, including the Legal Department. In other words, for civil-defence matters Simson merely replaced Jones as the man within the administration responsible for civil defence. Duff Cooper's object of achieving speed in decision and action was therefore nullified.

Fortunately, however, Duff Cooper's terms of reference to Simson of 31 December, published in the Press and widely issued within and without the administration, were never cancelled, while the Governor's more limited terms of reference were not published and, within the administration, were issued only to those departments mainly involved with civil defence. As a result, although he had officially no special powers of compulsion, by carrying copies of both terms of reference and producing whichever proved necessary if he were challenged, Simson was able to ensure that most of the urgently required protective measures were carried out and that many of the objects Duff Cooper had in mind were achieved.

At the end of December the Press in the United Kingdom published articles from a special correspondent in Singapore which repeated the scathing attacks made by the Singapore Press on the efficiency of the civil administration. As a result of these articles the Secretary of State for the colonies telegraphed to the Governor to know whether the local Press were stating the truth and to Duff Cooper for his comments. The replies he received, as might be expected, differed very considerably. The Governor, while agreeing that there were deficiencies, said the articles in the local Press made the most of them, and their appearance was due to the desire of the editor to ingratiate himself with Duff Cooper by indicating that it would be acceptable to the public if the latter were vested with authority in place of the existing civil government. Furthermore the people concerned were constantly critical of the local government. Duff Cooper, on the other hand, repeated much of what he had said in his letter to the Prime Minister of 18 December and gave a full list of the deficiencies in the civil-defence arrangements based on the findings of his committee. He made it clear that in his opinion the administration had failed to make adequate preparation for war, and that the Governor appeared to have lost his grip on the situation and instead of leading was being led.

The Prime Minister was at first inclined to blame Duff Cooper for not reporting the situation before war broke out, until it was pointed out that it was only after 10 December, when he was appointed Resident Minister, that Duff Cooper had any authority to look into Malayan affairs. He said that, if the report were true, it was most damaging to the Governor and it did not seem that he could continue in the post. He therefore made a suggestion that Sir Shenton Thomas should be replaced by a Military Governor (such as Vice-Admiral Sir Geoffrey Layton) and a new Colonial Secretary should be appointed. It had in the meanwhile been decided that, as a result of the establishment of ABDA Command, there was no longer the need for a

o

Resident Minister in the Far East. Orders had therefore been sent to Duff Cooper instructing him to return to London.

Before leaving Singapore Duff Cooper telegraphed to the Secretary of State for the Colonies saying that a widespread and profound lack of confidence existed in the administration, and that as a breakdown in it might well paralyse the fighting services, the time had come to make changes. The solution, he suggested, was that a state of siege should be declared and a Military Governor appointed. For this role he suggested Major-General Keith Simmons was the obvious choice. If, on the other hand, these measures were considered to be too drastic, Jones, the Colonial Secretary, should be replaced by Mr Hugh Fraser from Kuala Lumpur, who had done very well under war conditions.

On receipt of this message the Secretary of State for the Colonies, who considered it would be a mistake to change Governors in the middle of the emergency and was doubtful about the truth of some of Duff Cooper's detailed criticisms of the administration, decided to ask Wavell to advise whether the appointment of a Military Governor would assist in the defence of Malaya and if so who would he recommend. The Prime Minister was very much in favour of Duff Cooper's proposals for a change but also considered that it was first advisable to seek Wavell's advice.

On 13 January Wavell, in his capacity as Supreme Commander ABDA, paid a second visit to Singapore. He found that the Japanese had followed up the retreating III Corps much more quickly than he had expected, and told the Chiefs of Staff on the 14th that in his opinion the battle for Singapore would now be a close-run thing. That day Wavell received cables from the Prime Minister and the Secretary of State for the Colonies asking his advice on the matter of changes in the administration. Wavell immediately consulted General Pownall and Admiral Layton and interviewed Simson. From Simson he learnt of the difficulties he was experiencing in carrying out his task, the reluctance on the part of the Governor to make the changes in key personnel which Simson considered necessary if the civil defences were to be improved, and of Percival's reluctance to prepare defences in Johore or on the north of Singapore Island.[1] From his own knowledge and on the advice of Pownall and Layton, Wavell decided that if the Governor had strong backing he would be a good figurehead. He did not therefore recommend his replacement, provided that the Colonial Secretary was changed. He went on to say

[1] As a result of this interview Wavell once again urged Percival to get on with the preparation of defences on the north coast of Singapore Island.

194

that if he found the Governor, assisted by Fraser, failed to 'fill the bill' he would come forward with other suggestions.

As a result of this advice it was decided that Jones should be retired and replaced by Fraser. But when Sir Shenton Thomas heard of this decision he cabled London saying the decision was regarded in Singapore as the most grievous injustice to Jones, that it seemed both the Prime Minister and the Secretary of State had been misled, and urged that the matter should be reconsidered. However, the decision stood, and the change was made.

In retrospect, and bearing in mind that Sir Shenton Thomas remained in the United Kingdom on leave instead of returning to his post at a time when the danger to the colony had grown with the fall of France, it would appear that Jones was made the scapegoat for him. There is no doubt, however, that Jones, although an excellent and efficient civil servant, was so conservative by nature, or perhaps so ignorant of the probable effect of war on the civil community, that he was unable to adjust himself to the conditions which would exist after the outbreak of war. He therefore opposed measures which, though necessary in war, offended his views as a civil servant. Sir Shenton Thomas proved repeatedly to be a character far too easily swayed by the last person with whom he had been in contact. This characteristic was so marked that after the outbreak of war Percival always took a stenographer to meetings with him to record the discussions made and would not leave the building until he had the Governor's signature to them, for he knew from experience that after a few minutes' conversation with Jones the Governor would attempt to reverse the decisions already taken, should they not meet with Jones's approval.

Although he had the courtesy title of Commander-in-Chief of the Colony he had to govern, Sir Shenton Thomas had no military knowledge whatsoever,[1] and was inherently unable to grasp the problems with which an invasion of Malaya would confront him. Thus, backed by several senior civil servants who were anti-military, he failed to do so. In retrospect the Governor should have been replaced at the end of his first term of office by a man of forceful personality who could make his own decisions and stick to them. Such a man would either have ruled his Colonial Secretary instead of being ruled by him or, if he had found that Jones would not react, then he would have himself changed his Colonial Secretary. The unfortunate Jones would

[1] None of the civil servants who had been through the Imperial Defence College before 1939 had yet reached the necessary seniority to be considered for appointment as a Governor of a Colony.

then probably not have become the scapegoat in January 1942. It is, however, understandable that with the enemy nearing the gates of Singapore neither the British government, Duff Cooper nor Wavell wished to replace the Governor, and this view was in the circumstances of January 1942 probably correct.

19

The Third Phase of the Campaign: The Struggle for Johore

14–31 January 1942   *Map G, p. 183*

Before describing the struggle for Johore it is necessary to consider the plans the Japanese made for its occupation. The short lull resulting from the rapid withdrawal of the British forces to northern Johore enabled them to reorganize. Lieutenant-General Yamashita had two complete divisions with a total of seven regiments to operate on the west coast. He decided that *5th Division* would operate down the trunk road from Tampin towards Segamat while *Imperial Guards Division*, after concentrating in the Malacca area, would advance down the coastal road to force the crossings of the Sungei [River] Muar and the Sungei Batu Pahat (aided as necessary by amphibious landings) and to threaten the communications of any British forces opposing *5th Division* on the trunk road.

On the east coast *56th Regiment* of *18th Division*, having landed at Kota Bharu and secured the Kelantan airfields, had captured the Kuantan airfield. During its advance down the east coast it had been followed up by *55th Regiment* of the same division, which had been landed later. Yamashita now ordered *55th Regiment* (which had only two battalions) to relieve the *56th* at Kuantan and to move down the coast to capture Endau. Field-Marshal Terauchi (*Southern Army*) had intended that the balance of *18th Division* should be landed at Endau, but decided to cancel the operation, because the British forces had withdrawn so hurriedly from Kuala Lumpur, and because he was not satisfied that sufficient air superiority had been gained in that area to warrant the risk of the loss of transports. He therefore arranged for the balance of *18th Division* to be landed at Singora. In order to take the load off his long lines of communication, Yamashita requested that a number of administrative units required for use on the airfields in southern Johore together with stocks of ammunition, bombs and petrol should be landed at Endau when that port had been captured. This request was granted, and it was arranged that the Japanese navy would occupy the Anamba Islands and land the required administrative units at Endau on 26 January. Since Yamashita wanted *18th Division* fresh for his assault on Singapore Island, he ordered *56th Regiment* to move westwards by road from Kuantan to Kuala Lumpur and *55th Regiment*, after the capture of Endau and

Mersing, to move to Kluang by way of Jemaluang instead of advancing south towards Kota Tinggi and Johore Bahru.

On the British side General Bennett (Westforce) had only four brigades on the west coast with which to oppose the seven Japanese regiments. He was therefore outnumbered by nearly two to one. The adverse ratio was however even greater than it appeared, for 45th Indian Infantry Brigade was practically untrained and quite inexperienced. South of the Tampin gap the country was intersected by many roads, and in view of the weakness of Westforce no form of purely static defence offered any prospect of success. General Percival had by this time realized that the only chance of arresting the Japanese advance was to block the main roads and then, if possible, to take the counter-offensive against their flanks when they tried to overcome the road blocks. It was this form of defence which, had he concentrated his three divisions in northern Malaya earlier in the campaign, might, with the help of pre-constructed defences on bottlenecks on the main roads, have held up the Japanese in northern Malaya long enough for reinforcing formations to reach Singapore and be brought into action. But by mid-January it was too late. Westforce had a hopeless task, more especially as it was weaker than necessary and as Bennett had to control operations over a wide front with only his divisional staff. It would have been much better if Wavell had accepted Percival's original plan and not removed III Corps from the scene of action. What was required was at least a division on each of the two roads operating under III Corps' command.

A glance at the map of Johore on page 183 will show that the trunk road takes a wide sweep inland from Tampin, running east to Segamat some forty-five miles from the coast and then swinging back, so that at Yong Peng and Ayer Hitam it is only some seventeen miles from the coast. The communications of any formations fighting on the trunk road therefore had to pass through Yong Peng and Ayer Hitam. These two places, comparatively close to the coast, were therefore of vital importance, especially as it was known that the Japanese could outflank the defence by making amphibious landings at will. It seems that Bennett, who knew the area well, failed to recognize the importance of these two small villages, for he concentrated three-quarters of his force on the trunk road in depth and left the inexperienced 45th Indian Brigade, supported by only one field battery, to hold the crossings of the Sungei Muar and guard against further seaborne landings south of the river. This would have been an impossible task even for a highly trained brigade with its full quota of artillery support. To make matters much worse, he insisted that 45th Brigade must spread out over a front of some twenty-four miles along the river, with the left (Rajputana) battalion holding Muar and nine miles of the river and the right (Jat) battalion a further fifteen miles upstream, and that each of the forward battalions must locate two companies (about half its strength) to the north of the river. The reserve (Garhwali) battalion was located at Bakri with a company watching the coastline. Such dispositions courted disaster.

The Japanese plan on the coastal road was for *4th Guards Regiment* on the right and *5th Guards Regiment* on the left to advance on Muar on a front of some five miles. The *4th* was to contain the defence in Muar, while the *5th* crossed the river under cover of darkness and attacked the town from the east. As soon as the *5th* had crossed, the *4th* was to send a battalion by sea to land on the coast south of Batu Pahat with the object of preventing the British forces from using the coastal road when they withdrew. Once Muar had been occupied, the *4th* was to make for Batu Pahat along the coast road and the *5th* for Yong Peng along the inland road.

On the afternoon of 15 January the Japanese overran the two companies of the Rajputana battalion north of the river, apparently without a shot being fired and so completely that there were no survivors to tell what had happened. By 11 a.m. Japanese troops were on the north bank of the river opposite the town. That night, carrying some small boats found in the ricefields, a few Japanese crossed the river undetected and took back larger craft which had been moored on the south bank. In these *5th Guards Regiment* crossed, and at dawn on the 16th the regiment began its move on Muar from the east. It quickly overran the right-hand rear company of the Rajputanas, finding them unprepared, with their arms piled. They then cut the road between Bakri and Muar and attacked the town. The reserve (Garhwali) battalion tried to reopen the road but was forced back to Bakri with the loss of some one hundred men and its commanding officer. Muar was defended only by the headquarters and one company of the Rajputanas, and an Australian field battery. The latter stopped a Japanese attempt to cross the river in daylight but in the afternoon, attacking from the east, the Japanese overwhelmed the defenders of the town. The survivors made their way by a roundabout route to Bakri. Thus in the course of two days 45th Brigade had been driven off the river, its Jat battalion being cut off in the upper regions of the river, the Rajputana battalion being left with only two officers and a hundred and twenty men, and the

199

reserve (Garhwali) battalion having lost the equivalent of a company.

When the news of the utter defeat of his left flank reached Bennett, he realized that his communications were threatened. He therefore hurriedly sent the reserve battalion of 27th Australian Brigade (2/29th) from Gemas to Bakri. He did not however at the time grasp the seriousness of the situation. During the afternoon of the 16th information reached Percival that Japanese troops had been seen landing south of Batu Pahat. He immediately told General Heath to undertake the protection of Westforce's communications and ordered 53rd British Brigade (less a battalion), which had reached Singapore on the 13th after eleven weeks in crowded troop ships, to move to Ayer Hitam and there come under command of III Corps.

On 14 January, while the events described above were taking place on the coast, the Japanese *5th Division*, preceded by a battalion of infantry on bicycles and some tanks, had made contact with Westforce about six miles west of Gemas. Bennett had disposed 27th Australian Brigade at Gemas with 9th Indian Division behind it, 22nd Brigade being at Jementah to cover Segamat from the south and 8th Brigade at Segamat ready to take the offensive at an appropriate moment. These were sound dispositions had the left flank on the coast been properly defended. The 27th Australian Brigade had sent one battalion forward to the west of Gemas with orders to ambush any enemy forces approaching down the trunk road. In consequence the unsuspecting Japanese cyclists rode into the ambush and suffered severe casualties. Next day the Japanese attacked the main position of the forward Australian battalion but were held and lost a number of tanks. That evening, however, in accordance with Bennett's plan the battalion was withdrawn to the brigade's main position a mile to the east of the town. Throughout the 16th and 17th further Japanese attacks were held. Finding that he was meeting with fierce resistance on the trunk road, General Matsui, commanding *5th Division*, directed two regiments to outflank the Gemas defences by moving on Segamat through Ayer Kuning and Jementah. This formation made contact with 22nd Indian Brigade covering Jementah on the 18th.

On the west coast, in the meantime, as a result of the defeat of 45th Brigade, the threat to Westforce's communications was rapidly growing. At noon on 17 January at a conference attended by Bennett and Key (11th Division), Percival decided to make every effort to hold on to the Muar area and thus avoid a hurried withdrawal of the rest of Westforce from the Gemas–Segamat positions to Yong Peng and Ayer Hitam, since he felt that such a withdrawal would be extremely bad for morale. On the 18th he therefore authorized the transfer to 45th Brigade of another Australian battalion (2/19th from 22nd Australian Brigade at Mersing) replacing it there by the third battalion of 53rd British Brigade. He could not now afford seriously to weaken the defence of Mersing, for on the 14th patrols had contacted Japanese troops to the north of Endau.

Immediately after this conference Bennett ordered Brigadier H. C. Duncan (45th Brigade), now reinforced at Bakri by 2/29th Australian Battalion, to counter-attack to recapture Muar. A plan was drawn up, but as soon as the Garhwali battalion, ordered to attack Muar by way of the coastal road, moved forward from Bakri after dark that evening it ran into strong Japanese forces (*4th Guards Regiment*) already established on the coast road and was badly mauled. The counter-attack was clearly not feasible and was there-fore cancelled. Duncan then decided to hold Bakri until the Jat battalion, cut off in the upper regions of the Sungei Muar and out of touch, could rejoin. This played straight into the Japanese hands, as they quickly saw the opportunity of annihilating the British forces at Bakri between the Sungei Muar and the Sungei Batu Pahat. For this purpose *5th Guards Regiment* was ordered to contain and if possible surround the British forces at Bakri, while *4th Guards Regiment* (less of course its battalion which had landed south of Batu Pahat) was directed to occupy the Bakri–Yong Peng road between Parit Sulong and Bukit Pelandok, in an effort to cut 45th Brigade's line of retreat and incidentally to threaten Yong Peng.

Meanwhile, the isolated Jat battalion had managed to concentrate at Jorak, and on the 18th it regained contact by wireless with Duncan. He ordered it to move to Bakri on the 19th and decided he would have to hold on to the village until the battalion arrived. During the 18th, however, the Japanese attacked from the direction of Muar but without gaining ground, and 2/19th Australian bat-talion, speedily brought from the vicinity of Mersing by motor transport, arrived. Throughout the 19th the Japanese attacked 45th Brigade from the west and the south. All these attacks were repulsed, but the Japanese succeeded in establishing a road block two miles east of Bakri on the Yong Peng road, thus cutting the brigade's line of retreat. During the afternoon the two leading companies of the Jat battalion reached Bakri safely, but the rest of the battalion was ambushed, suffered heavy casualties (including its commanding officer and adjutant killed) and lost all its transport.

On 18 January Percival had learnt from his intelligence services that the Japanese forces consisted of *Imperial Guards Division* operating on the coastal road and *5th Division* on the trunk road. Up till that moment he had no idea of the strength of the enemy offensive in the coastal area, and it now became apparent that to hold on to Segamat would be to court disaster. Having discussed the position with Bennett that evening, he ordered the withdrawal of Westforce to the general line Kluang–Ayer Hitam–Yong Peng to begin at once. He realized that somehow or other he would have to hold the Japanese thrust in the coastal sector till the 24th, since Westforce could not possibly be clear of Yong Peng until that date. As Bennett could do nothing more to assist 45th Brigade and had his hands full in organizing the withdrawal of the formations from Segamat under heavy enemy pressure, Percival decided to regroup. He placed the coastal sector under Heath's command. Accordingly, on the morning of the 19th, General Key (11th Division), whom Heath had put in charge of the operations in the area, ordered 6th/15th Brigade (Brigadier B. S. Challen) to hold Batu Pahat, and 53rd Brigade (Brigadier C. L. B. Duke) to hold the Bukit Pelandok defile, which he expected the Japanese would attempt to seize. That afternoon Percival called another conference at Yong Peng with Heath, Bennett, Key and Duke. It was then decided that 53rd Brigade, brought up to full strength by a battalion (the Loyals) sent up from Singapore, should hold the Bukit Pelandok–Parit Sulong area and that 45th Brigade should withdraw from Bakri through it to Yong Peng.

This decision was taken too late, since *4th Guards Regiment* (less its battalion which had landed south of Batu Pahat and had disappeared in the thick country some five miles south-east of the town) had already occupied the five miles of road between the Bukit Pelandok and Parit Sulong with a battalion at each place. At about 1.30 p.m. on the 19th the leading battalion of the inexperienced 53rd Brigade, which was holding Bukit Pelandok with one company forward at Parit Sulong, was driven off the defile by a surprise attack. It was evident that, unless these two places could be reoccupied, the chances of 45th Brigade getting through to Yong Peng were negligible. The 53rd Brigade (at that time consisting of one British and one Indian battalion) therefore attacked the hills on either side of the road at the entrance of the Bukit Pelandok defile before dawn on the 20th. The attack was successful and the hills were occupied, but, before the brigade could reorganize the area for defence, a Japanese counter-attack recaptured it. Key therefore urged Duke to attack again on the 21st.

By 20 January Percival had come to the conclusion that only a miracle could save Johore and he issued a secret 'personal' letter to

Heath, Bennett and Keith Simmons. In it he asserted his intention to hold the Jemaluang–Kluang–Batu Pahat line for as long as possible, but gave an outline of his plan for the conduct of operations should events force a withdrawal through Johore Bahru to Singapore Island.

By the morning of the 21st, having successfully withdrawn from Segamat, Westforce was disposed with 22nd Brigade at Labis, 8th Brigade between Labis and Yong Peng and 27th Australian Brigade (now only two battalions) at Yong Peng. Realizing that the moves of Westforce now required careful co-ordination with those of 45th and 53rd Brigades and that the only communication with 45th Brigade was by Westforce's wireless, Percival again regrouped and transferred the control of both of these brigades back to Bennett. This left 11th Division with only 6th/15th Brigade at Batu Pahat. Having taken this decision Percival called another conference at Yong Peng early in the afternoon of the 21st to be attended by Heath, Bennett and Key. On his way to the conference Key went to see Duke and found that he had been unable to launch another attack on Bukit Pelandok earlier that day owing to the disorganization caused by the previous day's failure. At the conference Percival outlined his plans for the next stage of the battle. His intention, he said, was to hold the Jemaluang–Kluang–Ayer Hitam–Batu Pahat line for as long as possible, which needed three separate forces each with their own communications running back to Johore Bahru, all under command of III Corps. These were to be Eastforce (22nd Australian Brigade) to hold the Jemaluang area and to cover Kota Tinggi, Westforce, having rescued 45th Brigade, to hold the Kluang–Ayer Hitam area and cover the trunk road, and 11th Division, to which 53rd Brigade would be transferred, to hold the Batu Pahat area and protect the coastal road.

The rescue of 45th Brigade was, however, the first priority. To enable this to be done the Bukit Pelandok defile had to be recaptured and the road to Bakri opened. During the afternoon of the 21st Bennett, now responsible for the area, ordered Duke to attack the Japanese and recapture the defile. Duke arranged for the attack to be made at 5.30 p.m., but, as the enemy overlooked the whole area and surprise was impossible, accurate artillery support was necessary. Since this could not be organized in a hurry the attack was postponed first till 6 p.m. and then later till 9 a.m. on the 22nd. Early that morning the attacking troops were discovered by Japanese aircraft while on their starting line and heavily bombed and machine-gunned. Surprise having been lost, Duke wisely cancelled the attack and deployed his brigade for the defence of the road back to Yong Peng, for his brigade had no chance of regaining the defile and moving forward as far as Parit Sulong. Although Bennett later affirmed that the failure to make the attack was the cause of the loss of 45th Brigade, this is not so, for it was doomed from the moment that Percival decided at the conference on the 17th to try to hold on to the Muar area.

At Bakri Brigadier Duncan had been partially concussed during an air attack on his headquarters on 19 January and Lieutenant-Colonel C. G. W. Anderson (1/19th) had temporarily taken over command of 45th Brigade. He decided to break through the road blocks at dawn on the 20th and make for Parit Sulong, which he had been given to understand was held by 53rd Brigade. It was not till the afternoon that Anderson was able with difficulty and heavy loss to overcome the four strong road blocks which lay between him and his objective. The delay, caused by the need to mount an attack on each road block in turn, enabled the Japanese, supported by tanks, to attack the rearguard. Duncan was killed while leading a successful counter-attack to ease the pressure. After dark on the 20th, carrying its many wounded, the column crossed a stretch of open ground beyond the road blocks and about midnight reached the shelter of the rubber estate at Parit Sulong, only to find that the bridge was held by the enemy. The Japanese had occupied it without opposition that afternoon, for the company of the Norfolk Regiment, which on the 18th had been given the task of holding it, had since been out of touch with its battalion and without rations. Assuming he was isolated the company commander had decided on his own initiative on the morning of the 20th to withdraw his force and move across country to Batu Pahat.

The position of 45th Brigade, hemmed in between two enemy forces, was now desperate. An attempt to capture the bridge early on the 21st failed. Japanese forces following up from Bakri and supported by tanks and low-flying aircraft gradually forced the brigade into a small area west of the bridge. Casualties on the 20th and 21st had been very heavy. That evening Anderson tried under a flag of truce to persuade the Japanese to allow two ambulances carrying the most seriously wounded to pass down the road towards Singapore. His request was refused. Next morning two aircraft flew up from Singapore and dropped food and medical supplies on the brigade. Under attack all day the number of casualties rose alarmingly, and, when another attack on the bridge failed, Anderson destroyed his guns and transport and ordered the able-bodied survivors to make their way as best they could to Yong Peng, leaving the wounded to the care of the Japanese. To their eternal shame the Japanese massacred in cold blood all the wounded, except the very few, who survived by feigning death. In taking the action he did Anderson merely anticipated an order from Bennett to the same effect. The original strength of 45th Brigade had been around three thousand and of the Australians about fifteen hundred. Of these about four hundred Indian and five hundred Australian troops, including a number of walking wounded, managed to reach 27th Australian Brigade at Yong Peng during 23 January. So ended the first stage in the battle for Johore.

In addition to his duties as General Officer Commanding, Malaya, General Percival was forced from the beginning of the battle for Johore to act as an army commander. This was because of Wavell's decision to put General Bennett in charge of the battle and to relegate General Heath's III Corps to reserve. In order to take direct control of the battle Percival had to motor long distances to conferences in the forward area on the 17th, 19th and 21st. This meant that he had to work for at least eighteen hours a day, and so it was hardly to be expected that he could carry out his duties with full efficiency. At these conferences in the forward area, Percival arrived looking tired and worn and usually failed to take control. Bennett would then take the floor putting forward impracticable proposals until Heath would break in with a sensible suggestion based on sound military considerations, which Percival would accept and act upon.

The second stage of the battle for Johore began on 23 January, when Percival decided at a conference at Rengam to withdraw his forces to the general line covering Jemaluang–Kluang–Ayer Hitam but to continue to hold Batu Pahat. The 53rd Brigade was ordered to withdraw through 27th Australian Brigade at Yong Peng and then come under command of 11th Division. Once it was clear of Yong Peng (which would probably be during the night of the 23rd/24th) Westforce was to withdraw to new positions covering Kluang and Ayer Hitam. From the 24th, III Corps, as Percival had indicated on the 21st, was to take control of Eastforce, Westforce and 11th Division.

The weakened 53rd Brigade, though under considerable pressure from the enemy, managed its withdrawal with skill and by the morning of the 24th was at Ayer Hitam. It was then moved in lorries by way of Skudai and Pontian Kechil to Benut. When Heath reassumed control of the battle on the morning of the 24th, Eastforce (22nd Australian Brigade) was in contact with Japanese troops on the Sungei Mersing. Westforce was out of contact and disposed with 9th

Division at Kluang and 27th Australian Brigade at Ayer Hitam, while 11th Division was on the coastal road with 6th/15th Brigade in Batu Pahat (although the road between that town and Ayer Hitam was controlled by the Japanese), 53rd Brigade on the way to Benut and 28th Brigade at Pontian Kechil.

There was now little hope of staving off for long a retreat to Singapore Island, as Westforce on the trunk road was liable to be forced to withdraw since both its flanks could be turned. Japanese forces at Endau (which Percival estimated to be in divisional strength) could force 22nd Australian Brigade back towards Kota Tinggi and Johore Bahru, and *Imperial Guards Division*, already holding Bukit Pelandok and the Batu Pahat–Ayer Hitam road, was poised to isolate and destroy 6th/15th Brigade and then, opposed only by the balance of the weak 11th Division, would be in a position to move down the coastal road (possibly assisted by further amphibious landings) and move towards Skudai with the idea of cutting off Westforce on the trunk road. The position on the left flank on the west coast was the most dangerous, and it was to be the progress of *Imperial Guards Division* which was to force the hasty withdrawal to Singapore Island.

On 24 January Brigadier Challen (6th/15th Brigade) represented the danger of his position, which was not unlike that which 45th Brigade had faced at Bakri, and asked permission to withdraw to a position covering Rengit. His request was eminently sensible, but he was told to stay where he was. On the 25th, having discovered the enemy battalion concealed in a rubber estate near Senggarang, he reported that the Japanese not only were attempting to pin him down in the vicinity of Batu Pahat but also were preparing to cut the coastal road behind him. He therefore once again asked for permission to withdraw. Twice during the morning General Key sought Heath's permission to withdraw 6th/15th Brigade from the town, but on each occasion was told that he had to await the result of a conference which Percival was holding that afternoon. There was no doubt by that time that the brigade's position was parlous, since 53rd Brigade, moving north from Benut, had found that the Japanese had established road blocks between Rengit and Senggarang.

When Percival held his conference at Westforce's headquarters about 3 p.m., he learnt of the dangerous position on the coastal road and that Westforce had successfully repulsed enemy attacks at Kluang and Ayer Hitam. He then decided that 6th/15th Brigade was to withdraw to Rengit and Westforce was to withdraw some ten miles back along the trunk road and the railway. These positions were to be held till at least the night of the 27th/28th, and subsequent withdrawals would be made to previously selected lines which were to be held for fixed periods. Heath was to ensure that Eastforce conformed. The retreat to Singapore Island had begun.

Having received permission to withdraw from Batu Pahat about 5 p.m. on the 25th, Challen lost no time and was clear of the town by 4 a.m. on the 26th. During the morning he came up against the road blocks which the Japanese had established and, despite three attempts, failed to break through. The same morning Key, who had gone forward to Benut, arranged with Brigadier Duke that 53rd Brigade should try to break through to join hands with Challen. Not only was the hastily organized force sent forward by Duke ambushed and badly mauled, but after dark the Japanese occupied Rengit. The 6th/15th Brigade was now surrounded and there was no hope of the road being cleared. Since his position was quite hopeless, Challen destroyed his guns and transport, left his wounded under the protection—a useless protection, though he was not to know it—of the Red Cross and ordered his units to make their way across country to Benut as best they could. One column of some twelve hundred men, guided by police officers, reached Benut in a completely exhausted condition on the afternoon of the 27th. The rest of the brigade, coming up against an unfordable river, made for the coast west of Rengit. During the night Challen ran into a Japanese patrol and was captured. His brigade major, who was with the column which had reached the coast, found a small boat and managed to reach Pontian Kechil; thus Key learnt of the brigade's plight.

As soon as Percival heard of the situation he decided to evacuate the portion of the brigade cut off and marooned on the coast by sea. Between the nights of 28/29 January and 31 January/1 February two thousand seven hundred all ranks were rescued with some difficulty and taken by sea to Singapore. This was the only occasion during the campaign that the British forces were able to make use of their remaining sea power (two gunboats and some small craft). With 6th/15th Brigade cut off and the coastal road now protected by two weak brigades (53rd and 28th), Heath had no alternative but to organize a swift retreat to Singapore Island. He therefore issued a timed programme designed to ensure the evacuation of Johore by the night of 31 January/1 February. Eastforce was to withdraw from the Jemaluang area on the 28th, Westforce was to begin to withdraw gradually on the 27th and reach Kulai (where the trunk road and railway come together) by the 31st, and 11th Division was to cover the road junction at Skudai until Westforce was clear. The whole force was to cross the Johore Strait by the causeway on the night of the 31st/1st.

On receipt of these orders Bennett instructed General Barstow (9th Division) to withdraw his two brigades through each other down the railway, while 27th Australian Brigade withdrew down the trunk road. The 9th Division was to hold a position on the railway some three miles south of Rengam covering a cross track to the trunk road till the night of the 28th/29th, Sedenak till the night of the 30th/31st and Kulai till the night of the 31st/1st. The Australian brigade on the trunk road was to keep pace with 9th Division's withdrawal. Since the road running south from Kluang alongside the railway came to an end north of Layang, the transport of both brigades of 9th Division had to be moved across to the trunk road while this was still possible. Both Barstow's brigades were thus left without artillery, signal equipment or ambulances, and had to rely for support on such mortars as they could carry and on the railway telephone lines for communication and for everything else on what could be carried by the troops. On the afternoon of the 27th both brigades sent their transport away. The 8th Brigade then broke contact and withdrew through 22nd Brigade to Layang.

This move left Brigadier Painter (22nd Brigade) to hold his position for some thirty-six hours. He quickly realized that the Japanese could easily turn his right flank by using the many rubber-estate roads east of the railway, and therefore sought permission to move back to a position further south covering Layang village, where no such danger arose. In view of Bennett's specific orders that the cross tracks of the trunk road were to be denied to the enemy till 4 p.m. on 28 January, Barstow refused Painter's request. This and the fact that Brigadier Lay took 8th Brigade well south of Layang instead of holding a position immediately overlooking the village was to result in the final disaster in the battle of Johore—the loss of 22nd Brigade.

During the night of the 27th/28th not only was the railway bridge at Layang demolished without Barstow's approval, thus destroying the telephone communications with 22nd Brigade, but the Japanese also moved round Painter's right flank as he had feared and occupied Layang. Out of touch with Lay and realizing the danger of his position, Painter began to move south on the morning of 28 January. The same morning Barstow went forward to 8th Brigade and found out not only that Lay had withdrawn too far but that the bridge at Layang had been demolished. Anxious about the safety of 22nd Brigade, Barstow went forward up the railway to contact Painter and was ambushed and killed near Layang.

At midday 22nd Brigade unsuccessfully attacked the Japanese at Layang at the cost of some fifty casualties. Painter soon realized that he would be unable to break through and therefore decided to make a detour through the jungle to join 8th Brigade further south. Encumbered by wounded, without large-scale maps,[1] and completely out of touch with everyone, the brigade struggled on for four days, keeping clear of areas likely to be occupied by the enemy. On 1 February, when it had reached a point only some fifteen miles from Johore Bahru, the brigade, reduced to some four hundred exhausted men, found itself surrounded by Japanese troops, and Painter with the remnants of his brigade was forced to surrender. Some sixty men, who had become separated from the main body, did however manage to reach the Johore Strait and were found and taken to safety by hastily organized rescue parties.

On 28 January, before it became known that 22nd Brigade had been cut off, General Percival held yet another conference at III Corps headquarters in Johore Bahru. Both he and General Heath came to the conclusion that the extremely weak 11th Division could not be expected to prevent the Japanese *Imperial Guards Division* from reaching Skudai for very much longer. Since this would mean Westforce being cut off, it was decided to accelerate the withdrawal programme by twenty-four hours, and arrangements were made to cross the causeway on the night of 30/31 January. Westforce, always under heavy pressure on the trunk road, steadily withdrew, while repeatedly driving back attempts by *5th Division* to break through. By the morning of the 30th the force was holding a position just north of Kulai with 8th Brigade on the railway and 27th Australian Brigade on the road. That afternoon they broke contact and moved south of Kulai, from where they moved on across the causeway that night. They were preceded by 22nd Australian Brigade and followed by the remnants of 11th Division, which covered the Skudai road junction till Westforce was clear. An inner bridgehead position which had been held by the Argylls of 12th Brigade was then withdrawn and the whole of the garrison was back in Singapore Island.

*

Meanwhile, on the east coast of Malaya, from 21 to 25 January, 22nd Australian Brigade (Eastforce) had been in contact with a

---

[1] The maps of this area, specially printed, had been lost when the railway truck in which they had been packed fell into enemy hands on the Tampin–Malacca branch line. See chapter 16.

Japanese force (*55th Brigade* of *18th Division*) on the Sungei Mersing. It was on the evening of the 25th that Brigadier Taylor received the order to abandon the carefully prepared defensive position at Mersing and to fall back on Jemaluang. That night he withdrew as ordered, but organized an ambush on the road half-way between Mersing and Jemaluang. About midnight on the 26th/27th the Japanese, who as usual had quickly followed up, walked straight into the trap, which was then sprung. For the cost of some ninety casualties the Australians inflicted very heavy losses on *55th Regiment*, so much so that it appealed for help; Yamashita (*25th Army*) sent strong reinforcements from *5th Division* at Kluang, which reached Jemaluang on the 28th. By the time they arrived, however, Taylor was well on his way to Kota Tinggi. There was to be no further contact on this front, as *55th Regiment* had been ordered to move west towards Kluang.

On 26th January, while Eastforce was moving south from Mersing, the Japanese convoy bringing the administrative troops and stores required by Yamashita arrived off Endau, and the Japanese naval forces seized the Anamba Islands. A report reached Air Headquarters at Singapore during the morning that a force consisting of two cruisers, twelve destroyers and two large transports were off Endau.[1] Air Vice-Marshal Pulford's striking force now consisted of only thirty-six aircraft, twenty-four of which were the obsolescent Vildebeeste torpedo-bombers. Most of the aircraft had been operating during the previous night against enemy concentrations in central Johore and therefore had to refuel and rearm before they could be used again. Pulford organized a force of nine Hudsons and twelve Vildebeeste, escorted by twenty-three fighters, to attack the convoy in the early afternoon, but, since it was thought that the water off Endau was too shallow for the use of torpedoes, the Vildebeeste were armed with 250-pound bombs. Despite heavy fighter opposition, hits were scored on the two transports and on one cruiser and on barges ferrying stores to the beaches, but five of the slow Vildebeeste were lost.

A second attack was made later in the afternoon by three Albacores and nine Vildebeeste, escorted by twelve fighters. On this occasion one transport was hit, but the bomb failed to detonate. Enemy fighters shot down another five Vildebeeste, two Albacores and one fighter. In the evening five Hudson aircraft from Sumatra bombed troops and barges at Endau without incurring loss. It was a

[1] The force actually consisted of two transports and thirteen smaller craft escorted by four cruisers, an anti-aircraft carrier and six destroyers.

gallant effort especially on the part of the pilots of the obsolescent Vildebeeste, which had a top speed of only a hundred and thirty-seven miles per hour, and more especially as they were used as bombers instead of in their proper role of low-flying torpedo-bombers. The damage inflicted on the enemy was negligible and did not in any way compensate for the loss of the lives of the best-trained pilots in Singapore.

The Royal Navy also did its best to inflict damage on the convoy and its escort. Under cover of darkness on the night of the 27th/28th two old destroyers, the *Thanet* and the *Vampire*, attacked. Met by powerful modern Japanese destroyers the *Thanet* was soon sunk, while the *Vampire*, trying to cover the *Thanet* with smoke, was attacked by three destroyers and a cruiser. However, she succeeded in escaping and got back unscathed to Singapore. During the 26th and 27th a Japanese airfield battalion and a large quantity of ammunition stores and vehicles were landed at Endau, and the Japanese began to develop the Anamba Islands as an advanced base for light naval forces.

*

At the beginning of the battle for Johore, Air Vice-Marshal Pulford's average air strength was some seventy bombers and thirty fighters, but towards the end of January these were augmented by the fifty-one Hurricanes as they became operational. This small force was outnumbered by the Japanese by four to one. Every bomber, however, was used, mainly by night, to attack the Kuala Lumpur and Kuantan airfields to try to destroy as many enemy fighters as possible on the ground, and raids were made on troops and transport on the road south of Gemas and Muar, but again the effort was too small to have any serious effect on Japanese progress. When on the 18th Westforce was ordered to withdraw from the Segamat area, it was obvious that the airfields at Kahang, Kluang and Batu Pahat might soon be in enemy hands. Between the 21st and the 23rd the ground staffs of these airfields were evacuated and they were rendered unserviceable as far as possible. Since Pulford had now the use of only four airfields on Singapore Island and these were under constant and growing bombing attacks, he arranged to withdraw his bombers and his flying-boat squadrons to Sumatra, leaving only fighters on Singapore Island.

The fighters left on Singapore Island were constantly in action against the ever-increasing scale of Japanese raids on the airfields, the naval base and the commercial harbour. The first of the

Hurricane fighters was flown on 15 January, and by 20 January 232 Fighter Squadron, equipped with eighteen Hurricanes, was ready for action. Unfortunately the Hurricanes proved to be much less of an asset than had been expected, since not only were they slower and less manœuvrable than the Japanese Zero fighters below 20,000 feet, but their pilots were not acclimatized to Far East conditions and they were always outnumbered by enemy fighters. On the 20th three were shot down, on the 21st two, and on the 22nd five, together with four Buffalos. By the end of January twenty-six British fighters had been lost and ten damaged on the ground. What losses were inflicted on the Japanese between the 14th and 31st is not known, but at the time it was estimated that they also amounted to some twenty-six aircraft.

Nevertheless every raid was intercepted. This strained Pulford's resources to the utmost, especially from the 21st and the 30th, when the remaining three convoys bringing reinforcements to Singapore were due to arrive. Patrols were then flown far out on the route taken by the convoys from the Sunda Strait, and flying-boats maintained an anti-submarine patrol immediately south of Singapore. As the convoys neared the port they were given a close escort of six fighters, and other aircraft were held in readiness to meet a possible attack by Japanese naval vessels. On 22 January 44th Indian Brigade and seven thousand Indian reinforcements arrived, on 24 January the Australian machine-gun regiment and some nineteen hundred Australian reinforcements, and on 29 January (only two days before the final withdrawal to the island) the main body of 18th British Division (Headquarters and 54th and 55th Brigade with divisional troops). All these convoys arrived safely, but they reached Singapore too late to be used in the battle for Johore.

It will have been seen that in the battle for Johore one brigade was completely lost, and one, together with two Australian battalions, was reduced to a mere fraction of its strength, while the guns and transport of two brigades were destroyed to prevent them from falling into enemy hands. The formations and units which succeeded in reaching Singapore Island had all been badly mauled and had suffered severe losses. Although the Japanese had failed in their attempt to cut off and destroy III Corps in Johore, they had won a considerable victory and caused so much damage to the British forces that the chance of their being able to hold Singapore Island for any length of time was greatly reduced.

20

Planning the Defence of Singapore Island

January–February 1942   *Map H, pp. 218–19*

Having learned from liaison officers in Singapore that plans for a withdrawal to Singapore Island had not been prepared and no orders for its defence had been issued, Wavell sent General Percival a cable on 19 January instructing him to prepare the necessary plans in strict secrecy on the grounds that, as the battle had to be fought out in Johore, it was essential that no thought of further retreat should be in the minds of either commanders or troops.[1] The same day he cabled the Prime Minister warning him that, if the battle for Johore were lost, it was unlikely that Singapore Island could be held for long. The next day (20 January) Wavell flew to Singapore to assess for himself the progress of the battle for Johore. After discussing the position with Percival and Heath, he came to the conclusion that the British forces would shortly have to withdraw to the general line Mersing–Kluang–Batu Pahat and that there was every chance of their being forced to retreat to Singapore Island before long. He therefore ordered Percival to make strenuous efforts to prepare the island for defence, but to hold the Japanese in Johore until the convoys due on the 22nd, 24th and 29th with reinforcing formations had arrived at Singapore. Before returning to Java that evening Wavell told the Prime Minister and the Chiefs of Staff that a withdrawal to Singapore Island might soon become necessary and that defensive measures to repel an attack on the island from the north were negligible.

The receipt of this information in London produced quick and somewhat surprising reactions. The Prime Minister instructed Wavell on 21 January that the island was to be defended to the last and that there was to be no question of surrender until after protracted fighting among the ruins of Singapore City. A truly Churchillian instruction, but one which bore no relation to facts, since he obviously still thought of Singapore as a fortress with all-round defence. It would, in any case, have been neither practical nor humane for the beaten army of a colonial power to have fought to the bitter end among the ruins of a city whose population had been increased by the influx of refugees to more than a million Asians.

On 20 January the Chiefs of Staff had cabled Wavell that he

---

[1] It was this telegram that caused Percival to issue his secret and personal letter of 20 January. See pages 202–3.

should make all preparations possible for the defence of the island and suggested actions which he ought to take. Among many other things these included the diversion of strength from the south to the north and west coasts, the build-up of mobile reserves to deliver rapid counter-attacks and the development of switch lines in the interior to prevent the exploitation of successful landings. The next day they cabled Percival expressing their desire that the scorched-earth policy should be rigorously applied to the island, and that there should be no failure in denying to the Japanese anything that might be of value to them. It would seem that they too failed to grasp the many difficulties inherent in applying such a policy in a small and densely populated island.

It is evident that by 20 January Wavell foresaw that Percival would not be able to hold Johore. He had therefore to decide whether to try to hold Singapore Island or whether to put up a purely token resistance and divert to the Netherlands East Indies or to Burma the reinforcements on their way. There were four questions to be considered: the first, would the available formations withdrawn from Johore and reinforced by those arriving at the end of January enable the island to be held for a reasonable length of time; the second, if the island could be held for a reasonable time, would its retention help in the defence of the ABDA area; the third, if the island could be held for only a few weeks, would it not be better to divert elsewhere the reinforcing formations and units; and lastly, if he did decide in the interests of the ABDA area to divert the reinforcements, what would be the effect on world opinion and on the morale of the Singapore garrison.

He must have doubted whether the formations in Malaya, even if reinforced, could hold out for long on an island some twenty-five miles long and fifteen miles wide with some seventy-two miles of coastline, with virtually no air support and with the Japanese in control of the seas around it. The III Corps, including the reinforcements it had received since 8 December, had by 20 January lost a number of battalions; those that remained in being were all under strength and their morale had been lowered by the long withdrawal. Furthermore, it had lost a very large number of guns, quantities of transport and equipment and its strength could not be considered more than fifty or sixty per cent.[1] The 8th Australian Division had lost the greater part of two out of its six battalions and two of the

[1] Wavell did not of course know that during the withdrawal to the island 22nd Indian Brigade would be lost or that 6th/15th Brigade would lose all its guns, transport and equipment during the final stage of the retreat in Johore.

remainder had suffered heavy casualties. None of the formations and reinforcements due to arrive before the end of January was highly efficient. The Headquarters and two brigades of 18th Division had not been trained for war in close country and would be physically unfit after their long voyage, while 44th Indian Brigade would be no more effective than the ill-fated 45th Indian Brigade. Wavell could have had no illusions about the value of the seven thousand Indian reinforcements, for he must have known that to find them India would have had to scrape the very bottom of the barrel. Of the standard of the Australian reinforcements he could know little, but he must have known that Australia, having sent all her trained men overseas, would be unlikely to find highly trained troops. Wavell must have come to the conclusion privately that the defence would be overcome within a few weeks.

Wavell had concluded from the moment he took up his appointment that his only chance of holding the Japanese offensive was to prevent them gaining control of vital points for long enough to enable reinforcements to reach him. The successful defence of Singapore would contain three Japanese divisions and a sizeable air force, prevent them from being used elsewhere, such as Burma or the Netherlands East Indies, and provide time for the Australian corps and the armoured brigade, being sent from the Middle East and due to arrive in March, to reach the ABDA area. On strategic grounds the retention of Singapore for as long as possible was therefore desirable, and, in fact, Wavell later said that it would have made all the difference if it could have been held for a month longer.

The question which Wavell had to solve was whether the arrival of the reinforcements at the end of January would increase the ability of the garrison to hold out until the end of March. If that were possible he would be wrong to divert them. If on the other hand it was likely that the garrison, even if reinforced, could hold out for only a few weeks, would he not have been wiser to have diverted them either to Burma or Java? In the situation that existed Wavell could not possibly have foreseen Singapore holding out throughout March and militarily he must have seen that the right course would be to divert the reinforcements. He had, however, to consider the political effects. To have diverted the remaining reinforcing convoys would have been an admission of defeat which would undoubtedly have had serious political effects throughout the world, and in particular in Australia. Such action would also have brought the morale of the garrison almost to zero, and any chance of the garrison holding the island for even a few weeks would have disappeared.

215

While Wavell was wrestling with his problem, the Prime Minister, apprised of the fact that the battle for Johore was probably lost and that it was doubtful whether it would be possible to defend Singapore Island for long, had also to face the same problem. He evidently realized that to send the remaining reinforcements to Singapore might not prolong the defence of the island and that, if they were diverted to Burma, it might be possible to retain control of the Burma Road and contact with China. On 20 January he told the Chiefs of Staff that, although the reinforcement of Burma was a matter for Wavell to decide, they ought to express an opinion, saying, 'As a strategic object I regard keeping the Burma Road open as more important than the retention of Singapore.'[1] On the 21st, when it became absolutely evident that the battle for Johore was lost and that Wavell offered little hope of a prolonged defence of Singapore Island, the Prime Minister told the Chiefs of Staff that the question whether to abandon Singapore and concentrate on the defence of Burma and the Burma Road had to be squarely faced and put bluntly to Wavell. 'We may,' he said, 'by muddling things and hesitating to take an ugly decision, lose *both* Singapore and the Burma Road. Obviously the decision depends upon how long the defence of Singapore Island can be maintained. If it is only for a few weeks, it is certainly not worth losing all our reinforcements and aircraft.'[2]

Neither the Chiefs of Staff nor the Defence Committee were able to reach a conclusion, and they decided to take a day or two for further thought. On 22 January the views expressed by Churchill to the Chiefs of Staff somehow reached Australia, and her Prime Minister immediately cabled that, after all the assurances Australia had been given over the years that Singapore was impregnable, its evacuation would be regarded there and elsewhere as an inexcusable betrayal.[3] This cable hardened opinion against abandoning the island, especially in view of the fact that the Americans were desperately holding on in the Philippines. No instructions were therefore sent to Wavell, who was left to make his own decision, although the Prime Minister has since said, 'There is no doubt what a purely military decision should have been',[4] implying that the reinforcements should have been diverted to Burma.

While these discussions were taking place in London, Wavell had come to his own decision, which was to allow the reinforcements to reach Singapore. Once having made the decision he urged Percival to

---

[1] Churchill, *The Second World War*, Vol. IV, p. 47.   [2] Op. cit., p. 50.
[3] Op. cit., p. 51.   [4] Op. cit., p. 52.

fight to the bitter end and repeatedly sent him instructions to this effect. In retrospect Wavell's decision was the wrong one. The two brigades of 18th Division were unprepared for immediate active operations after their long voyage and the almost completely untrained 44th Indian Brigade and a large number of untrained reinforcements could not and did not affect the issue; they only went to swell the numbers of those who would be forced to capitulate. Their diversion to Burma, where they might have had time for training and acclimatization before the Japanese invaded the country, would have been the better answer. It was a great pity that the Prime Minister and the Chiefs of Staff, who clearly realized what was the right course, did not give Wavell the necessary instruction. As the Supreme Commander, ABDA, Wavell could scarcely have taken any other decision. The blame, if any, for the sacrifice of 18th Division must lie with the Prime Minister and his advisers.

*

The defence of Singapore Island against attack from southern Johore posed a difficult problem, since the northern shore of the island was too intersected by creeks and mangrove swamps for any recognized form of beach defence, while the small size and topography of the island made the launching of a counter-attack to drive out an enemy who had obtained a bridgehead somewhat difficult. The centre of the island, from a line on the west between the Sungei [River] Kranji and the S. Jurong to a line on the east running from the S. Seletar through Paya Lebar to the coast some miles east of Kallang airfield, was of vital importance. In it lay the city with its docks, half the fixed defences, all the reservoirs and the pumping station on which (since the pipe line from Johore was cut) the population of about one million depended for its water supply, the main ammunition as well as the temporary ammunition dumps, all the reserve food stocks for the garrison and the civil population, the oil storage tanks, hospitals and the remaining reserves of military stores. The importance of this central area had for long been recognized, and two defensive positions (known as switch lines) had been reconnoitred to cover it from the east and west should an enemy obtain a footing on the island. That on the east, known as the Serangoon line, covered the main reservoirs, Paya Lebar and Kallang airfield, and that on the west, known as the Jurong line, since it ran from the upper waters of the S. Jurong to those of the S. Kranji, covered the Bukit Timah area, the control of which was vital, for it contained the main storage depots.

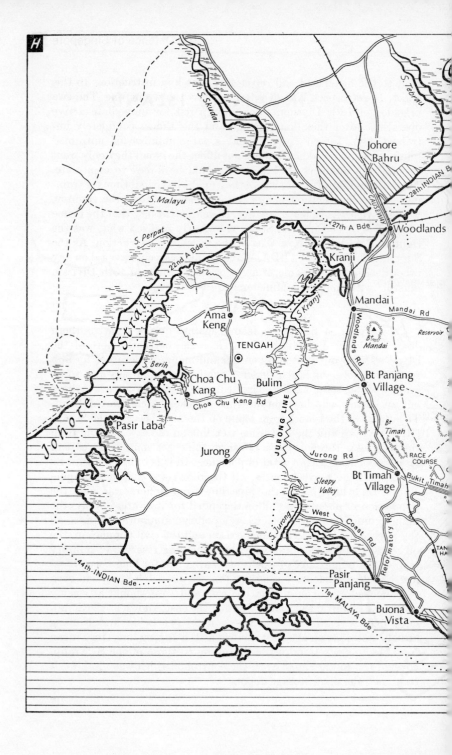

SINGAPORE ISLAND

Miles
0 ———————————— 5

Roads......... ═══ Tracks........ ─ ─ ─ ─
Railways... +++++ Pipeline...... ○ ─ ○ ─ ○
Rivers....... 〰 Swamp...... ═ ═
Hills .... Airfield .... ◎

NAVAL BASE
53rd Bde
Johore Strait
◎ SEMBAWANG
SELETAR ◎
55th Bde
Nee Soon
S. Seletar
S. Serangoon
54th Bde
Pulau Ubin
Changi
Reservoir
Paya Lebar
Thomson Village
Woodleigh
SERANGOON LINE
Bt Brown
KALLANG
2nd MALAYA Bde
SINGAPORE
S S V F Bde
Faber
Harbour
P. Brani
P. Blakang Mati

Since with the Japanese holding the northern coast of the Johore Strait an attack against the south coast was extremely unlikely, the areas which the defenders had to retain at all costs were first the Woodlands–Kranji area, to prevent the Japanese gaining a bridgehead which would have enabled them to repair and make use of the causeway for the passage of tanks, transport and supplies to the island, and second the two switch lines. Since the naval base was by this time useless the fixed defences at Changi and eastwards were of little value and could if necessary be destroyed and abandoned.

Before deciding on the defence dispositions, it was necessary for Wavell and Percival to appreciate the way in which the Japanese would be most likely to launch their assault on the island. The main Japanese lines of communication were the road and railway, which approached Johore Bahru from the north-west. It could have been assumed first, that they would wish to launch their attack as quickly as possible so as to give the defenders little time to prepare, second that they would, as they had done all the way down Malaya, make direct for their objective by the shortest route, third that they would want to gain control of the causeway as early as possible, and lastly that they would try to gain surprise by concealing their preparations until the last moment. The topography of southern Johore provided them with two lines of approach to the Johore Strait which were well supplied with road communications—the S. Skudai, S. Malayu and S. Perpat on the west and the S. Tebrau on the east of the causeway. From the former an attack could be launched on the north-west between the S. Kranji and the S. Berih to capture the Tengah airfield and then drive towards Bukit Timah. From the latter an attack could be launched on the area between the S. Seletar and Woodlands to capture the Sembawang airfield and again drive on towards Bukit Timah. Either assault, if successful, would have cut off the defenders of the Woodlands–Kranji area and have given the Japanese the eventual use of the causeway. It could have been appreciated that a direct attack on the Woodlands–Kranji area would have been made only as a subsidiary to the main assault either directed on the north-west or the north-east coast.

When Wavell paid Singapore a visit on 20 January he discussed with Percival the problem of defending the island should the garrison be forced, as then seemed probable, to withdraw from Johore. It was, no doubt, with the above factors in mind that he suggested that 18th Division, which would be the stronger formation, should be placed in the part of the island most likely to be attacked, which he thought would be the north-west coast, 8th Australian Division (by then with a strength of less than two brigades) in the next most dangerous sector—the north-east—with the Indian divisions, when reformed, as a central reserve. Percival replied that he expected the Japanese to attack on the north-east coast and therefore thought that 18th Division should be placed to meet that threat.[1]

Meanwhile, the situation was altered by the loss of 22nd Indian Brigade in southern Johore, by 6th/15th Brigade being cut off with the loss of all its equipment, by the fact that three of the units of 18th Division were not expected to arrive until 5 February, by which time the safety of the transports could not be guaranteed, and by the extremely poor quality of the Australian and Indian reinforcements which had been sent to Singapore. As early as 9 January, acting on Wavell's instructions given on his first visit (*see page 185*), Percival had ordered Major-General Keith Simmons to carry out a detailed reconnaissance of the northern coast of Singapore island on the basis of its being held by three brigades: one from the coast opposite the little island of Pulau Ubin to the S. Seletar, one from that river to Woodlands, and one on the north-west coast to the mouth of the S. Berih. It will be noted that the weight of the defence was to be east of the causeway, which proves that Percival thought early in January that this area constituted the greatest danger. He told Keith Simmons that, as the coasts were unsuitable for the normal form of beach defence, the plan in each brigade area was to be based on small defended localities covering approaches to the coast, such as rivers, creeks, road and tracks. These defended posts were to be supported by mobile reserves located so that they could operate against Japanese parties seeking to infiltrate through or around the forward posts.

No further steps were taken, however, until after his conversations and correspondence with Wavell. On 23 January he issued a firm order for the defence of the island. In it he divided the area into three sectors: Northern (east of the causeway but excluding Changi), Western (from the causeway along the north and west coasts as far as the mouth of the S. Jurong in the south), and Southern (the south coast from the S. Jurong to Changi). He allotted the Western sector to 8th Australian Division, the Northern to III Corps, and the Singapore garrison to the Southern with 18th Division, on arrival, in command reserve with the intention that it should later take over the

---

[1] In a letter to the author written after the war General Percival admitted that the statement in his book, *The War in Malaya*, to the effect that he expected the Japanese attack to be made in the north-west was incorrect and based on hindsight.

Northern sector, allowing III Corps to become the central reserve. He instructed Keith Simmons, assisted by Brigadier Paris and officers of 12th Brigade together with liaison officers sent back by the Australians and III Corps, to develop the defence plan, using the original reconnaissance as a starting point.[1] It will be noticed that this plan meant attempting to cover the whole seventy-two miles of coast line with the vital causeway area being divided between two formations. The junction between two formations always provides a weak link in the defence.

The state of affairs at the end of January, when Johore was evacuated, forced Percival to make changes in the dispositions (*see appendix*). He retained 8th Australian Division in the Western sector, giving it 44th Indian Brigade to bring it up to full strength. He brought 11th Division up to strength by giving it 8th Brigade from 9th Division, which he then broke up, and 53rd Brigade of 18th Division, so that it would consist of 8th and 28th Indian and 53rd British Brigades. He made III Corps responsible for the Northern sector with 11th Division and 18th Division, less 53rd Brigade, under command. He retained 1st and 2nd Malaya Brigade and the Straits Settlement Volunteer Force Brigade (the original garrison) in the southern sector. This left him as a command reserve with only 12th Brigade (one and a half battalions) and 6th/15th Brigade, which after its rescue he was attempting to re-equip. It was his stated intention that as soon as 6th/15th Brigade was ready it should return to 11th Division, which would allow 53rd Brigade to join its own 18th Division on the north-east coast.

As a result of these changes 18th Division was responsible for the coast from opposite Pulau Ubin to the S. Seletar, 11th Division from the S. Seletar to Woodlands (exclusive), and 8th Australian Division from Woodlands (inclusive) right round the twenty miles of coast to the S. Jurong. The three brigades of the original garrison were responsible for the south coast, and the command reserve was negligible. These dispositions placed five brigades to cover some fifteen miles of the coast east of the causeway and three brigades to cover some twenty miles west of the causeway, each with a normal complement of artillery support. It is evident that from these dispositions Percival expected the assault to be launched east of the causeway, contrary to Wavell's wise counsels.

These dispositions are open to criticism. By trying to defend the whole coast when it was obvious the Japanese would concentrate

---

[1] It is of interest to note that Percival failed to make use of the expertise available among the officers of the Chief Engineer's office.

on one carefully selected point, Percival was weak everywhere, no formation had any reserve for immediate counter-attack, the command reserve was too small to be of any value, no proper plans had been made to prepare the two switch lines for defence and the vital naval base–Woodlands–Kranji area was defended by two different formations. It will be noted that in making these dispositions Percival completely ignored the advice given to Wavell and him by the Chiefs of Staff on 20 January (*see page 213*). Once they had effected a landing the Japanese were thus given the opportunity of driving deep into the vital central area of the island before a reserve could be collected to check them.

It would have been sounder to have made one division responsible for the north coast from the S. Seletar to the S. Kranji, with a brigade in reserve at Mandai prepared to counter-attack north or east, one division responsible for the coast from the S. Kranji to the S. Berih, with one brigade holding the Jurong switch line or alternatively ready to counter-attack, and to have kept one division in command reserve in the Bukit Timah area. The SSVF Brigade and one Malaya Brigade could have watched the southern coast from the S. Berih to Kallang as long as the concentration of enemy shipping at the Anambas constituted a possible threat (*see page 211*), and could then have come into reserve as soon as the Japanese had shown their hand. The remaining Malaya Brigade could have held the Serangoon switch line. Such dispositions would have made it possible for the Japanese to have been met with a reasonable force in both areas liable to attack, would have provided the best defence for the vital central area of the island and would have given Percival a reserve immediately ready for action once the Japanese point of attack was known.

It was most unfortunate that Major-General Gordon Bennett was placed in charge of the Western sector, where it was highly probable that the Japanese would make their initial assault, as they in fact did. Personal ambition, it appears, dominated his outlook to the detriment of his duties as a divisional commander, and he was unable to contemplate with equanimity the possibility of spending the rest of the war as a prisoner. He therefore began to make arrangements with a couple of trusted staff officers, through the Sultan of Johore, to escape by a boat before the final surrender.

*

Let us now look at the problem of Singapore Island from the Japanese point of view. The pre-war plan had been that any assault

223

on the island ought to be made on the north-western coasts between the mouths of the S. Kranji and S. Berih. By the time *25th Army* reached the Johore Strait, General Yamashita's intelligence services indicated that the British expected the initial assault would be made on the naval-base area east of the causeway, and that their defences in that area were strongest. Yamashita therefore decided to launch his assault on the north-west coast with two divisions, to be followed shortly afterwards by a subsidiary attack immediately west of the causeway on the Woodlands–Kranji area. He concentrated the *5th* and *18th Divisions* in the S. Skudai–S. Malayu–S. Perpat area and *Imperial Guards Division* in the S. Tebrau area, and decided to launch the main assault on the evening of 8 February between 8 p.m. and midnight. The main assault was to be followed twenty-four hours later by the subsidiary attack. Between 1 and 7 February *Imperial Guards Division* was to attempt to divert the attention of the British to the east of the causeway by various means and to land patrols on Pulau Ubin island during the night of the 7th/8th. There was to be a heavy artillery bombardment carried out by all the available artillery (168 guns) to destroy forward defended positions, communications and artillery positions in the north of the island; this bombardment was to be spread over the area east and west of the causeway until the 8th, when it would be switched to the north-western area. The landing-craft, assault boats and rafts required for the assault were to be assembled or constructed and launched in the upper reaches of the S. Skudai, S. Malayu and S. Perpat and carefully camouflaged. To secure secrecy all civilians in a belt fifteen miles deep along the southern coast of Johore were forcibly moved inland.

Yamashita sited his advanced headquarters in the tower of the Sultan's palace from where he had a bird's eye view of the whole area to be attacked.[1] He gave the *5th* and *18th Divisions* Tengah airfield as their first objective and a north–south line through Bukit Panjang as their final objective. The *Imperial Guards Division* was to seize Mandai, then move eastwards along the Mandai road to Nee Soon and finally southwards to prevent the British garrison from falling back on Changi.

It is now known that *25th Army* was so short of ammunition by the time it broke through at S. Muar and forced the British to withdraw to the Jemaluang–Kluang–Batu Pahat line, that Yamashita

---

[1] This tower overlooked the whole of the north-western part of Singapore Island and was the obvious position for an observation point for the control of the Japanese artillery. Nevertheless, on orders from Malaya Command, the British artillery were not allowed to try to destroy it.

feared that the assault on Singapore Island would have to be seriously delayed while ammunition was brought forward from Singora down his long line of communications and over the many dozens of hastily repaired road and railway bridges. However what he required could perhaps be landed by the convoy due at Endau by 26 January and moved along the lateral road through Mersing and Jemaluang to Kluang. It was the importance of this road that made him hurriedly send reinforcements from *5th Division* to Jemaluang when 22nd Australian Brigade ambushed *55th Regiment* in that area. (*See page 210.*) Had the British been able to hold tenaciously on to the Jemaluang area, Yamashita's plans for the assault on Singapore would have been very considerably delayed.

*

After crossing the causeway all British military formations moved on 31 January straight to the areas they had been allotted for the defence of the island. As Wavell had ordered him to observe strict secrecy, Percival had allowed no work to be undertaken on preparing defences on the island. The plans prepared by Keith Simmons and his staff were therefore handed over to formation commanders to be put into effect. Since during the latter part of January the Japanese had bombed the island daily and within a few days of the evacuation of Johore began to shell its northern half, civilian labour became very scarce, and once again the weary troops had to set to work to dig or erect their own defensive positions. While engaged on this work formations and units had also to reorganize and absorb reinforcements to bring them up to strength.

It is wellnigh impossible for units to absorb untrained men when actively engaged in laying out and preparing defences, and the introduction of untrained men into units tends to reduce rather than increase their overall efficiency. Some of the Australian units were particularly affected in this way, especially the 2/19th and 2/29th Battalions, which had lost almost three-quarters of their original men at Bakri and Parit Sulong. Their reinforcements were totally untrained, so much so that one Australian described them as the corner boys of Sydney swept up and put into khaki and sent immediately to Singapore. The Indian battalions were affected to a slightly less degree, for it was possible to amalgamate battalions so that there were in a combined unit an adequate number of trained Indian officers and non-commissioned officers. When viewing the efforts of the garrison of the island to throw back the Japanese assault, it must be remembered that few units could be considered more than

Q

seventy-five per cent effective and many less than thirty per cent.

With twenty miles of the coast to cover, General Gordon Bennett placed 27th Australian Brigade (Brigadier Maxwell) with two battalions to cover the vital Woodlands–Kranji sector with a front of two miles; its third battalion (2/29th), which consisted mainly of untrained reinforcements and was not really fit for anything but a static role, he kept as a divisional reserve located in the Mandai area. He gave his strongest brigade (22nd, commanded by Brigadier Taylor) the eight miles of coast between the S. Kranji and the S. Berih. With this long length of coastline to cover Taylor had to deploy all his three battalions, placing his weakest (2/29th) on his left flank. He had no brigade reserve, so each battalion was instructed to keep one company in reserve. It was on his right and centre battalions (2/20th and 2/18th) that the whole weight of the assault by two Japanese divisions was to fall. The untrained and inexperienced Indian 44th Brigade was set the task of defending the ten miles of coastline from the S. Berih to the S. Jurong, the least likely to be attacked. The division was thus widely dispersed, there was no reserve capable of counter-attack and the Jurong switch line was left entirely undefended. If the Japanese were to attack west of the causeway, as in fact they did, the Australians had no hope of holding them. The fate of the island therefore depended on holding the Woodlands–Kranji area and on whether Percival could bring up reserves quickly enough to man and hold the Jurong line. He had, as already described, no reserves of any strength, and as a result, as will be shown, the Japanese reached the Bukit Timah and Bukit Panjang area some forty-eight hours after their initial landings.

General Heath, with two divisions and only fifteen miles of coast, was not so extended. He placed 18th Division on the right to cover with its two brigades (54th and 55th) some seven and a half miles of coastline east of the S. Seletar, and 11th Division in the seven-and-a-half-mile sector from the S. Seletar through the naval base to a point east of the causeway. This division was deployed with 53rd British Brigade on the right, 28th Indian Brigade on the left and 8th Indian Brigade in reserve near Nee Soon.

One method of defence which the Royal Engineers had produced was barrels of petrol to be placed in the water in the creeks and mangrove swamps and fired electrically and/or by tracer bullet, so that the water would be covered with blazing petrol. Numbers of these, also underwater obstacles, floating logs with barbed wire and car headlamps to illuminate the shore had been prepared and dumped on orders of the Chief Engineer in the Western sector before the final

226

withdrawal to the island, for it was there that the assault was in his opinion likely to take place. When this was reported, Command Headquarters ordered all these devices to be picked up and moved to the area east of the causeway, where they were partially installed but were of course never used. At the last moment orders were issued for their re-transfer to the west, but it was by then too late.

On 5 February the convoy bringing the rest of 18th Division and some Indian troops arrived at Singapore. Although covered as usual by fighters, it was attacked by Japanese bombers as it approached the island. All the ships escaped damage except the *Empress of Asia*, which owing to a semi-mutinous crew had fallen astern of the convoy. She received several direct hits, and caught fire, becoming a total wreck. Most of the troops were rescued, but the ship was carrying the guns of an anti-tank regiment and much equipment, all of which was lost. The *Empress of Asia* was the only ship among the many convoys reaching Singapore between 3 January and 5 February that was lost as a result of enemy action.

While the three divisions were preparing their sectors for defence, energetic steps were being taken to move stores and ammunition depots and dumps in the north of the island to safer areas, to destroy the naval-base installations,[1] to prepare the many large oil storage depots for destruction, to arm administrative units as far as possible so that they could defend themselves, to refit 6th/15th Brigade and to make preparations to carry out the scorched-earth policy ordered by the Chiefs of Staff.

Since their appointment in January the DGCD, Simson, and his deputy, Bisseker, had been taking what action they could to prepare the civil population to withstand the ever-increasing Japanese air attacks on the island, to help the Services and to prepare a scorched-earth plan in the event of a Japanese landing on the island.

Brigadier Simson was hampered from the beginning by his inability to induce the Governor and the senior Malayan civil servants to abandon the normal methods of bureaucracy and to realize the need for urgent action. Despite the Governor's orders to the Malayan Civil Service that speed was essential and that there was to be no passing of files, old methods were retained and no decision could be reached without the opinion of everyone concerned being

---

[1] The Royal Navy had withdrawn their technical personnel for shipment to Colombo at the end of January but had done little to render the base of no value to the Japanese other than by sinking the floating dock, damaging the dry-dock gates and sinking all auxiliary vessels. The task of destroying buildings, plant, machinery and oil tanks had to be undertaken by 11th Division.

227

obtained by letter, minute or committee meeting. This caused long delays at the very moment when quick decision and action were necessary. Simson was also hampered by the fact that no officer of the Malayan Civil Service would co-operate or work with Bisseker, who during 1940 and 1941 as an elected member of the Legislative Council had been severely critical of the administration's lack of preparation for war—criticism which, as has been shown, was entirely justified. In fact the Governor and senior officials brought repeated pressure on Simson to replace Bisseker by someone of their own choosing. Simson always refused to challenge Duff Cooper's choice of his deputy, more particularly as Bisseker proved an excellent man for the job.

As soon as he was appointed Simson called together with Bisseker on Jones, the Colonial Secretary, to obtain a building for use as their headquarters and to get his help to collect staff and office equipment. They met with a blank refusal couched most impolitely. In the circumstances Bisseker rented and furnished offices for the new organization at his own expense.[1] Simson soon realized that, if he were to carry out his task, he would have to short-circuit the official channels of the cumbrous administrative system and take action without permission whenever the importance of the matter in hand warranted such action. This he did, being greatly helped by the fact that Duff Cooper's much-published original directive to him with its wide terms of reference had never been cancelled, and by Duff Cooper's unswerving support so long as he was in Singapore.

Simson decided first of all that his most immediate and urgent problems were to persuade the Governor to evacuate all *bouches inutiles*, to provide labour and transport to meet the needs of the Services and civil organizations, to build physical protection for important buildings and installations against blast and fire risks, to prepare plans for the maintenance of municipal and public services (water, gas, electricity, conservancy and the burial of the dead) despite the scale of air attack envisaged, to increase the strength of several sections of the civil-defence organization whose numbers were considered to be inadequate for the task facing them, to organize the fire services (especially in the crowded Asian areas of the city), to provide shelters at points such as markets, food depots, hotels and workshops where large numbers of people were likely to congregate, to prepare denial schemes for broadcasting stations, workshops and other places which were likely to be of use to the Japanese and later

[1] When Duff Cooper returned to the United Kingdom in mid-January, DGCD took over his offices.

to organize the destruction of large stocks of wines and spirits.

Realizing that, if Singapore were to be invaded, it might not be possible to evacuate many of those whose presence would be an embarrassment to the defence or the many technicians and experts in the rubber and tin industries whose skill could be employed elsewhere during the war, Simson repeatedly urged the Governor to order all supernumaries, including wives and families, to leave Singapore in the empty transports which were bringing in the reinforcing formations. The Governor, who had already decreed that there should be no discrimination of race or creed for those who wished to leave voluntarily, declined to issue any such order, and the Chinese secretariat refused exit permits to the many Chinese who wished to leave the country, despite agreements between the government and representatives of the Chinese community that help would be given to those requiring passages.

This attitude on the part of the administration is all the more surprising when it is realized that, unknown to Simson at the time, the Chiefs of Staff had on 21 January drawn General Percival's attention to the fact that about a month earlier the Governor had been sent instructions from London telling him to evacuate as many *bouches inutiles* as possible and asking Percival to report the numbers already evacuated and details of future plans. It would appear that the Governor failed to make any attempt to carry out his instructions and that Percival (heavily involved in vital military operations) made no reply. The former had no excuse, but the latter had little time to approach the Governor on the subject or to frame a reply. The Governor's failure to obey his instructions resulted in many of the returning transports sailing almost empty and in a mad rush, with disastrous results, in the last days before the surrender.

It was important, if all the tasks facing him were to be carried out efficiently in the time that remained, that the DGCD obtained the full co-operation of the Chinese community. This co-operation had not at first been fully given because of the unpopularity of the senior officers of the Chinese secretariat. The Chinese had, however, offered their full support on 25 December 1941, but the administration failed to accept it. In the years before the war the secretariat had had to fight the influence of Communism amongst the Chinese community and because of this had taken a number of unpopular measures. Simson therefore urged the Governor to replace the two senior officials of the secretariat and suggested replacement by named younger Malayan civil servants who were *persona grata* with the Chinese. Despite considerable pressure later by Duff Cooper, Wavell,

Percival and influential Chinese as well as by Simson, the Governor remained adamant and refused to remove them. The Chinese on Singapore Island outnumbered the Malays very considerably and their co-operation was essential. However, although many Chinese did assist as paid labour, few gave their unstinted support to the war effort because of their dislike of the Chinese secretariat. These Straits-born Chinese already hated the Japanese for their attack on China proper, and a magnificent chance to use their patriotism and toughness both as guerrilla fighters and as labourers against the common enemy was lost by the Governor's stand to protect two of his officials who, no doubt excellent men under conditions of peace, were the wrong men in the wrong place in the crisis that faced Singapore at the end of 1941.[1]

Until the appointment of the DGCD the Services and the civil organizations had competed with each other for such labour as existed. As soon as all demands for labour and transport were centralized under Bisseker, the situation began to improve and it was possible to meet about three-quarters of the daily demands from all sources. Bisseker undertook to collect the labour and transport it to and from the site where it was required, but, once the labour was handed over, the employer became responsible for its supervision and for making arrangements for the safety of the workers in case of an air raid. Frequently supervision and protection was inadequate, and the workers on the site vanished for the rest of the day in the event of an air raid. As in January the weight of air attack grew, it became more and more difficult to get labour to work in such areas as the naval base, Singapore Harbour and airfields, all of which were regular targets for the Japanese bombers. As a result the Services and individual civilian organizations in these areas began once again about 20 January to rely on their own resources and to by-pass Bisseker.

This problem was discussed frequently in the War Council: some members advocated higher wages, compensation in case of injury, provision of meals at the site of work and air-raid shelters, while others proposed compulsion. Eventually it was agreed that a form of compulsion was necessary. The conditions and terms of employment were fixed after considerable argument on 26 January, but the

[1] Nevertheless a volunteer Chinese force known as 'Dalfora' was formed mainly from Chinese communists and fought well during the struggle on the island. Those who survived and managed to escape execution at the hands of the Japanese helped to form the core of the Resistance Movement in Malaya during its occupation.

Services were unable to pay the agreed rates without first obtaining approval from their Ministries in London. Thus, although a Bill giving compulsory powers to direct labour was rushed through the Legislative Council by 29 January, it was not till the 31st that the Services were given authority to fix the rate of wages and compensation which were necessary to attract a reasonable supply of labour. The passing of the Bill and the application of the new rates slightly improved the position, and it remained satisfactory until the Japanese landed on the island on 8 February. Everything then began to disintegrate, and compulsion became impossible.

Simson speedily made arrangements to provide some protection against blast for important buildings and to erect improvised air-raid shelters in the more populous residential areas and markets, but time was short and the work had to be carried out in the face of frequent air attacks. The civil-defence organizations, including the fire-fighting services, were augmented as far as possible, but little could be done to provide the extra men and equipment or to replace obsolete or worn-out equipment. (*See pages 191–3.*) Nevertheless, civil-defence volunteers of all races carried out their duties very well.

Simson gave a great deal of attention to the water supply of the city, since he realized that it might well prove to be the Achilles heel of the defence. Singapore was supplied from three large reservoirs located in the municipal catchment area in the middle of the island. The supply from these reservoirs was augmented from water piped from Gunong Pulai in Johore at the rate of ten million gallons a day. This pipeline ran for part of its twenty-seven-mile length above ground and was frequently broken by bombing. In fact it was repaired nine times between the outbreak of war and 27 January, when the pumping station in Johore was overrun by the Japanese. Nevertheless, when this supply ceased, the reservoirs on the island, fed by the catchment area, were still sufficient for a continuous, if strictly limited, supply for the swollen population of about one million, provided distribution could be maintained in face of constant air attack. Water from the three main reservoirs ran by gravity to the Woodleigh pumping station, from where it was pumped to two reservoirs perched on tops of hills within the city. These provided the necessary pressure for the city distribution system. Since a breach in these two city reservoirs would have brought distribution to a standstill, steps had been taken before the war to provide them with protection as far as was possible.

As Chief Engineer, Simson had been concerned with the water supply since August 1941, but from 1 January 1942 he, as DGCD,

231

assumed responsibility for all the water supply, although the municipal authorities continued the actual pumping and maintenance. Since in the event of war the municipal authorities would probably have been unable to cope with repairs to the distribution system without aid, twenty men of the Royal Engineers had been lent to the municipal maintenance staff in November 1941 to learn the layout and to assist with repairs if war broke out. On the outbreak of war this number was raised to sixty, and Simson increased it later to a hundred. Since there was no frost risk in Singapore, distribution mains were buried only a few inches below ground level and so were very vulnerable to breakages by even small bombs and shells. No plans of the distribution system between the city reservoirs and the houses existed. The whole system had been installed at the minimum cost and added to as Singapore expanded, and the layout was unsuitable for an area likely to be involved in war. Valves and stop-cocks were extremely few and far between, so that water could not easily be turned off from any one house or group of badly damaged houses. The only way to prevent large quantities of water running to waste was to close a valve perhaps half a mile or more distant, thus possibly stopping the supply to hospitals or other undamaged buildings where water was needed. To improve the system in this respect would have taken many months, involving labour, money, material and time which was not available. All that Simson could do was to organize parties to repair damage as it occurred and to ensure that the pumping station at Woodleigh remained in action. Despite all his efforts the failure of the water supply was to prove a vital factor in the decision to surrender.

Another serious problem which faced the DGCD's organization was the fact that the sixty-four transit sheds or warehouses in the docks had, against all recognized principles, been used as storehouses, and contained thousands of tons of flour, rice and other reserve food stocks. Since the docks were a legitimate military target for bombing, this concentration was a major error. It shows clearly that the civil administration and military authorities in the period 1939–41 had failed to envisage the conditions of war and to make the necessary dispersal of stocks. Throughout January efforts were made to disperse these vast stocks (for example, 12,000 tons of flour alone), but the lack of labour, alternative accommodation and transport precluded much being achieved under frequent bomb attacks. Since the docks were bombed several times each day, it is not surprising that by the time of surrender forty-six out of the sixty-four very large sheds and warehouses had been completely destroyed with their contents and all the remainder had been seriously damaged.

Arrangements were made for groups of Indians (Tamils) to bury the dead, a task which the Chinese would not undertake. In the Singapore climate quick burial was necessary to avoid pestilence. Throughout January burials averaged one hundred and fifty a day, excluding the many bodies buried under collapsed buildings or consumed by fire in the flimsy buildings in the villages outside the city. In February, when shelling was added to bombing, the dead were estimated at between four and five hundred a day.

Early in January the DGCD had recommended to the Governor that a phased programme to implement the scorched-earth policy should be drawn up and approved. It was not, however, until the 23rd (when Simson became a member of the War Council) that he could get any decision. By the end of the month it was agreed that public services (water, gas, electricity, and sewage) were to be left intact and that the civil administration would organize the demolition of rubber and tin stocks, radio stations and currency. Unfortunately some of the arrangements made by the administration broke down, and Simson had to take emergency measures in February using Royal Engineers and Public Works Department personnel. The Governor refused to sanction the destruction of some forty Chinese-owned engineering works, giving as his reason the need to maintain the morale of the Chinese community. He did however give Simson the authority to make plans to destroy the forty-seven British-owned engineering plants. The demolitions were carried out under the supervision of Lieutenant-Colonel McConechy who, until he joined the Volunteer Engineers, had been Chief Engineer of Selangar State, but they met with active opposition from some owners and/or agents. It was only the fact that Simson's original directive from Duff Cooper had never been cancelled that enabled McConechy to ensure that these plants were in fact demolished.

21

The Final Phase of the Campaign: The Fighting on Singapore Island (8-15 February) and the Surrender

Map H, pp. 218–19, and Map I, pp. 242–3

The Intelligence Branch in Command Headquarters at Fort Canning was reorganized between 18 and 20 January and put under control of a first-grade staff officer who had arrived from Great Britain on the 3rd. The new head of the Intelligence Branch found that no plans had been made to leave undercover personnel in Johore, but by the 20th it was too late to organize a fifth column behind the Japanese lines. And as there was no air reconnaissance available the only information which could be obtained about Japanese intentions was either by night patrols or by direct observation. Between 1 and 6 February the Intelligence Branch formed the view that the Japanese would probably attack the north-west coast of the island. General Percival was therefore urged to order 8th Australian Division to send patrols to find out what was going on in the S. Skudai–S. Perpat area. This he did, but he had to bring considerable pressure to bear on General Gordon Bennett before patrols were eventually sent over on the night of the 7th/8th. When the patrols returned they reported large enemy concentrations in the area between the S. Malayu and the S. Perpat. Their report was available to 22nd Australian Brigade by dawn on the 8th, but Gordon Bennett clearly did not know its contents when visited by Percival about midday on the 8th, and it was not until about 3.30 p.m. that a copy reached the Intelligence Branch at Command Headquarters. By that time the Japanese artillery bombardment had begun and it was too late for anything to be done. All that could be arranged was to shell the areas in which the patrols had seen Japanese concentrations.

The Japanese assault began after dark on 8 February on the front held by the over-extended 22nd Australian Brigade. Swift progress was made, although artillery fire sank or damaged a number of assault craft and the forward defended posts took a considerable toll of the enemy before being surrounded and overwhelmed. But once ashore the Japanese infiltrated steadily between the widely scattered defended areas and made for the neck of land between Ama Keng on the S. Kranji and the S. Berih, the capture of which was essential to enable them to debouch into the Tengah airfield region and to gain control of the road which led to the heart of the island. It was midnight on the 8th/9th before Brigadier Taylor could form any clear picture of events, and it proved to be a gloomy one. He told Gordon Bennett the obvious fact that he had no reserves with which to counter-attack and asked for reinforcements to be sent to him immediately. Gordon Bennett thereupon ordered his reserve (the weak 2/29th Battalion) to move to Tengah airfield and later in the night sent up the only other reserves he could lay his hands on—a company of his machine-gun battalion and a Special Reserve Battalion newly raised from the poorly trained reinforcements, the formation of which had only been completed that day. These were put under Taylor's command. It was not until 8.30 a.m. on the 9th that Percival transferred his only command reserve (the weak 12th Indian Brigade) to Bennett's command and ordered it to move to the vicinity of the Jurong switch line.

This was the moment for Percival to have re-created his reserve by concentrating 18th Division in the Bukit Timah area. He could have withdrawn 18th Division with safety, provided he had made arrangements to man the Serangoon switch line. He could also have withdrawn 1st Malayan Brigade from its task of defending the south coast; for, by 4 February, ABDA Command Intelligence Staff had told him that the Japanese convoy anchored off the Anamba Islands was destined for Palembang in Sumatra. They confirmed this view on the 7th and again on the 9th. By the 10th they knew that the Japanese had issued definite orders for the convoy to rendezvous in the Bangka–Billiton area on the 13th in preparation for an attack on Palembang.

By 9 a.m. on 9 February the Japanese had gained control of the Ama Keng neck, and the whole of 22nd Australian Brigade had lost cohesion. Taylor's right-hand battalion was completely isolated, but part of it cut its way out with heavy loss while the rest made its way across the S. Kranji towards Singapore. Nevertheless, with the reinforcing formations sent him, Taylor quickly organized a position running from the north-west of the airfield to Choa Chu Kang village. Behind this line he tried to reorganize the scattered remnants of his brigade. Realizing that he could not hope to hold this long and weakly held position in face of Japanese infiltration tactics at night, Taylor, who was out of touch with Gordon Bennett, decided to fall back on to the Jurong switch line. When Brigadier Paris (12th Brigade) arrived, Taylor asked him to hold the northern end of that line with the Special Reserve Battalion on his left, while Taylor himself organized what was left of his troops along the outpost position

235

to the Jurong line running approximately north and south through Bulim.

In the afternoon, while Taylor was reorganizing his badly mauled brigade and semi-trained reinforcements, Percival went forward to discuss matters with Gordon Bennett. They decided that 27th Brigade should continue to hold the vital Woodlands–Kranji sector, and that 12th Brigade, the reformed remnants of 22nd Australian Brigade and 44th Indian Brigade, which had been withdrawn from the south-west coast, should hold the Jurong switch line. Gordon Bennett issued the necessary orders, while Percival made arrangements for 6th/15th Brigade to move to the Race Course area, where it was to come under Gordon Bennett's command. He also ordered the destruction of oil storage tanks in the Woodlands area, and for III Corps to complete the demolitions in the naval-base area. Percival hoped that with this additional reserve Gordon Bennett would be able to stabilize the position on the Jurong line, but he still failed to create a new reserve with which to take the offensive. Finally, when he got back to his headquarters he prepared a secret and personal instruction for issue only to Heath, Gordon Bennett and Keith Simmons, in which he said that if the Japanese broke through to the Bukit Timah road, it was his intention to hold a close perimeter round Singapore City from Kallang airfield by way of the reservoirs in the centre of the island and Bukit Timah to Pasir Panjang on the south coast. On receipt of this secret and personal instruction Gordon Bennett issued the gist of it as an operation order to his brigadiers, an action which was quite unjustified and was to cause disaster.

Unknown to either Gordon Bennett or Percival, action was meanwhile being taken in the north which was to result in the loss of the Woodlands–Kranji area. Brigadier Maxwell (27th Australian Brigade), who as usual had his headquarters close to his divisional commander, was worried about his left flank and during the morning asked Gordon Bennett for permission to withdraw from Kranji and occupy a line that ran south-west from Woodlands. Gordon Bennett refused, but gave Maxwell permission to use his reserves to cover the left flank. Shortly after midday on 9 February, therefore, Maxwell told his two battalion commanders to make arrangements to deploy to cover the left flank; unfortunately he also told them that both battalions might later be withdrawn from the coast between Woodlands and Kranji.

During the day the Japanese artillery had switched to that area in preparation for the assault by *Imperial Guards Division* which was due to take place that night, and all communications in the area were cut. At 8.30 p.m. the Japanese launched their assault. Though suffering considerable losses they managed to obtain a footing ashore and drove the Australians back to Kranji village but could make no further progress. About midnight communications between Maxwell's headquarters and the two forward battalions were re-established and, although completely out of touch with the real situation on his front, Maxwell now told his two battalion commanders to put into effect the plan discussed that afternoon and to withdraw to a position which he had indicated near Mandai. Although Maxwell later maintained that he had Gordon Bennett's agreement to this move, no evidence to this effect is available. It is now known that, faced with stiff opposition and with burning oil on the water carried by the tide into the creeks from the oil tanks when they were destroyed, *Imperial Guards Division* sought permission to call off the attack. This unnecessary and unauthorized withdrawal not only exposed the right rear of 8th Australian Division but also exposed the flank of 11th Division.

While these unfortunate events were taking place in the north during the night of the 9th/10th, Gordon Bennett ordered Taylor to hold the Jurong line and placed under his command his last reserve, the weak 6th/15th Brigade. Consequently just before dawn Taylor withdrew his troops from the outpost line which he had held during the night, and by about 9 a.m. the Jurong line was held from north to south by 12th Indian Brigade, the remnants of 22nd Australian Brigade, the Special Reserve Battalion, 6th/15th Brigade and 44th Indian Brigade. During the hours of darkness all these formations had moved into an area unknown to them, and they had little idea either of the general plan or where the formations on their flanks were located. The fog of war had fallen on the defence with a vengeance. Two events then occurred which were to result in the loss of the vital Jurong switch line: shortly before dawn the Japanese began to send patrols forward towards their second objective; and the operation order, based on Percival's secret instructions, which Gordon Bennett had issued reached his brigade commanders. The order not only gave details of the sector which had to be manned by 8th Australian Division astride the Bukit Timah road, but also gave 22nd Brigade a sector immediately south of that road with 44th Indian Brigade in reserve. It went on to indicate that commanders might have to evacuate their existing positions, but did state that no action except reconnaissance was to be taken for the time being. However, Taylor interpreted the order as requiring him to man his sector in the inner-ring position forthwith. He therefore went back to reconnoitre the new position and ordered all the remnants of his original brigade to move back to the new line.

Meanwhile Paris (12th Brigade), who was out of touch with Gordon Bennett, sent out patrols to make contact with 27th Australian Brigade, which he presumed was still in the Woodlands–Kranji area. These returned with the information that the Japanese held the road junctions south of Kranji and that there was no sign of any Australians on the Woodlands–Bukit Panjang Road. Paris also found that his left flank was exposed and therefore decided to withdraw his brigade to the Bukit Panjang cross roads, from where he could prevent the Japanese from Kranji sweeping down on Bukit Timah. Thus by noon the northern part of the Jurong switch line had been abandoned.

At the southern end of the Jurong switch line 6th/15th and 44th Brigades were in position astride the Jurong road when at about 10.30 a.m. both brigadiers received the operation order from Gordon Bennett. Although their position had been heavily bombed and subjected to machine-gun fire during the morning, neither brigade had been attacked. But when the Japanese sent forward patrols, both brigadiers, who like Taylor had misread Gordon Bennett's order, began to withdraw towards the inner ring of defences in the neighbourhood of Reformatory Road. Thus by dark on the 10th the Jurong switch line on which the security of Singapore Island depended had been entirely abandoned. The loss of this line, the unauthorized withdrawal of 27th Australian Brigade and Percival's failure to reform his reserves on 9 February sealed the fate of Singapore.

No blame can be placed on 22nd Australian Brigade for its inability to hold the initial Japanese assault, for it was too weak and too extended. The failure to hold the vital Woodlands–Kranji area and the Jurong line must be laid squarely on Gordon Bennett's shoulders. As usual he had placed his headquarters far too far away from his brigades, he had made no attempt to go forward and see for himself what the situation in the forward areas was and, being almost completely out of touch with events, he failed to take control of the battle. He committed the reserves placed at his disposal piecemeal without proper orders and forwarded a secret instruction to his brigadiers in such a form that they were able to misread it and take action which was never intended.

Early on 10 February Wavell paid what was to be his last visit to Singapore. He and Percival drove straight to Gordon Bennett's headquarters, to be greeted by enemy aircraft bombing the building.

There they found that Bennett had little information about the position in the Western Area. He did not for example know that 27th Australian Brigade had withdrawn during the night of 9th/10th, which would appear to prove that he had not given Maxwell permission to take this action. Percival and Wavell then went on to Heath's headquarters, where they learnt that 27th Brigade had abandoned its sector, that 11th Division was using its reserve brigade (the 8th) to fill the gap north of the Mandai road which had been left exposed by Maxwell's withdrawal, and that the Bukit Timah–Woodlands road was open to any Japanese southward movement. The existence of a reserve in the Bukit Timah area was now even more urgent and Percival immediately told Heath to form a force of three battalions and concentrate it at the Race Course. Heath withdrew the reserve battalions of 54th and 55th Brigades and these, with 18th Division Reconnaissance Battalion, formed what became known as Tomforce, after its commander Lieutenant-Colonel L. C. Thomas. Percival also decided that 27th Australian Brigade should be placed under the command of General Key (11th Division), since its communications now ran through Nee Soon. But, pending Gordon Bennett's agreement to the transfer of the brigade, he sent a personal order to Maxwell to reoccupy and hold Mandai village. Percival and Wavell then returned to Gordon Bennett's headquarters, which they reached about 2.30 p.m., to learn that the Jurong line had been lost. Since the security of the Bukit Timah area depended entirely on the retention of the Jurong line (and of course Mandai village), Wavell told Percival to order Gordon Bennett to launch a counter-attack with a view to reoccupying it without delay.

There is little doubt that Wavell knew when he left Singapore in the early hours of 11 February that the base was lost.[1] Before he left he ordered the immediate transfer of the remainder of the RAF to the Netherlands East Indies and on his return to Java told the Prime Minister in a masterly understatement that 'the battle was not going well', but that he had given orders that there was to be no thought of surrender.

The Japanese had reorganized during 10 February, and after dark *5th Division* supported by tanks began to advance east along the Choa Chu Kang road, while *18th Division* moved up the Jurong road towards their second objective. Meanwhile, Gordon Bennett had prepared a plan for the counter-attack to regain the Jurong line. This was to be launched early on the 11th, from a starting line which all

---

[1] Wavell wrote in his dispatch, 'I left Singapore on the morning of 11th February without much confidence in any prolonged resistance.'

his scattered formations were to occupy after dark on the 10th. The plan was issued at 4.45 p.m. and all the brigadiers involved began to try to implement it, but there was such general chaos that no co-ordinated counter-attack could have been launched. Only fresh formations could have undertaken the task, and in the circumstances the counter-attacks could only end in disaster.

The night of the 10/11th was indeed disastrous. The advancing *5th Division* overwhelmed 12th Brigade after dark, and by midnight Japanese tanks and infantry had reached Bukit Timah, where, for-tunately for the defence, they halted. The *18th Division*, having met 22nd and 44th Brigades moving forward to their starting line, reached Reformatory Road and at dawn after a good deal of con-fused fighting also stopped. Both the Japanese divisions had reached their second objectives, and the difficulty of getting ammunition and supplies across the Johore Strait precluded a resumption of the offensive before the 13th. Had they continued their advance, how-ever, they could have split the defence wide open and occupied the city during the morning of the 11th.

Early on the 11th Gordon Bennett ordered Tomforce to counter-attack in order to retake Bukit Timah and Bukit Panjang. Initially the attack made some limited progress east of the road, but by mid-day it had lost its impetus and neither objective had been reached. While this attack was in progress Percival brought a battalion (2nd Gordons) from Changi and placed it under Gordon Bennett's orders, adjusting the boundaries between Western and Northern Areas so that the latter became responsible for all ground east of the Race Course. Heath immediately formed a second scratch brigade (which became known as Massy Force after its commander, Brigadier T. H. Massy-Beresford) and gave it the alternative tasks either of prevent-ing the Japanese from gaining control of Thomson Village and the pumping station at Woodleigh, or of filling the gap between Tom-force and the reservoirs. Almost at the same time Brigadier Maxwell (27th Brigade) told General Key (11th Division) that his brigade had been removed from the command of 11th Division and that he had received orders to occupy and hold Bukit Panjang. Key, who had previously ordered Maxwell to retake and hold Mandai village, was shocked to be told by Maxwell that he was no longer under his com-mand. Neither Percival nor Gordon Bennett issued any orders to this effect and there would seem to be little doubt that Maxwell acted on his own initiative because he wanted to get back under the command of 8th Australian Division. He was, however, out of touch with his two battalion commanders and had to send them orders to move on

Bukit Panjang by liaison officers and dispatch riders. Since some of the troops were already engaged in an attempt to recapture Mandai village, they had to disengage before starting to undertake their new task. With no co-ordination between the two battalion commanders, neither was able to make any progress, for the Japanese held Bukit Panjang in very great strength.

By the end of the day one battalion had skirted the Japanese positions and withdrawn to Tanglin and the other had withdrawn to a point on the road running north from Thomson Village. The fact that 27th Brigade had moved south left a gap on the western flank of 11th Division which Heath could not possibly fill. Realizing the danger in which his corps now stood, Heath decided that he had no alternative but to withdraw the entire corps from the north coast. The final demolitions in the naval-base area were completed by 6 p.m., and 11th Division then withdrew to a line running north-west covering Sembawang airfield and Nee Soon. During the afternoon of the 11th Percival, with Heath's agreement, ordered Massy Force to fill the gap on the right of Tomforce. Confusing as they were, by the evening these intricate redeployments produced a more or less continuous defensive position, running from the western end of the reservoir to the west of Thomson Village through the Race Course to Reformatory Road and then down to the sea at Pasir Panjang, which covered the western and northern approaches to the city.

That same evening a Japanese aircraft dropped copies of a letter addressed to General Percival, proposing that the garrison should surrender and giving the means by which Percival could notify Yamashita that he accepted the offer. Percival decided to ignore the proposal, but he clearly saw that the end was in sight, since he issued orders designed to prevent as much military equipment as possible from falling into Japanese hands.

*

On 12 February, in pursuance of Wavell's orders given on the night of the 10th/11th, the cruiser *Durban* and the three other British naval vessels still at Singapore sailed for Batavia escorting the remaining transports. The convoy carried the remaining air force ground personnel, the balance of the shore-based naval staff, a number of nursing sisters and some selected staff officers and technicians. Several ships received direct hits and suffered a number of casualties from air attacks, but the convoy managed to reach its destination. This was to be the last convoy to get away from Singapore.

R

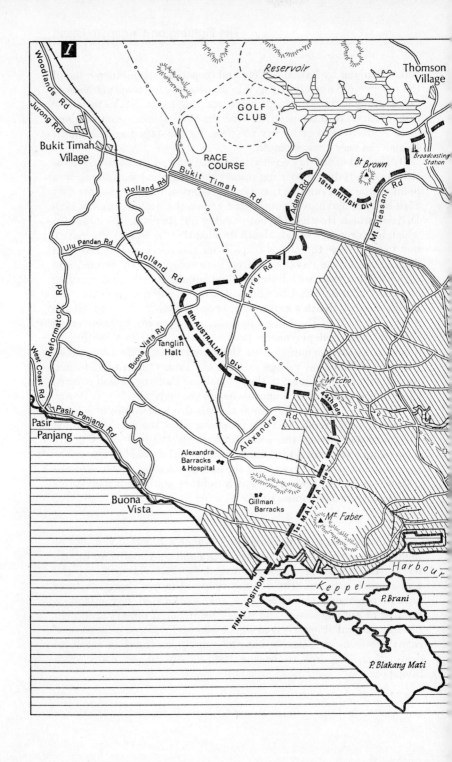

Paya Lebar

addell Rd

Woodleigh

11th INDIAN Div

2nd MALAYA Bde

Serangoon Rd

KALLANG
AIRFIELD

rt
ning

FINAL POSITION

SINGAPORE CITY

0   *Miles*   2

Roads ═══	Railways —+—+—
Rivers ∿∿	Pipeline o—o—o
Swamps ≈≈≈	Hills 🕸

Shortly before dawn on the same day *Imperial Guards Division* attacked 11th Indian Division in its positions covering Nee Soon, while *5th Division* attacked the Race Course area. By the afternoon Massy Force had been forced to withdraw to the general line of Adam Road–Farrer Road, and when he received the news of this Percival saw that there was a very real danger that the Japanese might break through on the axis of the Bukit Timah road and reach Singapore City. He therefore decided to abandon Changi and the north-east coast and to concentrate the whole garrison in a twenty-eight-mile perimeter round the city proper. Of necessity this perimeter was somewhat shorter than he had forecast in his secret instructions of the 9th. The withdrawal was completed during the night of the 12th/13th, and by dawn on the 13th the garrison was in position. The 2nd Malaya Brigade was on the right covering Kallang Airfield; on its left 11th Division covered Woodleigh; the 18th Division, now for the first time under its own commander, Major-General M. B. Beckwith-Smith, held a sector from west of Woodleigh to the Bukit Timah road; while 8th Australian Division with 2nd Gordons under command held the sector from Farrer Road to Tanglin Halt, and 44th Indian Brigade and 1st Malaya Brigade held the rest of the line to the coast.

There is no need to describe the fighting on the 13th and 14th in detail. On the 13th the Japanese forced back 55th Brigade of 18th Division, holding the Adam Road sector, for some thousand yards and made a salient in the perimeter. On the 14th the Japanese *18th Division*, having found that it could not drive in the Australians in its sector, moved south and launched an offensive parallel with the coast. This broke through the Buona Vista part of the perimeter, Alexandra Barracks and the hospital were overrun, and the Japanese massacred most of the medical staff and patients. By the morning of 15 February, 44th and 1st Malaya Brigades were holding a line on the outskirts of the city in the vicinity of Mount Faber.

*

Many problems faced General Percival and the civil administration after the Japanese had launched their assault on the island, and a chain of untoward events led Percival to surrender on 15 February. As soon as the Japanese landed, steps were taken to complete the destruction of the installations in the naval base which the naval authorities had left intact. On the 9th the Governor ordered the implementation of the civil denial scheme, and on the 10th, without informing Percival or Simson, he ordered the withdrawal of all

European technical staff from the Singapore Harbour Board installations. The withdrawal of these men brought this efficient organization almost to a standstill, and the army had to find men from its now exiguous resources to keep the docks working.

As may well be imagined, with the garrison precariously holding a perimeter in close proximity to the city outskirts the administrative situation was now becoming desperate. About a million Asians were hemmed in a semi-circle with a radius of some four and a half miles from the waterfront—an area of some thirty square miles—all of which became a legitimate target for Japanese aircraft and artillery owing to the concentration of military units and military transport of all kinds within the city boundaries. The garrison's food reserves were down to seven days owing to the loss of the Bukit Timah depots and petrol was scarce, but the reserves of ammunition, though low, were still adequate.

Although the Japanese were in possession of all the reservoirs in the middle of the island, they failed, either deliberately or inadvertently, to cut off the flow of water by gravity to the Woodleigh pumping station. Despite the fact that the pumping station was within half a mile of the front and was at times under fire, Simson ordered the staff there to continue pumping at all costs.[1] During the day the continuous bombardment of the city by both aircraft and guns caused so much damage to the water-distribution system that water from the reservoirs was mostly running to waste, and pressure had fallen so much that buildings, except those in the lower areas of the city, were without water.

At 2 p.m. on 13 February Percival held a conference at which all his principal staff officers and formation commanders were present. The possibility of organizing a counter-attack to recapture the Bukit Timah area was discussed but every one of the formation commanders stated that, owing to the exhaustion and poor morale of the troops, such an operation had no chance of success. Both Heath and Gordon Bennett advocated capitulation to save the population of the city from disaster, since they feared that if the Japanese troops entered it there would be scenes such as had occurred in many of the Chinese cities when the Japanese troops ran riot. Despite the gravity of the situation, Percival decided to continue the struggle in accordance with the orders he had received from Wavell.

Rear-Admiral, Malaya (Rear-Admiral E. J. Spooner), who was

---

[1] The engineer in charge of the pumping station remained at his post until the surrender and later kept the pumping station working on orders from the Japanese.

also at the conference, said that it was now necessary for all the remaining thirteen sea-going craft in the harbour to sail on the night of the 13th/14th, and that they could carry three thousand passengers. Since this was the very last opportunity for the evacuation of women and children and other selected people, the number of available passages was divided between the civil and military authorities. Morale in the Services had already begun to break down, and there were many armed deserters, mostly from recent untrained drafts, whose only desire was to find some means of leaving the doomed island. There were in consequence some ugly scenes as the deserters tried to rush some of the ships.

The departure of this last official convoy had been left too late. Although the Intelligence Branch at Command Headquarters had been told on 10 February that the Japanese shipping at the Anamba Islands had been ordered to rendezvous in the Bangka Strait on the 13th, as a preliminary to an assault to capture Palembang, most of the thirteen small ships, packed with women and children, were routed to pass through the very area where the Japanese were concentrating. Thus very few of them got safely to Java. Nearly all were intercepted and forced ashore, where most of their passengers and crew were massacred. These were, however, not the only craft to leave Singapore, for from about the 10th onwards a stream of small vessels moved south from Singapore and Malaya trying to make Sumatra or Java. Some carried soldiers who had been cut off on the mainland, and others deserters who had commandeered vessels and slipped away under cover of darkness. At least forty of the forty-four ships and small craft that sailed in these last three days were sunk by Japanese aircraft and naval vessels, but one of those which did reach Sumatra safely carried General Gordon Bennett. With two of his staff officers he had slipped away on the night of the 15th/16th without General Percival's knowledge and without appointing anybody to take his place.

In order to avoid the possibility of Japanese troops inflamed by alcohol committing outrages on the population such as had occurred in China, a systematic destruction of all intoxicants other than those required by the hospitals was ordered. By working round the clock for several days, teams from the Excise and Customs, from the Public Works Department and from the Royal Engineers, often assisted by Chinese and Indians, destroyed some one and a half million bottles of whisky and gin and sixty thousand gallons of Chinese spirit as well as much other intoxicating liquor.

During 13 February Percival told Wavell that resistance could not be maintained for more than a day or two, and asked to be given wide discretionary powers, since the stage would soon be reached when, in the interest of both troops and civil population, further bloodshed would be in vain. Wavell was unwilling to accept personally the responsibility for surrendering Singapore and in accordance with his instructions from the Prime Minister told Percival to continue to inflict the maximum damage on the enemy for as long as possible, if necessary by house-to-house fighting. Percival knew that, if the Japanese broke through his tenuous defence line and entered the city, with consequent street fighting, the large Asian population would suffer severely, for it was quite possible that the Japanese troops would get out of hand. There could have been little doubt in his mind on the 14th that, in the interests of the local population, surrender was the only possible course to take.

That day he went to the Municipal Offices to discuss with Simson the water-supply position. He was told that a check over the previous twenty-four hours had shown that two-thirds of the water being pumped from Woodleigh was running to waste, that the supplies would not last for more than forty-eight hours and perhaps less and that most of the municipality's Asian staff had failed to report for work that morning. Percival immediately agreed to another hundred Royal Engineers being brought back from the fighting line and placed under Simson's orders. He then visited the Governor, who pointed out to him the danger of an epidemic; but nevertheless Percival decided to carry on the struggle. Throughout the day the defences still held on with difficulty, but air attacks on the city increased and the situation became chaotic, with roads blocked and dead bodies lying everywhere. The water situation, however, seemed no worse by evening, and Percival therefore called for another forecast to be supplied by Simson next morning.

At 9.30 a.m. on 15 February, Percival again held a conference with all his commanders. Simson reported that repairs to the water mains could no longer keep pace with the damage, that five-sixths of the water being pumped was now running to waste, that the supply could not last for more than twenty-four hours and that once it had failed it would be many days before it could be restored. After a further review of the administrative situation, which had deteriorated sharply in the previous forty-eight hours, Percival told the conference that he could see only two alternatives: to launch a counter-attack to try to regain control of the food stocks in the Bukit Timah depots and the reservoirs, or to capitulate. All formation commanders once again reported that the state of the troops was such that a counter-attack was not feasible. In face of their unanimous views and since there appeared to be no solution to the water problem, Percival decided to capitulate. His decision was accepted by the conference without demur.

The decision having been reached, the method of surrender was discussed and Percival proposed that the cease-fire should be at 4 p.m. Heath objected strongly, saying that this would not give sufficient time for the first party of *parlementaires* to make their way through the lines, contact the Japanese to arrange for a subsequent meeting between Percival and Yamashita, and return. He suggested that 8 p.m. would be a more suitable time, but Percival insisted on 4 p.m., and orders were sent out to that effect.

Brigadier Newbiggin (the officer in charge of administration), Mr Hugh Fraser (the Colonial Secretary) and Major Wild (one of Heath's staff officers who spoke Japanese) then drove along the Bukit Timah road carrying a white flag and a Union Jack as specified by Yamashita on 11 February in his demand for surrender. When they reached the front line at the junction with Adam Road they left their cars and, with flags unfurled, walked some six hundred yards until stopped by a Japanese patrol, who disarmed them. Wild explained their mission and demanded to be taken to the Japanese main headquarters. After an hour's delay Lieutenant-Colonel Sugita of the Japanese General Staff arrived, and the British party handed him a letter from Percival. Sugita read it and then handed over a type-written letter which requested Percival to meet Yamashita at Bukit Timah at ——, the hour being left blank. Newbiggin agreed that the time should be 4 p.m. An appendix to the letter said that the British forces must lay down their arms and remain in their position from the time of the meeting, but said nothing about the Japanese themselves agreeing to cease fire. This point was raised with Sugita, who replied that the British were not the negotiators.

Sugita then handed over a large Japanese flag with orders that it should be displayed from the top of the Cathay Building as a signal to the Japanese that Percival accepted the condition and was on his way to meet Yamashita. Wild pointed out that it would be inadvisable to display the flag for more than ten minutes, for if left permanently displayed there might be incidents on the part of the Allied soldiery. After some argument Sugita agreed to the flag being displayed for ten minutes and the party, having been blindfolded, was taken back to the Bukit Timah road, given back their arms and returned to the city.

As usual heavy air attacks were being made on the city, and just as

248

the party reached Headquarters at Fort Canning a stick of bombs just missed the Fort. Newbiggin reported the result of the interview to Percival, and Wild was then told to go to the Cathay Building (which was III Corps Headquarters) and display the flag as arranged. Since it was then 3.30 p.m. Wild asked if he could be given orders about the time for the cease-fire, so that he could pass them on to Heath. He was told that orders had already been sent out. At 3.45 p.m. Wild hung out the Japanese flag for ten minutes as ordered. He then saw Heath and discovered that Percival had ordered the cease-fire for 4 p.m., as decided at the morning conference. Since he was to accompany Percival to the meeting with Yamashita to act as interpreter, Wild returned to Fort Canning, which he reached at 4 p.m., told Newbiggin, Percival and others present that III Corps had had no orders postponing the time of the cease-fire, and asked for orders to be sent out giving a revised time. Finding that his request was ignored, he approached Percival direct, saying that it would be unwise for the British to cease fire until the meeting with Yamashita had decided on the hour for a general cease-fire. This suggestion was also ignored, and Percival with his Chief of Staff and Newbiggin set off with Wild to meet Yamashita.

When Percival and his companions arrived at the front line of the Bukit Timah road it was well past 4 p.m., and some of the infantry of 18th Division had left their positions to close in on their battle headquarters in accordance with the order that the cease-fire was to come into effect at 4 p.m. The party was taken to meet Yamashita at the Ford factory at Bukit Timah, where they arrived at 5.15 p.m. The discussion on the terms of surrender began with a question from Yamashita about the time that Percival was prepared to cease hostilities. Despite the fact that he had already ordered his forces to cease fire as from 4 p.m., Percival gave the hour as 10 p.m. Yamashita insisted on 8.30 p.m., and when Percival demurred told him that the Governor would have to come out as a hostage unless the earlier time was agreed to. On this Percival gave way. Yamashita thereupon openly expressed his relief that 8.30 p.m. had been agreed and told Percival that his final assault on Singapore was timed to begin at 10.30 p.m. that evening. He added that if Percival had not accepted 8.30 p.m. he would have had only thirty minutes to call off the assault and might have failed to stop it. Now, however, he would have time to order his forces to stand fast. It was by this very small margin that the British forces, already ordered to lay down their arms, were saved from an overwhelming assault and from the entry of the Japanese divisions into Singapore, which might have resulted in much loss of life to the troops and civilians alike.

While the conference was taking place Wild managed to have a look at a Japanese map, which showed that the attack Yamashita had agreed to halt was to be carried out by a very strong force supported by armour and was to take place immediately east of the Bukit Timah road. This was the area where the infantry of 18th Division had begun to withdraw in accordance with the original orders issued by Percival and never cancelled.

At 6.10 p.m. on 15 February 1942 Percival signed the terms of surrender, which stated that the British Army would cease fire at 8.30 p.m. and with the exception of one thousand men who would be allowed to maintain order in the city until further notice should disarm themselves in the positions they occupied by 9.30 p.m. Thus ended the seventy-day campaign. The total British, Australian, Indian and volunteer manpower lost as a result of battle casualties and by the surrender amounted to 138,708, according to official figures.

In the circumstances that existed in Singapore City by the middle of February 1942, Percival was quite right to have surrendered, for the disaster to the million Asians in the city and to the troops would have been very great had the surrender been delayed by even a few hours. Yamashita did not allow his three fighting divisions to enter the city, which was occupied by small bodies of picked troops to keep order and enforce the terms of surrender and by technical troops to restore the public services in co-operation with similar technicians from the surrendered garrison. There were thus no excesses, and the control of Singapore passed from Britain to Japan with amazing smoothness.

22

Epilogue

Map B, p. 12

The Japanese, who had established an efficient espionage system in Malaya from the moment Britain had announced her intention of developing Singapore as a naval base, had accurately assessed the value of the British garrison and were confident that with a force of three divisions, with one held in reserve in Japan, they could overrun Malaya and occupy Singapore Island in one hundred days. As has been related, they gained their objective in seventy days and did not have to make use of their reserve division. The question must be asked why the defence collapsed so much more quickly than even the Japanese planners had estimated.

Without command of the sea and with such a weak air force that he could neither prevent an invasion nor support his troops in action, General Percival had no hope of holding north Malaya with one partially trained and inexperienced formation without armoured support. Time had to be gained somehow for the hurriedly collected reinforcing army formations and aircraft to reach Singapore, to be brought into action and to deliver a counter-offensive. Percival was well aware of this, as all his orders and instructions show. Nevertheless his conduct of the campaign was such that he failed to take the only two actions which might have given him the time he required. These were: first, to concentrate in the vital area west of the central range his forces which were at the outbreak of war scattered all over Malaya to defend the airfields, from which the RAF were supposed under the defence scheme to destroy the enemy before they reached the coastline; second, to make every effort to construct field and anti-tank defences at bottlenecks on the north–south communications and to ensure that the three approaches to Johore Bahru were covered by permanent defences on which to retire.

At the time that hostilities began it was obvious to all that the RAF with its 158 obsolescent aircraft, instead of the agreed minimum of 336 modern aircraft including a long-range striking force, would be unable either to carry out its task or to retain air superiority over northern Malaya. The continued dispersion of the army garrison in order to defend airfields which could not be used was therefore not warranted. Percival continued to attempt to deny the Japanese the use of airfields, instead of concentrating his forces to meet the main enemy thrust, which from the moment the Japanese had landed at Singora and Patani could clearly only be made down the western side of the peninsula. As a result the inexperienced and semi-trained 11th

Division, after its initial defeat at Jitra, was called upon to undertake a long fighting retreat without relief until, utterly weary and exhausted, it was overwhelmed by a handful of enemy tanks at Slim River. The consequence was the loss of central Malaya far sooner than would have been the case had another division been concentrated in that area as soon as the line of the Perak River had been abandoned. That this was possible has been shown in the preceding chapters.

The failure to concentrate resulted in the numerically inferior Japanese forces being able to defeat piecemeal the numerically superior garrison. Perhaps it was because Percival was a well-trained and extremely competent staff officer with little experience of command that he saw all the possible dangers and, unable to distinguish which of them was the most serious, could not decide where to concentrate his forces. His inability in this respect is also shown by his dispositions for the defence of Singapore Island. It must have been obvious to him that the Japanese would be forced by circumstances to select one area and one area only in which to assault the island, yet he discarded the advice given to him by Wavell and strung his available forces all round the island, leaving himself with no strong reserve with which to meet the enemy when the point of attack was disclosed. Even when the area of attack was known, he failed to concentrate to meet the danger in time, with the result that forty-eight hours after the initial assault the Japanese had captured the vital central portion of the island, and the battle was lost.

In 1941 it was considered both in London and Singapore that Japan was unlikely to go to war with Britain and the United States and that an invasion of Malaya was at least only problematical. Percival, therefore, even if he had wished, could not have embarked on the construction of defences other than those approved by the War Office at Jitra, Kroh and the beach defences at Kota Bharu, Mersing and on Singapore Island. He was bound by a defence scheme approved in London and was under War Office financial control which was so strict that many urgent measures required under the existing defence scheme were not completed when war broke out.

Once war had broken out, however, Percival's hands were free, and Duff Cooper was in a position to authorize any measure necessary to meet an emergency—and after the initial defeat of 11th Division at Jitra an emergency certainly existed. It should have been evident that III Corps would need every assistance that the available engineering sources could provide. But no action in this respect was taken or even contemplated in the first fortnight of the campaign.

After Kedah and Perak had been lost, General Heath asked that defences be provided at strategic points along the main trunk road on which his exhausted troops could fall back, and the Chief Engineer, Malaya (Brigadier Simson), did his utmost to persuade Percival not only to prepare field defences and provide anti-tank obstacles at all bottlenecks on the trunk road in Malaya, but also to allow him to organize the construction of more permanent defences in Johore to cover the approaches to Johore Bahru and the naval base against attack from the north. Percival however flatly refused to agree, as did the Commander of Singapore garrison, General Keith Simmons, giving as his reason for his refusal the explanation that such action was bad for morale.[1]

In retrospect, Percival's refusal to act on Heath's request or to accept his Chief Engineer's advice while there was yet time is all the more surprising in view of the fact that he had been principal staff officer to General Dobbie in 1937–8, had drawn up an accurate appreciation of the methods the Japanese might adopt should they invade Malaya, and had taken part in the decision to build defences in southern Johore to protect the naval base from the north— defences which were begun by General Dobbie but were abandoned by General Bond in 1939. (*See page 32.*) As he had stated in his appreciation of 16 December 1941, Percival realized that his object was the security of the naval base. (*See page 158.*) It would appear that with this end in view he should have been only too anxious to have defences prepared in Johore so that the Japanese, if they were to advance into that State, could be brought to a halt out of artillery range of the naval base; such defences would also have covered the main reservoir at Gunong Pulai, on which Singapore Island depended for a large proportion of its water supply. Yet he refused to have any action taken though he knew that the northern coast of Singapore Island was not defended and was in fact unsuitable for defence. (*See page 217.*)

A consideration which seemed to have escaped Percival's attention but which should have been perfectly obvious at the end of December 1941 (and this can be stated without hindsight) was that, should the Japanese succeed in reaching southern Johore, their forces would be at the end of a very long and unreliable line of communication, which could have only a very limited capacity. This was the moment

---

[1] See pages 168–9. Although General Percival did attempt to organize the PWD to build defences for III Corps his action was valueless, for he failed to mobilize the engineering sources available through his Chief Engineer. It therefore came to nothing.

to have attempted to force them to fight while at a disadvantage. Had defences been built in Johore covering Jemaluang, so as to retain control of the east–west road, and on the approaches to Johore Bahru along the trunk road and the west-coast road, there would have been a distinct possibility of holding the Japanese and bringing 18th British Division into action under favourable circumstances after its arrival. Furthermore the defence of this area would have been much easier and more satisfactory than the defence of the north coast of Singapore Island. It is now known that General Yamashita and his staff were very worried men towards the middle of January, because the Japanese formations were running short of ammunition. It was the British withdrawal from Mersing and Jemaluang that enabled the Japanese to land the essential supplies which they required for their assault on Singapore Island.

It seems evident that, while Percival paid lip-service to the need to gain time, he failed to take the only two actions which might have enabled him to do so. It was not until General Wavell insisted on defences being prepared on the north coast of Singapore Island that Percival took any action, and by then it was too late. Had defences been constructed in Johore in December and early January, there might well have been a chance for Singapore to survive for sufficient time for the Australian reinforcements from the Middle East to arrive. As it was, the weary garrison was forced to stand and fight in unsuitable terrain in northern Johore and when defeated was forced to withdraw back willy-nilly into Singapore Island, the defence of which for any reasonable length of time was not in the circumstances a feasible operation. It was these two errors in the conduct of the campaign which enabled the Japanese forces to achieve victory so much more quickly than they had ever deemed possible.

The loss of Malaya and Singapore Island is, however, attributable to a more fundamental cause than mistakes on the part of the British commanders. Even had they made no errors, Air Chief Marshal Sir Robert Brooke-Popham, Lieutenant-General Percival and Air Vice-Marshal Pulford could not have saved the naval base and the island in the circumstances prevailing at the end of 1941, and they cannot be blamed for the disaster. The basic cause lay in Britain's failure, for reasons dating back to 1919, to provide in advance of the outbreak of war with Japan balanced naval, land and air forces adequate to defend the area. (*See chapters 1–5.*) It can truthfully be said that the naval base was at least theoretically lost before the first sod had been turned, because of the British governments' actions between 1919 and the time the construction began in earnest.

There were, however, moments when vigorous action might have prevented the débâcle. Churchill and the Chiefs of Staff had it in their power, even after 1940, to ensure that Malaya could be held. They had the unenviable task of deciding which area of the Commonwealth should be strongly defended and which weakened in the general interest. There was no doubt that the security of the British Isles and the Atlantic trade routes had to be given first priority from slender resources. Since Russia had to be given aid, the choice lay between the Middle East and the Far East. The fate of Singapore was finally decided when early in 1941 the Prime Minister gave the Middle East priority over the Far East. In the prevailing circumstances and with the paucity of resources, no one can say his decisions were wrong, for some risk had to be accepted somewhere even if in a vitally important area.

It is, however, clear that Churchill failed to understand the problem of the defence of the naval base. To the end, he believed that Singapore was a 'fortress' with all-round defence capable of withstanding a siege, even if the Japanese held Johore, until relieved by the arrival of a British Fleet, and he failed to grasp the necessity for the defence of the whole of Malaya. Holding these views, he was prepared to gamble that United States naval power in the Pacific would provide a shield for Singapore, and that even were the Japanese to attack, America would join in the war and thus ensure eventual victory, whatever losses were suffered meanwhile. Had the Chiefs of Staff been able to disabuse the Prime Minister of the highly inaccurate picture of Britain's position in Malaya which he had built up for himself, he might have heeded Field-Marshal Sir John Dill's plea and altered the priorities between August and December 1941, thus saving Britain from humiliation.

As matters turned out, Britain did exactly what Sir Ian Hamilton warned her in a letter to *The Times* in 1924 was the worst possible course, viz. 'to put out at Singapore a half-way house and then half-garrison it'. The blame must be placed squarely on the shoulders of successive British governments whose decisions from 1919 to 1941 built up a chain which inevitably led to disaster. There is little doubt that had a Royal Commission been given the task of reporting on the loss of Singapore as promised by Churchill in 1942, its findings would have been very similar.

Appendix

British Malaya Command: 7 December 1941

Malaya Command	Lieut.-Gen. A. E. Percival
Singapore Fortress	Maj.-Gen. F. Keith Simmons
1st Malaya Inf. Bde	Brig. G. G. R. Williams
2nd Malaya Inf. Bde	Brig. F. H. Fraser
12th Indian Infantry Bde	Brig. A. C. M. Paris
8th Australian Division	Maj.-Gen. H. G. Bennett
22nd Australian Inf. Bde	Brig. H. B. Taylor
27th Australian Inf. Bde	Brig. D. S. Maxwell
III Indian Corps	Lieut.-Gen. Sir Lewis Heath
9th Indian Division	Maj.-Gen. A. E. Barstow
8th Indian Inf. Bde	Brig. B. W. Key
22nd Indian Inf. Bde	Brig. G. W. A. Painter
11th Indian Division	Maj.-Gen. D. M. Murray-Lyon
6th Indian Inf. Bde	Brig. W. O. Lay
15th Indian Inf. Bde	Brig. K. A. Garrett
Krohcol	Lieut.-Col. H. D. Moorhead
28th Indian Inf. Bde	Brig. W. St J. Carpendale
Penang Fortress	Brig. C. A. Lyon
Line of Communications Command	Brig. R. G. Moir

8 February 1942

Malaya Command	Lieut.-Gen. A. E. Percival
Singapore Fortress	Maj.-Gen. F. Keith Simmons
1st Malaya Inf. Bde	Brig. G. G. R. Williams
2nd Malaya Inf. Bde	Brig. F. H. Fraser
Straits Settlements Volunteer Force Bde	Col. Grimwood
Command Reserve	
12th Indian Infantry Bde	Brig. A. C. M. Paris
8th Australian Division	Maj.-Gen. H. G. Bennett
22nd Australian Inf. Bde	Brig. H. B. Taylor

s

27th Australian Inf. Bde	Brig. D. S. Maxwell
44th Indian Inf. Bde	Brig. G. C. Ballentine

III Indian Corps	Lieut.-Gen. Sir Lewis Heath
11th Indian Division	Maj.-Gen. B. W. Key
28th Indian Inf. Bde	Brig. W. R. Selby
53rd (British) Inf. Bde	Brig. C. L. B. Duke
8th Indian Inf. Bde	Brig. W. A. Trott
18th (British) Division	Maj.-Gen. M. B. Beckwith Smith
54th (British) Inf. Bde	Brig. E. H. W. Backhouse
55th (British) Inf. Bde	Brig. T. H. Massy-Beresford
15th Indian Inf. Bde	Brig. J. B. Coates

Japanese Twenty-fifth Army: 8 December 1941

Twenty-fifth Army	Lieut.-Gen. T. Yamashita
5th Division	Lieut.-Gen. T. Matsui
9th Inf. Bde	Maj.-Gen. S. Kawamura
11th Inf. Regt	Col. Watanabe
41st Inf. Regt	Col. Okabe
21st Inf. Bde	Maj.-Gen. E. Sugiura
21st Inf. Regt	Col. Harada
42nd Inf. Regt	Col. Ando
18th Division	Lieut.-Gen. R. Mutaguchi
23rd Inf. Bde	Maj.-Gen. H. Takumi
55th Inf. Regt	Col. Koba
56th Inf. Regt	Col. Nasu
35th Inf. Bde	Maj.-Gen. K. Kawaguchi
114th Inf. Regt	
124th Inf. Regt	
Imperial Guards Division	Lieut.-Gen. T. Nishimura
3rd Guards Inf. Regt	
4th Guards Inf. Regt	Col. Kunishi
5th Guards Inf. Regt	Col. Iwaguro
56th Division	

Note: The Japanese Order of Battle was not changed during the Malayan campaign.

List of Published Sources

Attiwell, K., *The Singapore Story* (Frederick Muller, 1959)

Bennett, H. G., *Why Singapore Fell* (Sydney, 1944)

Brooke-Popham, Air Chief Marshal Sir Robert, Dispatch on *Operations in the Far East from 17th October 1940 to 27th December 1941* (Supplement to the *London Gazette* of 20/1/48, No. 38183)

Butler, J. R. M., *History of the Second World War, Grand Strategy, Volume II* (HMSO, 1957) and *Grand Strategy, Volume III, Part II* (HMSO, 1964)

Churchill, W. S., *The Second World War, Volume II* (Cassell, 1949) *Volume III* (Cassell, 1950) and *Volume IV* (Cassell, 1951)

Cooper, A. Duff, *Old Men Forget* (Hart-Davis, 1953)

Gwyer, J. M. A., *History of the Second World War, Grand Strategy, Volume III, Part I* (HMSO, 1964)

Hasluck, P., *The Government and the People 1939–41* (Canberra, 1952)

Hough, R., *The Hunting of Force Z* (Collins, 1963)

Kirby, S. W., *History of the Second World War, The War against Japan, Volume I* (HMSO, 1957)

Layton, Vice-Admiral Sir Geoffrey, *Despatch on loss of H.M. Ships Prince of Wales and Repulse* (Supplement to the *London Gazette* of 26/2/48, No. 38214)

Maltby, Air Vice-Marshal Sir Paul, *Despatch on Air Operations during the campaign in Malaya and the Netherlands East Indies from 8th December 1941 to 12th March 1942* (Supplement to the *London Gazette* of 20/2/48, No. 38216)

Percival, Lieut.-General A. E., *Despatch on Operations of Malaya Command from 8th December 1941 to 15th February 1942* (Supplement to the *London Gazette* of 20/2/48, No. 38215) and *The War in Malaya* (Eyre & Spottiswoode, 1947)

Potter, J. D., *A Soldier must Hang* (Muller, 1963)

Stewart, I. M., *History of the Argyll and Sutherland Highlanders 2nd Battalion* (Nelson, 1947)

Tsuje, M., *Singapore, the Japanese Version* (Constable, 1962)

Wavell, Field-Marshal Earl, *Despatch by Supreme Commander of the ABDA Area on Operations in the South-West Pacific 15th January 1942 to 25th February 1942* (HMSO, 1948)

Wigmore, L., *Australia in the War of 1939–45, The Japanese Thrust* (Canberra, 1957)

Index

'ABC1' plan, 66
ABDA Command, 182, 186, 193, 214, 215
ADA Agreement, 67, 69, 109, 124
Adam Road, 244, 248
Admiralty, 15, 21, 26, 28, 35, 55, 56, 86–7, 122
Air Ministry, 15, 21, 28, 42, 44, 45, 88, 97
Air Observation Corps, 77
Air Raid Precautions, 77, 134
aircraft-carriers, 8, 114, 163
airfields, 14, 22, 28, 30–1, 102, 128, 136, 220, 224, 234–5; defence of, 41, 44, 46, 102–3, 104, 111, 113–14, 158–9, 160, 171, 172–3, 180, 186–7, 244, 251; evacuation of, 134–5, 137, 140–1, 160–1, 162, 172–3, 186, 197, 211
Albacore bombers, 210
Alexandra Hospital, 244
Alor Star, 31, 47, 54, 71, 97, 102, 108, 111, 114, 134, 136, 140, 141, 147, 148, 160, 188
Ama Keng, 234, 235
Amboina, 67, 69, 71
American Navy, 2–3, 8–9, 16–17, 23, 25, 58, 66; Pacific Fleet, 66, 68, 88, 182; Asiatic Fleet, 68–9, 137
Amoy, 26
amphibious operations, 31–2, 108, 112, 134–5, 165–8, 170, 174, 197–9, 206, 224
Anamba Islands, 127, 138, 197, 210, 211, 223, 235, 246
Anderson, Lieut.-Colonel C. G. W., 204–5
Anglo-German Naval Treaty (1935), 22–3
Anglo-Japanese Treaty (1902), 1, 8
anti-aircraft defences, 29, 104–5, 115, 134, 140–1, 161
Anti-Comintern Pact (1936), 24
anti-tank defences, 115, 116, 118, 143, 144, 150, 155, 157, 168–9, 176–7, 178–9, 251, 253
Argyll and Sutherland Highlanders, 2nd, 96, 152, 155, 178

armoured vehicles, 143, 144, 152, 153, 170. *See also* tank warfare
assault landing-craft, 165, 170, 224
Asun, 143, 144, 150, 153n
Australia, 7, 11, 13, 17, 24, 25, 26–7, 28, 35, 59–60, 67–8, 215, 216; War Cabinet, 73–4
Australian Army, 90, 91, 94–5, 212. *See also under* British Malaya Command
Auxiliary Fire Service, 77
Ayer Hitam, 198, 200, 205, 206
Ayer Kuning, 200

Babington, Air Vice-Marshal J. T., 39, 59, 73, 76; view of defence, 41, 44, 52, 58, 105; conflict with Bond, 41–2, 47, 52–3, 54, 55
Bakri, 199, 200, 201
Baldwin, Stanley, 13, 21
Baling, 152
Bandoeng, 182
Bangka Strait, 246
Bangkok, 126, 127
Barstow, Major-General A. E., 130, 136, 159, 172–3, 208
Bata River, 146, 147, 148, 149, 150
Batavia, 61
Batu Pahat, 107, 186, 199, 200, 203, 204, 205, 206, 207, 211
Beckwith-Smith, Major-General M. B., 244
Bell, Colonel Hayley, 30
Bengal, Bay of, 55, 56
Bennett, Major-General H. Gordon, 90, 140; builds up Australian force, 71–2, 105; role in defence of Malaya, 105–6; career and character, 131–3; responsible for eastern Johore, 174–6, 184, 185; given command of Westforce, 185–6, 198; and battle for Johore, 198, 200–4, 205, 208; prepares escape from Singapore, 223; defence of Singapore, 226, 234–40; advocates surrender, 245; escape, 246
Benut, 205, 206, 207

DATE DUE

GAYLORD			PRINTED IN U.S.A.